I0820960

How to Know Your Self

How to Know Your Self

The Art & Science of Discovering Who You *Really* Are

J. Eric Oliver

LIVERIGHT PUBLISHING CORPORATION
A Division of W. W. Norton & Company
Independent Publishers Since 1923

Printed in the United States of America
First Edition

For information about permission to reproduce selections from this book, write to Permissions, Liveright Publishing Corporation, a division of W. W. Norton & Company, Inc., 500 Fifth Avenue, New York, NY 10110

For information about special discounts for bulk purchases, please contact W. W. Norton Special Sales at specialsales@wwnorton.com or 800-233-4830

Manufacturing by Lake Book Manufacturing
Book design by Chris Welch
Production manager: Lauren Abbate

Library of Congress Cataloging-in-Publication Data is available.

ISBN 978-1-32409-523-1

Liveright Publishing Corporation, 500 Fifth Avenue, New York, NY 10110
www.wwnorton.com

W. W. Norton & Company Ltd., 15 Carlisle Street, London W1D 3BS

Authorized EU representative: EAS, Mustamäe tee 50, 10621 Tallinn, Estonia

1 2 3 4 5 6 7 8 9 0

For Thea, Martin, and Ethan,

my most beloved teachers

I rejoice in life for its own sake. Life is no "brief candle" for me. It is a sort of splendid torch which I have got hold of for the moment, and I want to make it burn as brightly as possible before handing it on . . .

—GEORGE BERNARD SHAW

These machines sometimes always breaking.

—ANONYMOUS SIGN IN AN OAKLAND LAUNDROMAT

Contents

Introduction

MY GRANDFATHER GREW UP IN GALVESTON, TEXAS, IN THE early 1900s. His old Victorian home did not have indoor plumbing nor did his neighborhood have sewage, so the family relieved themselves in a little shed around the back they charmingly called the "small house." This, in turn, was emptied every day by George, the driver of the equally endearing "honey wagon." George was an older Black man who spent his days steering a horse-drawn cart around the neighborhood, emptying pails of human excrement into its big copper tank. Most remarkably, Grandpa said that George always had a smile on his face.

This story haunts me. Southeast Texas is brutally hot and humid during the summer. It's the kind of climate that makes you feel parboiled the moment you step outside. The stench of the honey wagon must have been unbearable, and I don't even want to think about the flies. In this swampy oven, George didn't just have to handle his own crap (metaphorically speaking), but everyone else's as well. Yet he did this day in, day out, and, if Grandpa's memory serves, always with that smile.

So, how did he do it?

I can imagine two different scenarios. In one, George is an existential hero, a Camusian Sisyphus in overalls. Texas in the early 1900s was a viciously racist place, and George probably had few work options.

Maybe he had a family to support, and this was the only job he could find. But rather than wallow in despair, George is determined to rise above the misery, transcending his horrible circumstance through sheer force of will. So he drives and fills the honey wagon every day, but with a Stoic sense of dignity and pride—and maybe even a dash of joy. That's the inspiring spin.

But I suspect another story is closer to the truth. In this version, George also drives the honey wagon, but he hates it, every sweltering, stinking, fly-infested minute of it. Yet he never looks for another job because he can't imagine an alternative. He's gotten so accustomed to the smell, the nausea, and the fetid misery that it's come to seem weirdly natural. In this version, his smile isn't a reflection of some inner peace but an emotional camouflage, a way to hide his feelings and protect his dignity from the condescension of others. Yet beneath the smile, George suffers in silence, trapped in a terrible situation from which he can see no escape.

Either way, there are lessons here for all of us. Much like George, we all have to face challenges in life. Sometimes, these are unavoidable. We contract a disease, get abandoned by a lover, or endure Uncle Don's elaborate conspiracy theories at Thanksgiving dinner. And, like Version One George, it's up to us to meet these tests with a brave face and a positive attitude.

But this isn't where our story ends. For even on our best days, many of us are plagued with a nagging sense that things aren't as good as they could be. Sometimes this feeling is heavy, a real funk, a palpable fear or sadness. But more often our suffering comes in a softer form, a hushed feeling of discontent. It's that constant hum of tension and anxiety, like a distant radio playing static, the quiet disquiet of ordinary life.

This type of suffering is self-inflicted. We're typically the authors of our own distress. What's worse, we're also usually blind to this fact. We may have a vague sense that something's off and that things aren't as good as they should be. Yet, that's typically as far as our self-awareness takes us. Too often, we've gotten so used to our misery that we can't imagine anything else. We've been pulling that honey wagon for so long that we've forgotten that life could be any different. Either way, we struggle, lost in a fog within a fog.

But why is this the case?

According to history's wisest thinkers, the answer lies with the self. One of these sages was none other than my high school English teacher, Mrs. Malone. She was a brilliant, imposing woman, the kind of teacher who could silence us just by clearing her throat. She opened our muddled teenage minds to the genius of Dostoevsky, Dickinson, and Hemingway, and we students revered her. One day, she wrote "know thyself" on the blackboard. Distilled in these two little words, she said, was the collective wisdom of the ancient Greeks, those marbleized founders of Western civilization who, when not inventing democracy or wrestling in the nude, spent their time doling out cryptic advice. If we wanted to lead a happy and meaningful life, Mrs. Malone said, we would need to heed their guidance; we'd need to know ourselves.

During my bumpy adolescence, I took her advice to heart. And so began a lifelong quest to know this elusive self. Over the following decades, I devoured scores of books on Buddhism, existentialism, and positive psychology. I sought wisdom from priests, gurus, and even Turkish rug sellers (who, oddly enough, often have a surprising amount of insight into spiritual matters). I dipped my toes into self-help, twisted myself into various yoga poses, saw a parade of therapists, dabbled in psychedelics, and even subjected myself to long, silent meditation retreats where the highlight of the day might be the sound of someone's growling stomach. In short, I did my best to tick off every box on the spiritual seeker's bucket list.

Yet, for all this effort, I remained unsettled. If I wasn't chasing some peak experience, my life often felt like it lacked meaning. Even as I was achieving professional success, I was less sure of myself than ever. I was doing all the "right" things—whatever that means—but the deeper fulfillment I was grasping for always seemed beyond my reach. Like trying to catch a shadow, my self-knowledge often seemed to come up short, and this heavy, stinky honey wagon always seemed to be dragging me down. Eventually, it dawned on me that my quest had some fundamental problems.

First off, it turns out the Greeks didn't have a word that meant "self" as we know it today. If they really carved "know thyself" onto the ancient temple at Delphi, as the legend says, it probably meant something more like "know thy place." In other words, "know thyself" was another way of saying, "Hey, you're about to enter a sacred building. Put down your wine, put on your best tunic, and, for Zeus's sake, stop fooling around!"

Funnily enough, "know thy place" is actually great advice. In fact, for most of human history, these were probably the best three words you could live by. Our ancestors typically existed in small groups tightly bound by custom and tradition. Famine, violence, and death were always close by. If you wanted to survive, you embraced your role and played your part, and the group protected you in return. Life wasn't about finding your inner truth but about keeping the wolves at bay, sometimes literally.

But that doesn't apply to us today. We no longer teeter on the brink of survival. Released from our ancestors' dogmas, we now enjoy the liberty, or perhaps the burden, to figure out what makes us happy, who we should love, and what our life's purpose should be. In this sense, we're freer and more isolated as individuals than at any other point in human history. And so, "know thy place" has evolved into the more introspective "know thyself" we often hear today.

All of this, however, still leaves us with a second problem: What exactly is this self we are supposed to know? The answer isn't straightforward. Take philosophy. Here we have some of history's greatest minds, people who have spent thousands of years contemplating the meaning of existence. Surely, they'd have a solid description of what we are. But in all that time, they've agreed on, well, practically nothing. Worse still, their metaphysical reflections are often very unclear.

Consider the example of Søren Kierkegaard. He's one of the big names in philosophy, a profoundly spiritual and earthy thinker. Yet, when defining the self, he famously declared it to be "a relation that relates itself to itself or is the relation's relating itself to itself in the relation." Hmm. Okay, technically, that might be correct, but it doesn't illuminate much about our experience of being, aside from confirming that it's subjective. The same goes for the obscure musings of most other philosophers, too.

So if philosophy isn't helpful, perhaps we can find better answers in psychology. For if anyone can tell us about the self, you'd think it would be the scientists of the mind. Unfortunately, psychology doesn't deliver the goods either. Sure, it offers us thousands of wondrous experiments, colorful brain scans, and intriguing theories about what makes us tick. Yet these ideas mainly exist in pristine isolation, like puzzle pieces that remain unconnected to the larger picture. Modern psychology tends to zoom in on one tiny fragment of the self at a time, and it's not always clear how these fragments come together into a cohesive whole.

Well, if the West is failing us, then perhaps we could look to the great wisdom of the East. For millennia, Hinduism, Buddhism, and Taoism have grappled with the subtleties of existence. Buried within their ancient tomes is a treasure trove of insights about the human condition. Surely, these sages and gurus must have cracked the code on what or who we are. But alas, even these venerable traditions can't agree on the nature of the self; in fact, the self is one of the very things that divide them.

Here, then, is the dilemma of our modern lives. Most people I know struggle with a nagging sense of anxiety, a great uncertainty about their purpose, and a heavy honey wagon always in tow. But it's not clear what they (we) can do about it. They may read a self-help book, or find a guru, or go to therapy, but they continue to struggle because they don't understand what is behind it all. Why are those "Seven Habits" so highly effective? What is the real "power" of positive thinking? How does therapy actually work?

These questions have no apparent answers. We still don't have a clear understanding of the self and no single version seems to explain it all. As a result, we fumble about from system to system, unclear which path is the most useful for modern life. Searching for the self today is like asking a group of fifty people for directions and getting fifty different suggestions in fifty different languages.

For a long time, this was exactly where I found myself—stuck groping about for self-knowledge and never finding a single, satisfying way forward. Then, in 2003, I took a job as a professor at the University of Chicago. It's one of the world's great universities, and if I wanted to find answers to the big questions in life, this seemed like an ideal place to look. Another draw was their laissez-faire approach to teaching. They generally let their faculty design whatever courses we want for some of the brightest students around. Inspired by this golden opportunity, I cobbled together a class that reflected my eclectic interests in Buddhism, psychology, philosophy, and neuroscience. My wife, Thea, wryly suggested I name the class Stuff I'm Interested In, but I opted for the more respectable title of The Intelligible Self.

I wasn't entirely sure how the class would go, but the students really liked it. So I kept offering it year after year, and it eventually became one of the more popular courses on campus. I've had innumerable students tell me how the class changed their lives—in a good way, I should add—and it changed me, too. Over the past twenty years of teaching this class, I've found a much better way of living in my own skin.

Meanwhile, as word of the class spread, I found myself talking about it with many curious adults who would inevitably ask me for a book recommendation. This was a bit awkward because I didn't have just one; I had hundreds. Here then, I thought, was an opportunity to do something useful. Perhaps I could write a book that brought together all this scattered wisdom on how to know the self. Maybe I could combine the insights from the world's greatest minds with the hands-on lessons I've developed in my life and class. And so, *How to Know Your Self* was born.

This book explores what the self is, why it often malfunctions, and what we can do to make it work better. We'll investigate what's going on behind the scenes of our ordinary awareness. We'll explore the mysteries of energy, language, consciousness, and free will. We'll look at morality, history, and psychedelic drugs. We'll learn about the science behind our minds and the power of myth and story. And ultimately, we'll confront the big question: How can we live better?

But before we go any further, a quick warning: This book is an odd hybrid. It's part applied philosophy, part popular science, part intellectual history, and part "thinking person's self-help" book. The logic behind this strange mixture goes back to my class. When I first started teaching The Intelligible Self, we focused mostly on ideas. We pored over great philosophical texts, grappled with cutting-edge scientific theories, and debated the finer points of psychology, Buddhism, and quantum physics, sometimes all at once. While these discussions were intellectually stimulating, they often felt sterile. The class was more head than heart; a seminar on the self that dodged the very selves in the room.

Then, one year, I decided to try a different approach. Instead of simply regurgitating Freud, Nietzsche, and the Buddha, I asked my students to reflect on what these august thinkers told them about *themselves*. The results were astonishing. Suddenly, the course came alive with personal stories, psychological insights, and confessions. Friedrich Nietzsche wasn't just some nineteenth-century grouch; he became a mirror for grappling with their own moral hang-ups. Sigmund Freud wasn't just a guy with a mother fixation; he became a crowbar for unpacking their inner conflicts. The class transformed from a dry academic exercise into something messy, raw, and deeply meaningful.

This book takes a similar approach. We're going to start with some esoteric scientific topics like energy, entropy, and evolution. These subjects may feel remote at first, but stay with them, for they will be crucial for knowing our place and purpose in the universe. However, as the chapters progress, our focus will shift inward, moving from the universal to the personal. We'll begin seeing how we can interpret our life stories, how we can pinpoint our own problems, and how we might let go of them.

The goal here is not just to understand ourselves; it's to see how we can live better. And by living better, I'm not talking about the obvious things like getting a toned body, earning more money, or the other consumeristic promises of a happy life that you find in some self-help books. I'm talking about something more subtle and profound. I'm talking about a radiant experience that resides below your ordinary awareness. The true aim of knowing yourself is to open your consciousness up to this innate luminescence, an experience of being that is defined less by ego and identity and more by flow and equanimity. So, I invite you to join me on what I hope will be an illuminating and entertaining tour of this wonderfully complex, fascinating experience that we call a self.

1

Essence

I WAS BORN AND RAISED IN HOUSTON, TEXAS, THE SON OF A truck driver and a homemaker. I spent my twenties in California, my thirties in New York, and have lived in Chicago for the past two decades. I'm the (usually) happily married father of two teenagers. I enjoy surfing, yoga, dancing, and talking about interesting ideas with curious people. So that's me.

Or is it?

While these traits may give a rough snapshot of who I am at this particular moment, they don't capture the full picture. They don't reveal my quirks (which are numerous), my darkest secrets (which are more a light shade of gray), or that parade of awkward moments that trail behind me (which I generally try to forget). These words certainly don't encapsulate my experience as a living, breathing being. In short, none of these descriptors truly gets to the heart of what makes me, well, *me*.

The ancient philosophers of Greece recognized this problem and, being ever inventive, came up with a different way to describe themselves. Instead of simply being an Athenian or a shoemaker or something mundane like that, they said that, at their deepest core, they were composed of two fundamental parts. First, there was the body, a blubbery mass that lusts, rages, and sobs until it eventually decomposes into a blob of rotting flesh; physical life in ancient Greece clearly had its challenges.

But they also saw something else, a pristine element that was less prone to farting and cramping. This was the mind, and the ancient Greeks venerated it. They viewed it as the part of us that thinks and contemplates the world's great truths, the constant thread linking every moment of our conscious experience, the golden ticket to eternity.

The idea that we are composed of a separate mind and body came to be known as dualism, and it has been widely adopted by thinkers, theologians, and life coaches across the ages. It also aligns with how most people intuitively understand themselves. This is usually the case with me, too. I, for one, strongly identify with my body—I definitely spend too much time fretting over the muffin top that used to be my abs. But I also feel like there's something else, some ethereal quality to "me" observing my body from afar, an inner soul that feels singular, stable, and even eternal.

But these notions are illusions.

Dualism relies on our intuitions to describe us, and intuitions, to be frank, are unreliable guides to reality, even on our best days. Consider the body. Our senses tell us that we're a solid mass, constant and unchanging, but this is a gross misperception. In reality, we are a swirling collection of atoms and molecules, constantly moving, always changing, and mostly composed of empty space. Despite all appearances, we are actually about 99.9999999 percent emptiness. When it comes to the body, there's almost no *stuff* there. Instead, we are something far more subtle, a luminescent phenomenon that defies easy comprehension: We are energy.

If we want to get to the heart of what makes us, well, *us*, then we'll need to look past not just our fleeting identities and social markers but the comforting but misleading notions of body and mind. We'll need to delve into the deeper forces at work behind this existence. We'll need to see what it means to be comprised mostly of energy. And while this idea may sound a little mystical, don't worry, I'm not going to talk about chakras or harmonic vibrations or anything gooey like that. Instead, we're going to start our journey with a little exploration of how science explains the mysterious forces that compose us.

The Atomic You

If you were to ask a group of physicists to describe themselves, they'd likely say that they are collections of atoms. These are folks who spend a lot of time thinking about atoms, after all, so the response makes sense. And, in a fundamental way, they are right.

Atoms, as you undoubtedly know, are the building blocks of the universe. The Earth, the sun, the cosmos, and you . . . are all made up of atoms. That breath you just inhaled? It had twenty-seven sextillion atoms within it (that's about two and half times greater than the number of stars in the entire universe). Your lunch had even more. And your body? It's home to about seven octillion atoms—that's seven followed by twenty-seven zeros, if you're counting, though I wouldn't recommend trying it as it would take 222 quintillion years. The sheer multitude of atoms within us is incomprehensible.

Atoms come in ninety-two natural varieties, and they can merge together into an even wider number of combinations called molecules. The three most important atoms for our purposes are carbon, hydrogen, and oxygen. They comprise about 93 percent of our body's mass, with the rest of us being made up of nitrogen, calcium, and a few other trace elements. The reason why so much is oxygen and hydrogen is simple: You're mostly made of water. In fact, about two-thirds of you is the molecule H_2O, the legacy of life's aquatic origins.

So there you have it. You and I are a vast conglomeration of just a few types of atoms and molecules. But if this picture leaves you feeling a bit underwhelmed, as if you've just found out you're made mostly of the same stuff as a swimming pool, you're not alone, for these facts don't tell us very much about ourselves. They don't explain why we're afraid of intimacy, why we can't resist buying things we don't need, or even how to win friends and influence people. Nor do they say what makes us any different from all the other carbon-, hydrogen-, and oxygen-based stuff in the universe. But let's not give up on atoms just yet. If you look into the science of atoms, you'll find that it reveals three important secrets about what, exactly, you are.

1) Atoms are eternal, but we are ever-changing.

Atoms are very persistent things. Unless they get caught within a star, a black hole, or the occasional nuclear bomb, they will generally hold themselves together forever. Most of the hydrogen atoms that are part of you originated near the beginning of the universe, and most will be around at the end. In this regard, most of "you" is actually billions of years old and will continue to exist well after your death. An atom's indestructibility also means it gets recycled a lot. Every sip of water, every bite of food, every breath you take is essentially a hand-me-down from rivers, clouds, plants, or some other creature that had the pleasure of hosting those atoms before you.

This atomic exchange also means that you are never the same from moment to moment. With each breath, your body is transferring sextillions of atoms and molecules from your surroundings into you and vice versa. In the time it takes you to read this sentence, quintillions of atoms that were part of you are now gone, and quintillions of atoms that were elsewhere are now part of you. The sheer number of particles coming into and out of us is truly staggering. At the atomic level, there isn't a firm boundary between you and the world or even a fixed materiality that is you. Instead, you're more like a molecular subway car, constantly being replenished with a shifting array of atomic passengers.

This also means that, at any given moment, we are made up of stuff that was once part of someone else. Atoms not only circulate through us, but they circulate through other people all over the world and throughout time. In other words, a lot of "you" has been pre-owned by other human beings. And this has some fun benefits, for odds are, some tiny part of you was also once part of someone great like Jane Austen, Mahatma Gandhi, or Groucho Marx. Of course, the flip side is that part of you may have been once part of Genghis Khan, Joseph Stalin, or Pol Pot. So, in this very micro sense, we have had many, many "past lives," even if they aren't always so ennobling.

An even more enchanting fact is that the carbon atoms that comprise us were themselves born from stars. Carbon atoms bond easily to other atoms and molecules, so they make a terrific material for creating living things. However, carbon atoms don't form easily in the matter-making processes of the universe; they need exceedingly high pressures to be created. This type of pressure only occurs toward the end of a star's life cycle. As stars age, they cool, which compresses their helium atoms into carbon atoms. When a star eventually explodes in a supernova, it disperses its carbon atoms across the cosmos. As Earth formed, it accumulated many of these residual carbon atoms, which, in turn, formed the basis of life on this planet. So yes, my fellow hippies, we are stardust. Or even more romantically, we are made from the last gasps of dying stars.

Unfortunately for such starry-eyed notions, atoms are the only thing about us that approximates immortality. This odd fact is ironic, considering the classical view is to think of the body as temporal and the soul as immortal. In reality, it is almost the opposite. The body, or at least the atoms that temporarily comprise it, is the only lasting thing about us.

2) We are (mostly) energy.

Atoms are really, really tiny. To give you a sense of how small an atom is, imagine this: It would take about 840 quintillion hydrogen atoms to fill a sphere the size of a poppy seed. And just so we're clear, 840 quintillion is a lot. Although the space that atoms occupy might be minuscule, their actual mass is even more absurdly small. The particles inside an atom are so incomprehensibly tiny that they are almost beyond our capacity to describe, so let me try to put them into perspective with another image.

Imagine you blew up a hydrogen atom to be the size of Earth. Yes, that's an outrageously large amplification, but bear with me. Even at this gargantuan scale, the atom's nucleus would be only the size of a basketball, and its solitary electron would be comparable to a peppercorn. Picture it: a peppercorn materializing around a basketball with such speed as to create the appearance of an entire planet. That's essentially an atom—a vast amount of space with just a smidgen of actual stuff.

What this also means is that you and I are mostly empty. When it comes to us, there's hardly any "stuff" there at all. It's mind-boggling when you think about it. If you could somehow compress all of the human race, eliminating all the empty space, we would easily fit into a box the size of a sugar cube (though it would weigh a staggering

1.3 trillion pounds). What we perceive as our bodies, this seemingly solid mass, is actually an intricate dance of tiny particles moving around each other so quickly that they create the illusion of solidity. In reality, we are vastly, impossibly empty.

But, if we're mostly empty space, why do we feel so solid? The overly simplified answer is that we are not really made up of mass; we're mostly made up of energy. Atoms are energy systems. They have electrical forces that bind their protons to their electrons like a sort of subatomic Velcro. These same electrical forces also push away anything that tries to get too close. Under certain conditions, atoms can overcome this repulsion and link up, forming molecules. In most cases, atoms keep their distance, repelling each other like magnets with matching poles. It's this energy, both within and among your atoms, that gives you the impression of being solid and distinct. But here's the cosmic punchline: you're neither. You're not really a solid being; you're far more diaphanous. You are energy.

3) We are a potential.

But if we're mostly energy, then what exactly is energy? This is where things get a bit foggy. Most scientific definitions of energy are tantalizingly vague. Physics textbooks, for example, often describe energy as "the potential for something to happen," "the ability to do work," or "the capacity to do things." These are all phrases that could just as easily describe my teenagers on a Saturday morning as they could the fundamental essence of the universe. Energy also comes in various flavors, like light, gravity, and electromagnetism, but these expressions are about as intuitive to our ordinary minds as trying to smell the color blue. Energy is not really a "thing" in the way we typically understand things. It's without substance but takes form, discrete yet continuous, boundless yet law-abiding.

Our inability to describe energy arises from the ineffability of reality itself. The ambiguities are both big and small. On the cosmic scale, our universe is mind-bogglingly enormous. Even with all our sophisticated telescopes, we have observed only a tiny fraction of its content, which, let me repeat, is inconceivably huge. It's not just that there are "billions and billions of stars," as the popular astronomer Carl Sagan used to say; it's that the universe is mainly composed of dark matter and dark energy, phenomena that we can't even perceive. In other words, we've charted only a tiny smidgen of a vast cosmos that itself is ever-expanding, the essence of which is profoundly and indescribably weird.

Then there's the microscale, which is equally baffling. We know that protons and electrons are made of subatomic forces and particles that have been given playful names like quarks and gluons. But how these particles acquire mass is still something of a mystery. Scientists believe it has to do with how they interact with latent energy fields, but much of this is still in the speculative realm of quantum physics, where the laws of common sense are on permanent vacation. Just as our understanding of the vastness of the universe is limited, so too is our grasp of the minutiae within us.

Adding to the confusion is the fact that most forms of energy exist outside our intuitive comprehension. Take the example of light. Common sense tells us light illuminates our surroundings, but what exactly is doing the illuminating? Physicists say light is a massless particle (a photon) and a wave, but how can something be both a particle and a wave? How can something exist without mass? When you stop and think about it, light, like most forms of energy, is incredibly hard to fathom.

Our inability to understand energy is not our fault. Our brains evolved to solve problems our ancestors encountered in the wild, like where to find bananas or how to avoid getting eaten. They didn't evolve to comprehend the true nature of energy, let alone the fundamental nature of reality. The fact that the rare genius is even capable of imagining things like infinity, collapsing space-time, or multidimensional universes is more of an unintended by-product of our curious monkey brains than anything else. Nevertheless, much of what physicists like Albert Einstein or Stephen Hawking tell us about the universe defies our ordinary intuitions.

So how then can we know ourselves as beings of energy? This is a tough question to answer. When I ask my smarty-pants colleagues over in the science buildings how they know energy, they often invoke abstract concepts, laws, or equations like $e = mc^2$. In other words, they know energy primarily through this esoteric body of knowledge known as physics. But our dependency on these equations for understanding reality raises its own question: Is energy, like math, something we have discovered or something we have invented? The answer, weirdly enough, is not clear. It may seem self-evident that energy is out there for us to discover, for it exists all around us. But we understand energy through abstract concepts and equations, which are definitely human creations. In this way, energy itself, at least as we know it, is a human invention.

With this weird thought in mind, let me offer my very quick and admittedly naive description of what energy is. Energy is the currency of reality. Beneath the surface of what we experience—matter, sound, light—lie vast, invisible fields, subtly humming with potential. Think of these fields as the quantum undercurrent that comprises the universe, where particles appear as brief sparks or waves, like ripples forming on a still pond. Every action, from flipping a light switch to singing karaoke, is energy morphing from one form to another.

While these energy fields are mainly invisible to our senses, physics gives us rudimentary tools to describe them through equations and experiments that trace these invisible ripples. The underlying nature of the universe is subtle and often counterintuitive (as quantum mechanics and relativity remind us), and we still haven't figured it all out, even as we describe its various parts.

But even this description is pretty vague, and it doesn't tell us much about our bodies as energy systems or ourselves, for that matter. If we really want to know ourselves as energy systems, we'll need to understand a strange property of energy at the core of what we are: entropy.

The Great Unraveling

When scientists began exploring the nature of energy in the nineteenth century, they stumbled upon two key facts that would forever change our understanding of the universe. The first was that energy could never be created or destroyed, only transformed. This discovery, which they grandly named the first law of thermodynamics, basically means that every time you do anything—whether it's eating a hamburger, running a marathon, or simply blinking—you're pulling energy from one source and converting it into another. Our very existence can be described as the continual transformation of energy from food and oxygen into the proteins and chemical processes that keep us alive, a constant reminder that you are literally what you eat (and drink and breathe, too). In many ways, we are just way stations for energy that is shifting from one form into another, a kind of living recycling center.

But when we're transferring energy, we are also changing its suitability for potential use. This leads to another important observation: Under normal conditions, energy is constantly degrading in form, becoming less and less available to carry out high-level functions. This is the second law of thermodynamics, something scientists call entropy. Entropy is the degradation of energy from a higher potential into a lower one.

Entropy is a difficult concept to grasp, but I like to explain it with the example of a bunch of logs stacked in a fireplace. The logs are energy storehouses carved from trees that were built upon captured energy from our sun. They are in a low state of entropy, and there are many things they could possibly do. For example, if I set them on fire, the logs will burn, releasing their stored energy through heat and light. And while we take this for granted, turning wood into light and heat is a nifty trick.

Eventually, however, the fire burns out, the temperature drops, and the light fades. What's left? A pile of ashes, some smoke, and quickly dissipating heat. All that energy, once neatly packed into the logs, is still around, but it's now so disorganized and dispersed that you couldn't make another log out of it, much less a fire. The energy endures, but it's in a degraded form, a shadow of its former self, kind of what it feels like to be in middle age.

A similar process is currently happening in our universe. The universe began in its highest form of energy capacity (or, awkwardly stated, in its lowest state of entropy). The moment immediately before the Big Bang was indeed the greatest "potential for something to happen." It was the potential for an entire universe to spring into existence.

Since then, the universe has been on a slow but steady decline, a long, drawn-out unwinding of that initial potential. It's the cosmic equivalent of going from a five-star gourmet meal to cold crumbs, a process that continues to this day. Our universe no longer has the juice to create another Big Bang, and with each passing eon, it has less and less energy to form new stars and galaxies. At some point, it'll stop making them altogether.

But this degradation isn't happening uniformly. Instead, the energy in our universe is breaking down in a somewhat clumpy way. Rather than being evenly spread out, energy is coagulating into different forms. One of the ways this clumping happens is through the formation of atoms and molecules, which then interact to create centers of gravity, radioactive waves, shifting nuclear forces, and other forms of further clumping. All the visible things in our universe (galaxies, solar systems, stars, and us) are just the "clumps." We're part of a random, uneven distribution in the unfolding energy that makes up our universe. So, in another sense, you could say we're all just a bunch of random globs of energy.

Like those burning logs, these clumps are also breaking down. Everything in the universe is headed toward the lowest potential for something to happen. Thankfully, it's taking a bit of time to get there. It's like a flowing river with all sorts of eddies, trickles, and stagnant pools that find their languorous way to a calm lake. Eventually, our reality will be mostly inert, a cold, dark, and essentially motionless place dotted with trillions of black holes. When you gaze up at the stars, you're witnessing a vast, gradual undoing.

This cosmic dissipation is reality's clock. According to physicists, entropy is one of the only things in the universe that consistently moves in a unidirectional way. Once energy becomes disorganized, it won't ever spontaneously put itself back together, something very much like a teenager's bedroom. So, in a way, entropy defines time for us. It marks the sequence of cause and effect in the universe.

Entropy is also where the self begins. We're not just beings of energy; we're beings of energy that actively resist entropy. The self is all the processes that enable this resistance to happen, and this fact distinguishes us from the nonliving parts of the universe. Planets may rotate, and stars burn bright, but neither is pushing back against the great degradation of the cosmos. We, however, are different. We are clawing back against the entropic tide, and it is this fact that ultimately defines the self.

Knowing Your Essence

When I was young, I believed that "knowing" myself meant unlocking some ultimate truth about the universe, the cosmic code behind the mysteries of existence. I think this notion came from reading a few too many pseudoscience New Age books. You know the type. Some dude, and it was always a dude, claimed he'd cracked the grand cosmic puzzle and was now "one with the universe." Usually, these self-proclaimed gurus would drape themselves in the lingo of some esoteric Hindu philosophy or an obscure pseudo-theory of physics. Naturally, being a dude myself, I believed I could achieve the same thing. All I had to do was find the truth beyond my ordinary perceptions. Maybe this insight would come from an ancient Vedic tome, a powerful meditation session, or even a great acid trip. Whatever the method, I too could understand ultimate truth and become enlightened.

I now realize this is a youthful fallacy. Our human brains just aren't wired to fully comprehend the nature of reality or even ourselves, for that matter. At our core, we are energy, and energy is really hard to understand. Most of what we "know" about energy is just a set of placeholders, concepts we've concocted to make sense of something far more complex than our minds can grasp. Whether it's chakras, harmonic vibrations, entropy, or the famous $e = mc^2$, all are constructs we've invented. They represent our best attempts to translate the staggering reality we inhabit into something our limited brains can handle. But even with all our sophisticated science and elaborate religions, these interpretations can never fully capture what's going on. They're just words and equations, and these will always be a little bit off, a glimmer of the real thing. To know energy and ourselves is always to know a human invention, not the full truth.

This idea is not mine alone. It shows up across human history. It's at the heart of Buddhism. It is found in the Tao as well. In the Western tradition, it's described in Plato's famous allegory of the cave, where he says we are like prisoners bound in a cavern who can see only shadows dancing on the wall before us. Because we know nothing else, we assume that the shadows are real. But we never see them for what they are: dim representations of a far more vivid reality that cast them, a reality that we never directly perceive.

Of course, we are not entirely in the dark, especially when it comes to science. Recent discoveries in physics offer a much brighter depiction of the energies that comprise us. With time, our understanding of these forces will deepen. But for now, we're still working with a scientific picture of our essence that's more suggestion than certainty. Science might give us a clearer image of our being than our ordinary perceptions, but it's still not entirely in focus.

So, where does that leave us in our quest for self-knowledge? For now, we'll have to work with what we've got. Hopefully, these descriptions of energy can provide a sufficient approximation of what's happening within us. And for our purposes, that should be enough. Because, unlike what I believed in my youth, transcendence doesn't require a total understanding of reality. As long as we can see well enough, we can grope our way forward.

2

Self

SOCRATES, THE ANCIENT GREEK PHILOSOPHER AND EARLY pioneer of self-knowledge, spent his days roaming the marketplace in Athens, pestering anyone who'd listen—or couldn't escape—with probing questions like: What is life's purpose? How do we find meaning? How do you know what's true? Not surprisingly, this made him less than popular among his fellow citizens, most of whom were busy doing things other than contemplating their essence. In ancient Greece, "know thyself" usually meant "know thy place," and most people didn't want to question it. Eventually, their patience with Socrates's endless questions wore thin, and in a warning to all other navel-gazing philosophers, they condemned him to death.

Yet Socrates's fate hasn't stopped his questions from resonating through the ages. They remain as vital as ever. Before we start probing into our purpose and meaning, however, I think we should start with a different question, one that Socrates probably never thought to ask: What is the difference between you and a glass of water?

At first glance, the answer is less than you might think. Your body is made up of mostly water, and it's not like the H_2O in the glass is fundamentally different than the H_2O coursing through you. A molecule is a molecule is a molecule, as Gertrude Stein might have said had she been a chemist. What's more, if you drink that glass of water, its molecules will promptly become part of you. Yet, despite this fact, we persist in believing we're something special, for unlike the inert liquid in the glass, we are alive. But what does it actually mean to be alive?

The answer is more elusive than it first seems. The line between living and nonliving is blurrier than you'd expect, and the scientists who think hard about this question are far from unanimous about where it lies. Many qualities we associate with life show up in the nonliving world. Take reproduction, for instance. We typically think of life as something that reproduces itself, yet crystals can grow and replicate their structures with an efficiency that would make rabbits blush. Or maybe life is anything with DNA, the celebrated blueprint of all living beings. But viruses also have DNA, and whether they qualify as being "alive" is still up for debate.

Ultimately, the real difference between living and nonliving things lies not in what they *are* but in what they *do*. And it all goes back to energy. The glass of water and you are both energy systems, but the glass is a closed system. It's just sitting there, inert, waiting for something external to act upon it, like a thirsty human. You, on the other hand, are an open energy system, a perpetual-motion machine of sorts, constantly regenerating yourself. Yes, both you and the water glass will eventually succumb to entropy's relentless pull, but only one of you is actively resisting that fate.

The fight against entropy is not just life's defining feature; it's also where the self begins. As we venture further into the self, we'll discover that it all revolves around a simple but profound fact: We are life forms, and life forms are distinguished from everything else by their resistance to entropy. Planets, stars, and water glasses inevitably degrade over time, yielding to the second law of thermodynamics. Life, however, doesn't go quietly into that entropic night. It fights back, constantly regenerating and reproducing itself.

The self is the expression of this fight. Everything that makes you *you*—from the microscopic cellular machinery humming away beneath your skin to the grand epiphanies that light up your mind—is an articulation of these life-sustaining systems. Your experience of self, right here and right now, is rooted in intricate processes mediating between your life force and the rest of the universe. To get a better sense of these heady notions, let us turn to the person who first came up with the best answer to the question of what it means to be alive.

The Life Force

At first glance, Erwin Schrödinger is not the kind of person whom you would think could tell you much about yourself. Born in Vienna in 1887, he is most famous for figuring out how to determine the position of an electron. This was one of the most challenging puzzles in physics, eluding even great minds like Albert Einstein and Niels Bohr. After locking himself away for several months, Schrödinger devised a solution, now called, appropriately enough, the Schrödinger equation. It's a very complicated mathematical scheme, but it basically describes the material fabric of the universe using statistical probabilities, what physicists now call a wave function. In lay terms, Schrödinger's equation gives us a way to measure reality. This work was so pathbreaking that it earned him the Nobel Prize, and it is now at the center of quantum physics.

Schrödinger's curiosity, however, wasn't limited to electrons. He also loved thinking about philosophy and nature, contemplating deeper spiritual questions, fighting against Nazism, and exploring sex with lots of women not named Mrs. Schrödinger. It was his political actions, not his sexual dalliances, that eventually forced him to flee Austria for Ireland in the mid-1930s. During this exile in Dublin, he turned his formidable mind to one of the most challenging questions of all: What is life?

Schrödinger's answer was deceptively simple, and it offers us a crucial way to know the self.* Life, he said, is an energy system that pushes back against entropy. It's an energy process that keeps itself organized even as the rest of the universe is coming undone. Life does this by taking energy in from its surroundings, which physicists call free energy, and then using this energy to sustain itself. Schrödinger called this resistance negative entropy.

---

* Schrödinger also talked about other aspects of life, like the existence of DNA, but I'm just focusing on the entropic part.

But rather than using this awkward term (or, even worse, negentropy), I like to describe the resistance to entropy with a more poetic phrase: *the life force*.

The term *life force* probably sounds familiar, if not somewhat mystical. One can find similar notions throughout human history, most notably in the Indian idea of prana and the Chinese concept of qi. The French philosopher Henri Bergson popularized his own vision of a mystical life force called the élan vitale in the early twentieth century. And, of course, there is "the Force" from the *Star Wars* movies. These ideas are not dissimilar to what I am describing, for they, too, connect life with deeper energy processes, but prana, qi, the élan vitale, and "the Force" are based on supernatural energies. They are spiritual conceptions.

My definition of a life force, however, is one based on science, the second law of thermodynamics to be precise, and it is something observable in the natural world. Following Schrödinger, when I use the term "life force," I'm referring to the ways that living creatures resist entropy. The life force is composed of three crucial elements: what I like to call food, sex, and death. Anything that is alive must do the following three things:

1. It must draw in energy (thus, consume food).
2. It must replicate itself in a way that allows for evolutionary development (this is sex).
3. It must protect itself against harm (I like to describe this as death because it's more fun to say than survival).

Nonliving things may perform one or two of these processes but don't perform all three. Stars, for example, perpetuate themselves through atomic fusion (food), but they don't reproduce (sex). Crystals may reproduce (sex), but they can't protect themselves from external threats (death). Living creatures, by contrast, are animated by all three processes of food, sex, and death. For all its mystical connotations, the life force is simply a colorful way to describe these combined processes, a swirling eddy slightly reversing the flow of the more significant entropic stream of the cosmos.

Another way to think of the life force is like a self-perpetuating fire, a phenomenon that exists through sustained, reactive chains. You can see this in your body. Every moment, innumerable chemical reactions are taking place within each of your trillions of cells. These reactions are your cellular metabolism, the living equivalent of fire. Your cells use oxygen and fuel (in our case, a molecule called adenosine triphosphate, or ATP) to keep "burning." The sense you and I have of ourselves at this moment is the by-product of this ongoing chain of chemical fires. Our life force will keep burning as long as our cells can metabolize energy, reproduce, and protect themselves from death. As living beings, we genuinely are energy systems.

The Origins of the Self

All this talk about the life force naturally leads to the big question: How did it all begin? The short answer is . . . we're not entirely sure. Although we now have some plausible scientific theories about how life started, we'll probably never know precisely what the first life form looked like. Early life was too fragile to leave a fossil record, and it likely underwent many changes before anything durable enough to fossilize came along. There probably wasn't a single moment when life began. Scientists now think that several life processes emerged independently in various places at different times; instead of using just one "spark" to light up, life probably needed many. So, barring any religious conjecture, we can't locate any particular moment of life's creation.

If we're itching to pinpoint a starting point for life as we know it, we'll have to fast-forward a few million years to a creature scientists have affectionately named LUCA, which is short for last universal common ancestor. LUCA was a microscopic, single-celled organism, a modest little bacterium that fit snugly into the backwater of a primordial ocean. But don't let its modesty fool you. LUCA was the ultimate ancestor. Biologists have identified over 350 genes that all life forms share in common. This diverse lineage includes everything from slime molds and toadstools to grand oak trees, whales, you, and me. These shared genes trace us all back to LUCA. By reverse-engineering the rates of genetic mutations, biologists estimate that LUCA lived about 3.7 billion years ago. Somewhere on that early Earth, LUCA was doing its thing, blissfully unaware that it would one day be the ancestor of every living being.

And most importantly for our purposes, *LUCA also had a self.*

Now, this idea may sound strange at first. After all, we don't usually think of microscopic bacteria as having selves in the way we think of ourselves as having selves. LUCA didn't have any thoughts or a personality. It didn't dream or reflect on the world. It wasn't even aware that it existed. To the untrained eye (albeit one with an extremely high-powered microscope), it probably looked more like a tiny balloon of chemicals than a living being.

But LUCA was alive, and it contained the rudimentary foundations of the same self-processes that exist in us today. In the past 3.7 billion years, there was never a point when creatures had no selves, and then, suddenly, bam!, selves appeared. Every living being has had some form of self, and all of their selves are elaborations on the one that first existed in LUCA. And yes, that includes us. Everything that makes you and me who we are traces back to LUCA.

Here then is the most important idea in this book: *the self is a set of processes that negotiate between our life force and reality.* It's all the ways we living creatures get food, have sex, and resist death. Or, to use another analogy, the self consists of all those routines and behaviors that keep the flame of life alight.

What's more, this self is something we share with all other living beings. In simple life forms such as bacteria, the self is mainly concerned with basic housekeeping tasks like DNA replication and metabolism, essentially the bare minimum needed to keep the life force going. In complex creatures like us, the self is expressed through more elaborate ways, such as our thoughts, behaviors, and even culture. But regardless of whether we're talking about a humble bacterium or a concert pianist, the self is constantly engaged in the same fundamental struggle: pushing back against the disorganization and chaos of the universe.

This description of the self may sound odd, for it contradicts how we commonly think of ourselves. By my definition, the self is not a thing. It's not our ego, material body, or even our self-perceptions. It's not the constant stream of thoughts and worries in our heads. It's not our various identities or even this feeling of a soul that we intuitively carry around.

These experiences are certainly parts of ourselves and play crucial roles in keeping us alive and functioning. Because they dominate our consciousness, we tend to mistake them for the whole package, assuming that these outer layers represent the entirety of who or what we are. But our thoughts, identities, and consciousness are not the self, just a part of it. They are more like the crust congealing on top of a far more dynamic, energetic maelstrom churning beneath our conscious perception. The self goes far deeper than we commonly assume.

What this also means is that our essence is something much different than what our intuitions tell us. In simple terms, we are not things; we are *processes*. A good way to see this is by considering one of philosophy's great conundrums: the Ship of Theseus paradox. The puzzle starts with a story of ancient Greece. According to legend, the Athenians wanted to memorialize their fabled hero, Theseus, by preserving the ship that brought him home from his battle with the Minotaur in Crete. So they moored his ship in the harbor, where presumably it became a popular tourist attraction.

Over the years, the ship began to rot. As its various planks, ropes, and oars fell into disrepair, the Athenians replaced them. Eventually, every part of the ship had been swapped with something new. Then, some smart-aleck philosopher named Plutarch came along and wondered: If all its parts are no longer original, how can we still call this vessel the Ship of Theseus? Enlightenment philosopher Thomas Hobbes, an even smarter aleck, further wondered what you might call a new ship that was constructed from all the original, discarded parts.*

The Ship of Theseus paradox also applies to us. We all feel we are the same person we were as children. We carry our childhood memories and a profound sense of continuity with our past. Yet nearly all our bodies' cells and parts have been replaced or rebuilt over time. If the stuff that is you is continually being swapped out, are you still the same person you were years, weeks, or even minutes ago?

---

* I'm in debt to Sean Carroll for this reference.

Let me offer a simple answer: Yes! This is because, if you consider all the ground we've covered so far, "you" were never defined by your materiality to begin with. We are not merely the stuff within our bodies. All the molecules, proteins, and amino acids that comprise us are just vehicles. The only continuity of our lives is the *process* of cellular regeneration, replication, and renewal within the boundaries we naively think of as ourselves. The true continuity of being is our life force and the self-processes that keep it burning, the ongoing flame of life's fire.

This takes us back to our quest for self-knowledge. It's common for us to think of ourselves as things. I, for one, spent much of my youth thinking that if I could just get a handle on this self, then all my problems could be solved. But I was thinking of myself as some kind of solid, unchanging entity. I now realize that was a mistake. As the revolutionary designer Buckminster Fuller observed, we are not nouns; we are verbs. There will never be a point where I can say, "Oh, I have myself figured out. Now everything will be great." Life doesn't work that way. The self is not a static object to be mastered; instead, it's a far more dynamic process that is always changing. To better understand what that process is, let us revisit the ancient Greek philosophers and answer what they considered to be life's most important question: What is my purpose?

3

Purpose

WHEN I WAS TWELVE YEARS OLD, I ABANDONED MY CATHOlic faith. At the time, I had plenty of reasons for doing this: the scandals within the Church, my family disintegrating, and God's apparent indifference to my fervent prayers for a Houston Oilers Super Bowl appearance. But ultimately, my decision boiled down to church doctrine. The whole notion that some "heavenly father" created me only to watch me suffer through life seemed implausible, if not downright sadistic. My church's God seemed less like a loving deity and more like an absentee landlord who occasionally left passive-aggressive notes on the fridge. So, one day, I just stopped believing in Him or any other god for that matter.

Leaving the Church had its perks. I could let my mind roam in new directions and no longer endure the weekly pre-Communion hunger pangs. But atheism, I quickly learned, came with a significant downside. Suddenly, my life felt like it lacked any meaningful purpose, and the looming specter of death inflicted me with a chronic terror. As if to rub salt in the wound, Kansas's hit song "Dust in the Wind" was constantly looping on the radio, taunting me with its depressing reminder of my inevitable mortality. For the next two decades, I fretted constantly about death—it was like being trapped inside a Woody Allen movie but without all the crackling one-liners.

For many people, this existential terror may sound familiar. Once you leave behind your parents' religion, the question of life's purpose can become vexing. And without the comforting certainty of church doctrine, a reliable answer can be hard to find. So where do we nonbelievers locate meaning in life?

The answers vary. Some people I know dodge the question altogether, focusing on just getting through the day and distracting themselves with their chores and smartphones. Others take a more proactive approach, deliberately creating a purpose for themselves by helping people in need, writing a novel, or running a marathon. My neighbor seems to find life's purpose in picking up all the loose garbage on our street every week, something the rest of us on the block deeply appreciate.

While all these pursuits are undoubtedly gratifying, they are not what really gives our lives their meaning. Instead, religion, helping others, and obsessive neighborhood beautification are all indirect ways of doing something that *is* our true purpose: finding an optimal way of being.

This idea is not as narcissistic or shallow as it first sounds. It actually goes back thousands of years and is found in most spiritual and philosophical traditions. A classic example comes from the ancient Greek philosopher Aristotle. With his characteristic logic, Aristotle said that if you want to know anything's purpose, you must first recognize its function. Take, for instance, a hammer. Its function is to smash things. Therefore, a hammer's purpose is to excel at smashing. The ancient Greeks were really into this idea of excellence. The purpose-driven hammer should thus be sturdy, reliable, and robust.

Aristotle believed this same principle applied to us. If we want to find our true purpose, a state the Greeks called eudaemonia, we must identify our function and strive to be excellent at it.

Now, in theory, our function is straightforward. As I already mentioned, each of us is a life form, an energy system trying to perpetuate itself across time and push back against entropy. Like all life forms, our function is to keep the fire of life burning. But mere survival isn't enough, because mere survival is not excellent. To truly fulfill our function, we need to thrive. We must keep our energy flowing brightly and steadily and help those around us do the same. In short, we need to optimize the self.

And how do we achieve this self-optimization? This is where we need to be careful. Self-optimization is a term you hear a lot today, typically from some "bros" in the tech or crypto community explaining how they enhance their three-hour regimen of cold plunges, rhythmic breathing, and circuit training with various nutritional supplements that you too can enjoy for the low price of $49.99 a month.

This, however, is not the type of self-optimization I am referring to. Instead, self-optimization goes much deeper than this. It starts with the two central operating principles of the self: *order* and *vitality*. Order refers to the information and routines we employ to resist entropy and maintain the flow of energy. Vitality represents the energy flow itself, which can vary in intensity depending on the conditions.

The optimal self finds the right configuration of order and vitality. It creates an order that is best suited for its environment. It also expresses its vitality in a regular and efficient percolation. And it strives to keep both in balance: A self with too much order is stifled and overburdened; a self with too much vitality is wasteful and incoherent. Continuing with the "life as fire" metaphor, order is like the fire crew, the team that holds the fire in one location, feeds it fuel, and keeps it from burning out of control. Vitality, by contrast, is the intensity, brightness, and heat of the flame.

Biologists have a word for this balancing act between order and vitality: homeostasis. It's the thermostat of life. Homeostasis ensures that living beings always return to their ideal energy range. For example, if you get too cold, homeostasis kicks in, and you shiver to warm up. If you're low on fuel, homeostasis makes you hungry, which causes you to seek out food. It keeps your energy in check, helping you maintain the steady rhythm of life. It is absolutely essential for a well-functioning self, for self-optimization is about keeping close to our ideal homeostatic set point.

This is all good news. Thanks to both Aristotle and modern science, we now have a clear purpose for our lives: Find and sustain the right homeostatic balance between order and vitality within ourselves!

Sounds simple enough, but here's our challenge: We are incredibly complex beings. Over billions of years, life has evolved many intricate ways of making order and expressing vitality. We humans have further complicated matters by developing elaborate languages, cultures, political systems, technologies, and economies. Balancing order and vitality as a modern human is no simple task.

If we want to optimize ourselves, we'll need to understand the various layers of self that make us who we are, because the self isn't just one process; it's many. This is an idea that's easy to overlook. It is intuitive to think of the self in the singular, a solitary being, a me. Yet this is not the self. Rather than having a single self, we are comprised of many selves, each existing in a series of concentric elaborations. Like Russian nesting dolls, we expand outward from inner, hidden layers; open one, and you'll find another inside. This experience of being that we enjoy arises from these different selves, all working simultaneously and not always in sync.

In the pages ahead, we will explore these various layers of being, but let me offer a brief, general description here. In my simple model, the self consists of five layers (or nesting dolls if you want to stick with the analogy). They build upon each other as follows, starting from the center:

1. The cellular self
2. The animal self
3. The linguistic self
4. The egoistic self
5. The transcendent self

That, in a nutshell (or a nesting doll), is you and me. However, in this model, we also see the real challenge of meeting our life's purpose. Optimizing the self means not just balancing order and vitality within each layer of your being, layers that are often invisible to us; it means balancing order and vitality *among* the different layers as well. The task of the transcendent self is getting all of these layers to act in harmony.

And this reveals a dilemma of our modern lives: Our pathway to transcendence is often unclear. Most traditional cultures use religion and custom to find balance between order and vitality. When I gave up my Catholic faith, I wasn't simply letting go of my religion; I was letting go of a primary way that I found order in a vast and chaotic universe. It was a system that my ancestors had relied on for nearly two thousand years, something that helped them know their purpose and place in the world. Giving all this up, I was relinquishing the ballast that had kept them in balance. But for me, this ballast, with all of its dogmas, strictures, and implausible assertions, seemed like an insufferable burden that was only weighing me down. So I let it go and started on a lifelong quest to find a new way of rebalancing myself at a higher elevation. While it took me several decades to realize it, this journey would eventually lead me to the innermost layer of my being, the tiniest nesting doll at the core of who I am, the cellular self.

4

Foundations

IF ANYONE SEEMS TO HAVE OPTIMIZED THEMSELVES, IT IS MY friend Julie. Professionally, she is a dynamo. She was her high school valedictorian, got a PhD from MIT, and founded a thriving consulting firm. Personally, she does even better. Julie has a loving marriage, two wonderful children, and a wide circle of devoted friends. In her spare time, she teaches yoga, volunteers at her church, and belts out karaoke classics like she was born to headline at the Apollo. Julie is also soulful, funny, and courageous. She's that rare person who truly makes the world brighter just by being in it.

And yet, for all her brilliance, Julie has a monumental challenge, or as I sadly now say, had. When I met her, Julie was battling stage 4 ovarian cancer, and in December 2022, she passed away. Even now, writing this sentence years later, I feel a painful grief at her loss.

In Julie's life and death, however, we can also find a deeper truth: The self is far more than we commonly perceive. We tend to equate the self with the visible and tangible aspects of our being. We typically know ourselves through our achievements, relationships, failures, and so on. This view comes with the comforting illusion of control. If things aren't going as we want, then it's because *we* are failing, as though the self is limited to what we can see and consciously shape.

But Julie shows how this is not entirely true. For all her wisdom and vitality, she faced a challenge no amount of discipline or grace could overcome. Her fatality did not come from the outside; it came from within. Cancer was a hidden but inescapably natural part of her self.

Julie's story also highlights a profound fact: We are not simply the person we see in the mirror or usually perceive in our minds. In reality, we are something far more complex. We've already seen a little of this from physics, which describes us as an energy system. But biology has some secrets to reveal about us as well. From a biological perspective, we are collections of cells, the fundamental units of life. Trillions of these microscopic entities work ceaselessly to keep us alive, doing what living things have done since the dawn of life—resisting entropy and maintaining the precarious balance of order and vitality. When that balance falters, as it did in Julie's case, everything else unravels. And this has an important lesson for us: If we want to optimize ourselves, we need to start with the deepest layer of our being, the cellular self.

The Life of the Party

Cells were first discovered in 1665 by the English scientist Robert Hooke. A polymath, architect, engineer, and all-around genius, Hooke was fascinated with seemingly everything in the natural world. His pathbreaking research straddled topics ranging from the nature of light to how memory works. He was also, by most accounts, brooding, spiteful, and egotistical. He greedily claimed credit for nearly every scientific advance of his day, including Isaac Newton's theory of gravity. Legend has it that Newton hated Hooke so much that he conveniently "lost" Hooke's portrait at the Royal Society, an act that was the eighteenth-century version of cancel culture.

Yet, for all his failings, Hooke was a brilliant researcher and inventor. He crafted one of the first working microscopes, and with this wonderful device, he began peering into the composition of all kinds of things. While examining a sliver of cork, he noticed it was made up of numerous boxlike structures. He named these little boxes "cells," which was derived from the Latin term *cella*, a word that translates as "small room" and is the origin of the English term *cellar*. Soon, researchers began seeing cells everywhere, from sections of skin to drops of pond water, and by the 1830s, it became clear that cells were the fundamental units of life, what biologists now call cell theory.

But it turns out Hooke's term, *cell*, was not very apt. If Hooke had either a better microscope or perhaps a more agreeable personality, he might have come up with a different descriptor. Peer inside a living cell and you will not see an empty chamber sparsely populated by a few pieces of furniture; instead, you'll find something more like a crowded, raucous party.

Like any good party, cells are demarcated by a boundary enclosing all the fun—in this case, a semipermeable lipid membrane. This membrane acts like a bouncer's velvet rope, letting only desirable guests in and keeping undesirable ones out. Inside the cell, floating about in a gelatinous cytosol fluid, are a myriad of different chemical elements called organelles (so it's really more like a pool party). These organelles, like any party guests, are busy interacting with each other, transferring energy, and expelling waste.

The host of the cellular party is DNA. It orchestrates the creation of the cell's many structures. It determines the party's size, shape, and raucousness. It also needs to keep the party going, and it does this by replicating itself, a process biologists call mitosis. Or, to further abuse my analogy, it's as if the hosts of every party regularly decide that it's time to break off into two identical parties to keep the fun alive.

Now, occasionally, there are errors in the copying process based on random mutations that can occur along the strings of DNA. Usually, these mutations have no effect. Sometimes, however, they lead to a catastrophic system failure (a terrible party). And sometimes, they produce new structures that benefit the cell and make it thrive (an even better party). This pattern of genetic replication and random mutation is the driving force of evolution and a central part of your life force.

DNA is the instruction manual for creating all living things, the foundational way the self creates order. And what a manual it is. Your DNA comprises two tightly spiraled strands of over three *billion* molecules. These molecules combine into sequences called genes, like letters coming together to form words and sentences. These genes are then translated by ribonucleic acid (RNA) to create the proteins that comprise your living tissue.

Woven into this tiny structure of DNA is an enormous amount of information. If you unraveled a single DNA strand, it would measure over six feet long and contain as much information as all the books in an average neighborhood public library. And if you unraveled all of the trillions of DNA strands in your body and wove them together into a single, microscopic thread, it would circle the Earth many times over. In everything from its elegant double-helix structure to its incredible programming power, DNA is truly a marvel of nature.

Small wonder, then, that it has acquired such a mystique since it was discovered in the 1950s. Because a person's DNA is unique, we often identify it as intrinsic to ourselves. And this is understandable, for if there is any physical part of my body that has a claim to be "me," it's probably my DNA. Not only is it responsible for creating my body, it determines everything from my eye color to whether or not I enjoy cilantro. Ever since scientists figured out how to sequence it, DNA's descriptive power has only grown. Companies like Ancestry.com and 23andMe now use our DNA to trace our "life story" and tell us all kinds of distinctive things about ourselves. Given all of this, it is deeply seductive to believe that somewhere, locked within DNA's intricate double helixes, are the secrets of our very being.

Equating your essence with your DNA, however, would be a mistake. Although your particular DNA coded for the individual that became you, there is nothing exceptional about your DNA compared to the DNA of anyone else or any other animal. Not only do you share about 99.9 percent of your DNA with the rest of humanity, but you also share about 70 percent with tapeworms.

Your DNA is an array of at least twenty thousand genes or possibly much more. This embarrassing ambiguity arises because a lot of your genes are noncoding ones, and their function is unclear. Yet, regardless of their number, the genes in your DNA are not permanent partners; rather, they are a somewhat arbitrary and temporary collection of coding routines. Although your cells use the information in your DNA to make your body, the genes that have created you are not inviolable nor fixed as a set. Some genes only get activated if triggered by something in your environment, and some only express themselves in combinations with other genes. Genetic science is very complicated, and much of it still remains a mystery.

What's more, your genes have no plans to stay together after you are gone. If you have a child, you'll only give them half of your genes. If you have another child, you'll pass on a different set. Your DNA (and your life, it turns out) is just a way station for a chance mélange of genes floating about the larger biome. These genes don't identify as a collective entity and are indifferent to whether their fellow genes within your DNA are passed on to future generations. You are simply a vehicle that will possibly allow some of these genes to replicate. In other words, just as a chicken is an egg's way of making another egg, so we too are our genes' way of making another set of genes.*

This takes us back to the most important fact about cells—their primary purpose is to sustain the *process* of life. Their individual parts are merely vehicles. DNA, for instance, has no life force by itself. If you take it out of a cell, it would be a bunch of inert molecules (or something to be left as incriminating evidence at a crime scene). This fact also holds true for all the other parts of your cells: Nothing within your cells can live alone. Life only occurs when the cell's elements begin *acting in concert* in a fantastic cacophony of chemical reactions. Going back to the party analogy, a great party isn't made by simply having a hot DJ, a yummy buffet table, or any particular guest, even if they claim to be the "life" of the party. A great party occurs when these elements interact together, creating something effervescent. This is the essence of your cellular self.

Cellular Thriving

But what, then, does all of this mean for optimizing ourselves? At first glance, it's not exactly clear. "Keep your cells in homeostatic balance" is not a very inspiring motto for living. It's not nearly as appealing as

* This phrase was first popularized by the nineteenth-century writer Samuel Butler and then reinterpreted in genetic terms by the biologist Richard Dawkins.

"do what you love" or "follow your bliss." As pearls of wisdom go, it's clearly at the back of the string.

Moreover, it's not self-evident how we can make our cells work better. We can't feel them or see them with the naked eye. If we didn't have microscopes, we wouldn't even know they exist. Our cells are also autonomous. They mindlessly follow the dictates of their genetic code regardless of what we want them to do. Usually the only time we notice them is when they malfunction. However, that doesn't mean we are helpless. If we look more closely at how our cells thrive and break down, we can find some important clues about how we can optimize ourselves.

For most of human history, the biggest challenges for keeping your cells healthy were getting food, finding shelter, and avoiding death. Like all other life forms, our ancestors' first purpose was merely to stay alive. They accomplished this task by foraging for produce, scavenging from carcasses, and hunting almost anything that moved. They lived in small bands and tended to be widely dispersed. And they seemed pretty healthy. Your average Paleolithic forager had a nutritious diet and was physically robust even if their life span was much shorter and far less comfortable than ours. Infectious diseases and cancers were probably rare. From the fossil record, it looks like the most significant danger was, far and away, violence from other people.

Around ten thousand years ago, however, this began to change. The advent of agriculture, trade, and urbanization fundamentally altered how we live. This proved to be a mixed blessing. On the one hand, civilization greatly expanded our physical capacities and allowed us to dominate the planet. We could now build fantastic pyramids, temples, and cathedrals. We created art, dramas, and poetry. We discovered great medicines and how to make ice cream. On the other hand, it also paved the way for the proliferation of all kinds of nasty toxins, viruses, and bacteria. Infectious diseases soon became the primary cause of death for most people living in large towns and cities. The story of human civilization could just as easily be told as a tale of disease and pestilence as it is of great monuments and culture.

And this has only gotten worse over time. Consider the effects of industrialization. From pesticides to plastics, many of our most significant innovations over the past two centuries are extremely harmful to our bodies. We now live in an era where one of our biggest challenges is protecting our cells from ourselves.

Yet, thanks to a host of scientific discoveries, we now have some better ideas about how to do this. When biologists began deciphering the chemical properties of cells in the 1930s, they figured out what all the various molecules in our bodies were up to. They began to see how metabolism works, how cells reproduce, and what contributes to aging and diseases like cancer. And, across all of these different studies, one villain kept popping up again and again: free radicals.

Free radicals are molecules that carry around an extra, unpaired electron in their outer shell. They come in many varieties and affect us in different ways, but they all share a joint mission: They will always try to steal the electrons of other molecules to balance themselves. In doing this, they can cause severe damage to your cells. Going back to the party analogy, free radicals are like the drunken, obnoxious lech who tries to hit on everyone else's girlfriends, leading to fights and general mayhem. Left unchecked, free radicals can accelerate aging, wreck DNA, and cause a wide range of diseases. In the cellular festival of life, they are the ultimate party crashers.

The problem with free radicals isn't simply that they exist; free radicals are naturally abundant in your body and are a by-product of normal metabolism. The problem is when your body gets too many of them. A prime example of this is cancer. Cancer occurs from mutations in DNA that lead a cell to grow and reproduce uncontrollably. By "selfishly" taking too much of your body's energy, cancer cells can end up destroying you. And cancer is often caused by having too many free radicals in your system.

Your cells, however, have a natural defense: antioxidants. Antioxidants are molecules with a distinctive property; they can easily give up an extra electron without becoming unstable. This means they cancel out the harmful effects of free radicals. If free radicals are the villains of our cellular drama, antioxidants are the heroes that come to our rescue. Antioxidants come in a wide variety of forms, and they are common in many vitamins, minerals, and organic compounds. Anything healthy for you to eat, like organic fruits and vegetables, has lots of antioxidants.

And here is where we see the possibility of doing something to optimize our cellular self (and create some fantastic multilevel marketing opportunities along the way). After all, if we want to protect our cells from the ravages of modern toxins and disease, then it only seems logical that we should consume lots of antioxidants. And what better way than through some green superfood powder made from a patented blend of algae, ashwagandha, and ten other obscure ingredients? Thus it's no coincidence that self-optimization and nutritional supplements always seem to show up in the same places, for the two seem to go hand in hand.

Unfortunately, there's a hitch to this simple plan: We don't know precisely how antioxidants work. In the past thirty years, there have been a lot of scientific studies on the benefits of health supplements, and almost all of these have come up with null results. Some supplements, if taken in large doses, can even be harmful. Ironically, if you consume too many antioxidants, you may reduce your body's natural defenses that come from having a base level of free radicals. What's more, the benefits of antioxidants may not come from individual compounds like vitamin C but from combinations of different compounds working together. The truth is, we don't really know.

All we can say for sure is that no magic pill can protect our cells against the toxic hazards of modernity. Nor is there any evidence that taking large amounts of vitamin C will keep you from getting a cold or cure any disease. Maybe, at some point, we will develop effective gene therapies that will eliminate disease and forestall aging. It seems like we're on the precipice of such technologies, but then again, it also seems that we've been on this cusp for decades, so who knows?

In the meantime, if you want to optimize your cellular self, there is a much more straightforward path, and it's probably advice that you already know:

1. Eat a modest diet of fruits, vegetables, and whole grains.
2. Avoid refined carbohydrates, saturated fats, red meats, and processed foods.
3. Don't smoke, abuse drugs, or overconsume alcohol.
4. Exercise regularly.

5. Get plenty of sleep.
6. Maintain regular social contact with people you love.

Here, the scientific evidence is abundantly clear: People who follow these guidelines live longer, look younger, and have less disease than people who don't. So, hooray! We now have our first, clear purpose in life—if we want to optimize ourselves, we need to adopt a healthy lifestyle. Self-optimization starts with taking care of the basics.

Unfortunately, this commonsensical advice is often hard to follow. Nearly everyone I know struggles to eat right, exercise regularly, and get enough sleep, and this includes myself. I know the things I'm supposed to be doing to make myself healthy, but I usually find it hard to do them. And I'm lucky. I don't live in poverty, I'm not commonly subject to discrimination, and I enjoy a lot of physical security. Most people in the world don't even have these basic freedoms. So, going back to Aristotle, our life's circumstances often make our life's purpose a little more complicated. If our first purpose is to live a healthy lifestyle, our second purpose is to figure out how to follow the first one.

5

Evolution

ONE OF MY FAVORITE PLACES IN THE WORLD IS THE REMOTE Escalante canyonlands of southern Utah. Escalante is a place where time itself seems to stretch and shift, measured not in hours or days but in eons. Its massive plateaus are etched with winding slot canyons that expose the Earth's geological strata like the pages of an ancient book. At night, the sky erupts with the dazzling glow of the Milky Way. The total effect is both humbling and awe-inspiring. Sitting around the campfire in this special place, the same question inevitably pops into my head: "Why am I here?"

For most of human history, this question had a simple, reassuring answer: *I am here because the gods made me*. Our ancestors, also gathered around their own campfires and staring up at the same stars, wove intricate stories about their origins. These myths didn't just satisfy their curiosity; they provided a roadmap for existence, offering explanations for their place in the cosmos and a guide for how to live. Nestled in the comforting certainty of these tales, they were free to focus on all the rituals and rites they believed they needed to keep their creators happy. And this is how it has been for most of human history.

Today, however, things are different. The warm glow of our ancestors' mythic campfire stories has been replaced by the cold, fluorescent light of scientific inquiry. Over the past few centuries, science has unraveled the intricate threads of those ancient tales, replacing them, strand by strand, with evidence-based facts. While this shift has brought countless technological advancements, it also leaves us with a problem: The modern scientific origin story undermines the very question that motivates it.

Consider a brief synopsis. About 13.8 billion years ago, the universe sprang into existence in a moment we call the Big Bang. Over time, matter coalesced into stars, galaxies, and solar systems. About nine billion years later, the Earth formed, and soon after came life. LUCA, the last universal common ancestor, set off the evolutionary journey that, billions of years and countless twists of fate later, gave rise to you and me. Or at least this is how most people understand the scientific story of why we are here.

But this is not what the science really says. If you look at how evolution occurs, you'll see that we are neither the culmination of some grand life process nor even really distinct from this life process at all. We are not singular entities so much as accidental collections of parts, tangled participants in the broader tapestry of life. The boundaries between each of us and the rest of life are fuzzy, and there is not so much of a "me" as a "we" that asks questions about its origins. In other words, if I ask modern science, "Why am I here?" it will tell me that there's not really an "I" that exists in the first place but something more like a spark in a greater fire. This shift in perspective—seeing ourselves not as separate individuals but as interconnected participants in life's grand experiment—is the key to understanding not only where we come from but also what we truly are.

Reconsidering Our Origins

In the middle of the 1800s, the dominant origin story of European society was one that is still widely accepted today: We are here because God intentionally created us to rule over all other living things and celebrate His glory. For most Europeans, this wasn't just a bedtime story; it was the bedrock of their worldview. It not only told them why they existed, it validated their feelings that they were at the center of the universe and superior to all other life forms. Anyone who challenged this story was harshly criticized and ridiculed, if not tarred and feathered, or worse. Then, along came a mild-mannered scientist who upended it all.

Charles Darwin was an improbable revolutionary. The son of a prosperous doctor, he was a rather shy yet respectable member of England's polite middle class, a proper gentleman as it were. But beneath this genteel exterior, Darwin harbored an obsessive passion for the natural world. Bubbling within him was an insatiable curiosity about everything from rock formations to beetles, which he collected with an odd enthusiasm. Finishing college and uncertain of what to do with his life, Darwin secured a spot on the HMS *Beagle*, a royal sloop tasked with charting the South American coastline. Officially, Darwin came on as a gentlemanly dining companion for the ship's captain. In reality, it was a golden opportunity for him to explore the tropics and catalog their many wonders. He was in gentleman-nerd heaven.

And this is where things got a bit complicated. During his travels, Darwin observed many natural phenomena that didn't quite align with the biblical tales he'd been raised on. He found fossils of marine life perched improbably high in the Andes Mountains, discovered the fossilized bones of extinct mega-mammals, and noticed curious patterns in the distribution of bird and turtle species. For Darwin, these observations didn't fit neatly with the biblical narrative of creation. Something else was clearly at play.

When he returned home, Darwin busied himself by writing respectable books on geology, ocean atolls, and barnacles—actually, several books on barnacles, if you can believe it. But the idea of evolution gnawed at him, preoccupying him in a way that was both intriguing and terrifying. Eventually, he formulated a theory of evolution by natural selection. Then, gripped by a fear of what havoc this idea might unleash on his otherwise quiet life, he tucked the manuscript away in a desk drawer, where it languished for the next fifteen years. It was only when a fellow scientist, Alfred Russel Wallace, approached Darwin with his own identical theory of evolution that Darwin felt compelled to release the book we now know as *On the Origin of Species*.

Most of us have a basic grasp of Darwin's theory of evolution, and usually, it goes like this: Life began with a humble little one-celled creature. Over time, some of its descendants decided to up their game; one sprouted a body, and another developed fins and gills. Before you knew it, some adventurous amphibian crawled out of the primordial soup onto land. This pioneer eventually morphed into a lizard, which evolved into a mammal, shed its fur, started walking upright, and, voilà!, became us, the pinnacle of evolution, complete with mom jeans and midlife crises.

This is the version of evolution you often see on posters, bumper stickers, and *New Yorker* cartoons. It's a story of progress, where each stage is an upgrade from the last, kind of like the iPhone of life. It's a tale where each creature is a distinct entity, evolving into another, culminating in the ultimate life form: humans. Since we're the authors of this story, it's no surprise that we cast ourselves in the leading role, with all other creatures playing their supporting parts. But this isn't how evolution works. In fact, this version is misleading in almost every regard.

To understand evolution, we need to revisit the life force. Remember, life's only purpose is to resist entropy; essentially, to keep the party going as long as possible. Life does this primarily by replicating its genes, those microscopic segments of DNA that organize living tissue into various parts. Like nearly all forms of transmission, genetic replication inevitably produces some errors in the copying process. If a random genetic typo results in a trait that helps the life force keep going (or at least doesn't hamper it), that genetic quirk sticks around; if not, it gets tossed into the wastebasket of history. It's a system that is cold, relentless, and indifferent to whatever the genes are actually coding for in the wider world. This, in brief, is the modern version of Darwinian evolution.

It also means that life has no grand plan, no master blueprint. If we map out life's history, we see growth and innovation, but we also see dead ends, U-turns, and a whole lot of trial and error. Life's evolutionary journey isn't a straight line; it's more like a twisted, knotty tree with innumerable branches. We're just one little leaf, not the final, definitive flower. And more importantly, the story of evolution isn't a neat progression from one creature to another. Instead, it's the messy tale of many creatures, often merging and mingling, occasionally creating something new, but all expressions of the same underlying life force.

It all starts with microbes. For about three billion years after LUCA came into existence, life on Earth was a microbial monopoly. These tiny, one-celled creatures may have been small, but they were the ultimate survivors, outlasting numerous global catastrophes, ice ages, and even the odd asteroid. For most of Earth's history, they were the only living game in town, and even today, they're still going strong. Microbes make up more biomass than all the other creatures on Earth combined. Sure, our world has impressive whales, elephants, and redwood trees, but, at its core, Earth is still a predominantly microbial planet.

But it's not an entirely microbial one, and this is due to a separate domain of life, the eukaryotes, the forerunners of all later animals, plants, and fungi. For their first two billion years, our eukaryote ancestors were also pretty straightforward in form, primarily microscopic one-cell creatures. Think of an individual slime mold, and you'll get a picture of what our early eukaryote forerunners looked like. However, they also had some essential differences that distinguished them from their bacterial cousins.

One of these was mitochondria, which are essential for understanding a hidden secret about the self. At first glance, mitochondria may not seem that special, just another little organelle within our cells. But mitochondria are notable because of one incredible fact: They have their own DNA. This is worth reflecting on for a moment. Within each of your cells are many little creatures with entirely different genes than the ones that program you.

The best theory for this curious situation was championed in the 1960s by the biologist Lynn Margulis. She hypothesized that one of our earliest eukaryote ancestors ingested an ancient bacterium, and rather than destroying it, the two creatures developed a symbiotic relationship: The host cell protected the mitochondria while the mitochondria helped the host process energy.

This is an odd-sounding hypothesis, but it has a profound implication: You and I are not a single species; we are not even two different species. Instead, we are composed of two entirely different *domains* of life! At the cellular level, we are an amalgamation of two distinct life forms.

And our biological entanglements don't stop there. We are also deeply interconnected with other species. Consider your microbiome, the teeming zoo of microbes that call your body home. Right now, your body is hosting over a trillion different creatures. This microscopic menagerie includes over a thousand species of bacteria, protozoa, and fungi, all of which are swarming on your skin, in your hair, and especially in your gut. These little guys help you digest food, fight off infections, and produce essential vitamins. And they can make up to five pounds of your body's weight.

Much of what you intuitively perceive as you, in fact, is not really "you" at all but a lot of tiny creatures that are feeding off of you and rendering some valuable services in return. But in a way, these creatures are "you," because you could not live very well without them. In other words, our DNA is only partly responsible for making us what we are. Numerous other species have a hand in it (or actually not a hand, since they don't have hands, but you get my point).

And this takes us back to our common misperceptions about evolution. It's easy to think that all creatures are standalone entities, with more complex animals being "better" than simpler ones. There is a part of me that stubbornly believes I'm superior to a frog, which is, in turn, superior to a bread mold. I think I got this notion from those early depictions of the tree of life, where humans were placed at the very top (or even worse, the depictions of the evolution of man, which always seem to culminate in an upright-walking white guy).

But this is a vain conceit. In reality, nature doesn't care about our sense of superiority. Life isn't a race to the top; it's a chaotic free-for-all with no clear finish line. The story of life is just as much about frogs and bread molds as it is about us. We're not the inevitable stars of the show. We're just minor actors in a very long, weird play.

This realization is why Darwin kept his theory of evolution a secret for so long. Most origin stories cast humans as the grand finale of divine creation, the pièce de résistance of God's handiwork. My Catholic upbringing, for instance, said that God created humans as something special, the only beings that he expected sacrifices and prayers from. Not only that, God kept meticulous tabs on my actions, like an obsessive cosmic accountant. Therefore it was natural for me to believe that if I took up so much of God's attention, I must be an important creature.

Darwin's theory of evolution, however, abruptly derails this ego trip. It reveals that our entire existence is nothing more than an accident, a genetic roll of the dice. It demolishes our sense of biological and cosmological superiority. This also makes evolutionary theory one of the most provocative ideas of all time, for it toppled us from our self-constructed perch on the pinnacle of life. And, in a more subtle way, it upends the very idea of an "I" at the center of it all.

A Greater Self

Before I was married, I would occasionally venture deep into the wilderness for solo backpacking trips. Camping alone in the wild is an odd cocktail of serenity and terror. One feels more connected to nature but also like a mouse in a room full of cats. Every rustle of leaves and snap of twigs is a vivid, high-definition experience, and your adrenaline surges as if you're in the world's longest horror movie. For me, the tension always ramped up at night. Lying in my tent, bombarded by the nocturnal cacophony, my mind would craft increasingly elaborate fantasies involving hungry bears, prowling cougars, and the occasional axe-wielding maniac. It was usually hard to fall asleep.

One night, however, I decided to take a different approach. Instead of treating every rustle and chirp as a prelude to my untimely demise, I interpreted them as friendly greetings. I imagined all the night creatures were saying, "Hello, Eric!" in their own way. And wouldn't you know it, everything changed. Suddenly, I wasn't a lone camper about to be mauled by a bear; I was the guest of honor at nature's midnight soiree. The nocturnal sounds, which had once set my nerves on edge, now felt like a soothing lullaby. I drifted off to sleep, cradled by the chorus of the wilderness, feeling more at peace than I had in years.

This experience led to a revelation. I am not simply an isolated, fragile being clinging to a solitary existence; instead, I'm part of a much larger life force. Every living thing flows from a single source, a common ancestor. Over billions of years, LUCA's descendants, through a series of genetic mutations and evolutionary experiments, have formed into all the plants, fungi, microbes, and animals we see today. But underneath this staggering diversity lies a simple truth: We're all just different expressions of the same, original life force. Yes, we are all unique, but we are part of the same ongoing process of life as well.

While this might sound wonderfully poetic and vaguely mystical, it's also a bit of a mixed bag. On the plus side, it means you're never truly alone. You're not only carrying lots of different life forms within you, you're also part of a cosmic family that includes everything from the towering redwoods to the humble housefly. Every living being you encounter is a distant cousin, a fellow traveler on this haphazard ride called life. If you're ever feeling lonely, there's no need to look to distant gods or mystical heavens for connection. The life force surrounds and penetrates us; we just need to open our perceptions to it.

But this interconnectedness also means that you and I don't matter all that much in the grand scheme of things. And that's a bit of a gut punch. Just as no single leaf is essential to a tree's survival, your particular existence isn't all that crucial to life as a whole. Life is remarkably redundant and resilient. Even if humanity decides to self-destruct through some cataclysmic doomsday event, microbial life will likely shrug and keep on thriving.

Moreover, the rest of life is as indifferent to us as we are to it. While I might have fancied that the nocturnal creatures in the wilderness were extending a warm welcome, in reality, they couldn't have cared less. Given the chance, many would gladly have made a meal out of me. Life, it turns out, is an endless buffet, and sometimes you're the entrée. Once we strip away all our myths, aspirations, and inflated egos, we're just another tiny flicker in life's ongoing fire, doing our part to keep it burning until we're eventually recycled as nutrients for the next round of combustion. There's nothing particularly sacred or special about us.

This final realization isn't exactly a feel-good story. It's like reading about the end of the universe, it's bleak. Nobody wants to hear that they don't matter or, worse, that they exist only to propagate some mindless gene sequences. I know I don't. But facing this grim truth, perhaps I should be asking another question: Why am I so obsessed with my importance in the first place? Where does this feeling of "I" even come from? To answer these questions, we'll need to look a little more closely at the evolution of animal life.

6

Animal

ASIDE FROM ESCALANTE, ONE OF MY OTHER FAVORITE places is the Hall of Antiquities within New York's Metropolitan Museum of Art. Its light-filled rooms overflow with priceless statues from ancient Greece and Rome. Most of these depict spectacular images of heroic figures, often with perfect proportions and rippling muscles, mighty in their physicality, the embodiment of the optimized self. But wandering among these stony incarnations of Hercules, Pericles, and Achilles, I can't help but notice one glaring fact—they all have tiny penises. Here are these guys, all chiseled like Greek gods, but each is packing something that makes you wonder if they just stepped out of a frigid Aegean Sea.

These diminutive phalluses are not a reflection of Greek prudery. Greek myths are filled with lurid stories of fantastic debauchery, and Greek pottery is often painted with pornographic scenes in which the men are impressively endowed. Nor are tiny penises even a convention of Greek sculpture; the statues of their mythical satyrs, for example, are always crafted with massive erections, and this porn-star potency is also why you don't usually see satyrs in the family-friendly parts of the Met.

Instead, the tiny penises are a deliberate artistic choice. The Greek sculptors wanted to depict civilized man, even the strongest among them, as mighty in his rationality, someone in full command of himself.

So, despite his outsized physical prowess, the typical hero has a penis that looks like it's still waiting for puberty. For the ancient Greeks, the animal self was something to be kept on a very short leash.

And this is how it has been across most of Western history ever since. From the early days of antiquity through the rise of Christianity, Europeans have been highly conflicted about their animal natures. They believed they were distinguished from the beasts by their rational minds and pristine souls, making them unique among God's creation. By contrast, their animal parts were base, foul, and impulsive. From this point of view, the animal self is the wellspring of our sinful natures, our grossest impulses, and our darkest desires. Whenever we do something wrong, it is the animal parts of ourselves that inevitably come to blame.

I know this is how I used to feel about myself. I was brought up with some ardent shame about my bodily functions. My family, teachers, and seemingly every adult I knew told me, either explicitly or implicitly, that I would need to control my impulses if I wanted to be a good person. Whenever I overate or masturbated or lazed about all day, I inevitably felt remorse and shame. And most people I knew felt the same way.

This, however, is a woeful mischaracterization. If you step back and view your animal self through the grand lens of evolution, you'll see that you are far more nuanced than a slovenly creature preoccupied solely with fornication, defecation, and gluttony. Our animal self is something far more extraordinary. It's at the foundation of consciousness and our experience of self. It is the source of our thinking, the part of us that maps out reality and predicts what's coming next. It's also the source of our most elevated behaviors, enabling our most sublime feelings of love, generosity, and compassion. Our animal self is the source of this feeling of "I" that each of us carries around.

If we want to know ourselves, we'll need to know our animal selves. Sounds logical, but this also comes with a big challenge: Our animal self is mind-bogglingly complex. It is the product of eons of evolution and innumerable biological parts. Describing the animal self could take volumes. So, to keep things manageable, I'm going to stick to a simple path. Instead of leading us on a grand excursion into our animal past,

I'm going to focus on four critical points of interest that are most relevant to knowing our selves. Although this won't describe every aspect of your animal self, hopefully, it will give you a better sense of where this feeling of "I" comes from, at least more than you'll find by wandering among the ancient Greek statues in the Met.

Coherence

It's your child's first band concert. You're begrudgingly sitting there, trying to smile encouragingly as you listen to what can only be described as an enthusiastic interpretation of what music might sound like if played by cats in heat. And, in this screeching moment, a crucial fact reveals itself: The most essential part of any musical group performance isn't just hitting the notes; it's getting everyone to hit the right notes at the right time together. Even if your child is the little Marsalis in the trumpet section, it won't help if you can't hear her above the din. In any group performance, coherence is everything.

A similar rule applies to ourselves. If any part of our biological orchestra starts playing out of tune, we begin to fall apart. This, however, raises an intriguing question: What keeps our biological orchestra playing in harmony? In other words, if I'm made up of trillions of individual cells, what transforms this biological rabble into a coherent experience of "I"?

The answer, surprisingly enough, can be found in how we eat. Stick with me on this one. The major kingdoms of multicellular life (plants, fungi, and animals) are distinguished by how they obtain the energy they need to survive. Plants, for example, get their energy from sunlight; they're basically nature's solar panels. And this has some interesting implications for them. Because sunlight is everywhere, plants don't need to move around to get energy. Most plants don't even have a fixed body plan; they grow toward the light, a slow-motion stretch that lasts a lifetime. Animals, on the other hand, are more like energy scavengers. We get our fuel by ingesting other living things, which puts us on a different evolutionary path.

To see how this started, let's go back to the first multicellular animals that appeared around 600 million years ago. These creatures likely resembled tiny sponges, simple beings with no bones, muscles, or skin. They were the couch potatoes of early life, staying put, waiting to suck up any food that drifted by, and living a very laid-back existence. And sponges don't have a single self, at least not in the way we think of a self. Sponges are more like a loose collective, a commune of cells that hang out together because it's convenient, much like a bunch of kids who grow up together on the same street. For example, you can put a sponge through a sieve, and its cells will reassemble into smaller, perfectly functional sponges. Despite its singular reference, a sponge doesn't have any sense of being an "I."

But these sponge ancestors also faced a problem: If the plankton they survived on moved just a few inches away, they would starve. If they wanted to be more adaptive, they would need to figure out how to move.

Enter the jellyfish, our earliest mobile ancestor. Jellyfish are different from sponges, not simply because they move around but because they have specialized cells and body parts dedicated to helping with this movement. One of the most important of these new cells was a neuron, a specific type of cell that allows animals to coordinate their movements and sense the world. But neurons didn't just help jellyfish move about; they also did something far more important—they started knitting together a rudimentary sense of self.

The evolution of jellyfish was a decisive moment in the history of life. No other creatures have a self quite like we descendants of jellyfish. For example, you can cut off part of a sponge or a plant, and it'll keep on living, but try that with a jellyfish, and you're left with a sad blob of jelly.* And this goes for us as well. Our cells have sharp divisions of labor. We are *intra*-dependent beings. In other words, you can't create a copy of somebody by grafting their arm onto another person. Because our cells are so specialized, they have to work together as a whole if we are to survive.

This is where coherence comes in. Coherence is how we animals

* Sponges and many plants can regenerate or propagate from fragments because their cells are totipotent (capable of differentiating into any cell type).

turn our vast collection of specialized cells into a unified, functioning whole. It makes you more than just a sack of cells; it makes you an "I" from a "we." But it's important to remember that coherence doesn't simply happen. It results from cellular collaboration, a collective effort that started with a jellyfish ancestor and continues in you today. That feeling of self you enjoy is the orchestra of your cells playing in harmony, a melody that has been in the works for eons. And, like any good symphony, it's the result of a lot of practice, evolution's way of fine-tuning the multicellular self into a singular whole.

Tempo

When I was isolated during the COVID-19 pandemic, I started learning the piano. As I began to plunk out a few songs, Thea noticed that I seemed to be performing a lot of sad ones. She started to worry that I was depressed, or at least it was depressing for her to hear me play piano so badly. I reassured her that I wasn't consciously selecting melancholy pieces; I was playing slowly because it was easier. The strange thing about music is that even a cheerful melody can sound like a funeral dirge if played at a snail's pace. In music, as in life, tempo makes a difference.

The same principle applies to ourselves. Like a song, our animal self moves through time, guided by a rhythm set by millions of years of evolution. And it all started with one of our earliest animal ancestors: worms. At some point long ago, some jellyfish evolved fully enclosed bodies and became worms. This allowed them to do marvelous things like burrow into the protective depths of the seabed. But an enclosed body also posed a new challenge: How could they get nutrients to their interior cells?

Evolution's answer was a circulatory system. Mouths and guts, hearts and lungs, blood flow and breath—all these life-sustaining features trace back to the innovations of our great-great-great-grandworms.

These evolutionary upgrades, however, did more than improve their survival chances; they also anchored these worms in time. It all began with the rhythm of breath and heartbeat. The emergence of a circulatory system meant that animal life was no longer dictated by random chance but was instead governed by a steady rhythm. This pulse marked each moment of existence. Consider yourself for a moment. What do you hear if you sit quietly and listen to your body? The constant thrum of your heartbeat and your breath's gentle ebb and flow. Like an orchestra with a conductor, the self is ordered to a pulmonary beat.

But that's not the only rhythm we follow. The animal self also follows the cadence of hormonal cycles. And most animals have daily routines—feeding, resting, and so on—tied to the Earth's rotation. This circadian rhythm is why we get hungry at noon and sleepy at midnight. In this way, our bodies are synchronized with the spinning of the planet itself.

And then there's memory, the grandest way we're shaped by time. Memory is the body's way of storing information, an internal filing system that helps us navigate the world. Memory exists in many forms. Scars, DNA, and language are all forms of memory, but the most important ones reside in our neural networks. And this type of memory is ancient, tracing back at least as far as our worm ancestors.

Memory also stretches us through time. With memory, our present self is constantly shaped by our past actions, just as our current actions will influence our future selves. This happens in both obvious and subtle ways. Take, for instance, the poor judgment of an imprudent teenager (I'm not naming names here) who gets spectacularly sick one night from drinking too much bourbon. Not only will the trauma of that event linger in memory, but chances are, this unnamed person will avoid bourbon in the future, even when they're fully capable of moderating their intake. The faintest whiff of that sweet, brown liquor still provokes a physical recoil, forever linking them to the residue of that teenage misjudgment.

This is *learning*, and learning also situates us in time. The lessons of our past echo into our future. All our current thoughts, emotions, calculations, and identities are shaped by prior experiences embedded within us. Some of these, like the unpleasant encounter with Jim Beam, are vivid, but most are lodged deep beneath our conscious awareness. We may not remember the first time we said "monkey" or tasted chocolate, but these experiences are integral to who we are now. And it is our memories that help define the individual that is each of us.

Another crucial aspect of memories is that we are constantly making them. Every moment we are alive, we are forging a memory. It may be a short-term impression that quickly fades away, or it may be a heavy stamp that lasts decades, but either way, the patterns of action and reaction we are currently having will inevitably alter our future lives. In some Eastern traditions, this process is characterized as karma, the idea that our current actions have implications for our future selves because of the habits of mind they teach. We'll explore the subtleties of this idea in later chapters, but for now, let's note that memory and karma not only originate in the deepest levels of our animal self, they also have a fundamental impact on this feeling of being an "I."

Certainty

What makes some pop songs so irresistibly catchy? Everyone has their own peculiar taste in music, but certain songs transcend personal preferences and become instant hits, dominating airwaves and burrowing into our brains like relentless earworms. Their secret? Predictability, with just the right dash of surprise. Popular songs often feature simple, repetitive themes that are easy to hum along to, with a hook that either delights or torments or sometimes both. But here's the twist: If a song is too predictable, it's boring; if it's too unpredictable, it's improvisational jazz (ack!). The songs that hit the sweet spot of just predictable enough are the ones that become our reliable pleasures or our unforgettable tormentors.

But predictability isn't just the secret to pop music's success; it's also a fundamental aspect of our animal selves. Brains evolved to be pattern-finding machines, a trait that traces deep into our evolutionary history. To understand where this began, let's travel back to about 540 million years ago, during the Cambrian explosion. This was when life on Earth diversified at an astonishing rate. Creatures began sporting hard shells, multiple limbs, and even backbones, setting the stage for the dazzling array of life forms we see today.

One of the most crucial developments during this period was the evolution of perception. Perception is about seeing and creating internal maps of reality. Early animals, like worms and jellyfish, had only the crudest maps. They could sense light and detect a few chemicals, and that was about it. However, during the Cambrian period, many animals began to develop more advanced sense organs and bigger, more complex brains to process all this new information. Together, this gave them more specific depictions of the world. Indeed, it was the enlarged brain that was making the more detailed maps; the newly formed eyes, ears, and noses merely provided better cartographic tools.

This "mapmaking" ability radically changed animal life. Most plants and fungi live at the mercy of their environment. They may slowly react to changes around them, but they can't anticipate any sudden shifts. Animals with advanced perception are different. They not only perceive the world but also predict and prepare for what might be coming next. Their brains are what neuroscientists today call prediction machines, which greatly increase their bargaining power with reality.

But perception didn't just help our ancestors navigate the world; it also laid the groundwork for something more profound: sentience. As animals began to perceive the world around them, they also started perceiving themselves. This sentience originated in two early forms of perception: pain and pleasure. Pain is the body's way of saying, "Hey, something's wrong here!" while pleasure signals, "Yes, keep doing that." Both are extraordinarily adaptive and ancient. As soon as animals started sensing the world, they likely began feeling "good" or "bad" about the things they encountered.

And here's where things get interesting. Once animals started feeling pain and pleasure, they moved beyond simply recognizing their reality; they began evaluating it. Objects and events were no longer just "things"; they became "good things" or "bad things" based on how they made the animal feel. This applied to themselves as well. Animals felt differently depending on whether they were hungry or fed, sleepy or rested. In short, they began experiencing the world and themselves in a subjective way.

With perception and sentience in the mix, our animal ancestors then took another step. Not only did they now interpret the world and generate feelings, they also started generating feelings about how they were interpreting it. If their map of reality was clear and accurate, they felt great; if their map was incomplete or fuzzy, they felt terrible.

Here is the secret of pop songs: They fulfill our intense desire for predictability. As long as we animals can discern regular patterns, we're more or less content. In fact, predictability allows us to endure a lot of discomfort. Numerous studies have shown that lab animals will adjust remarkably well to unpleasant treatment from their human experimenters if their shocks, stings, or other tortures come at regular intervals. But if these shocks and stings have no pattern, the poor creatures quickly descend into despair, adopting what psychologists call learned helplessness. Give an animal unpredictable shocks, and it will collapse into a feeble depression; make those shocks regular, and it'll adjust to the new reality.

The intense need for certainty is an underappreciated part of our animal self. We often think of our animal instincts as wild, impulsive forces driving us to act without thought, immune to reason. But most animals are far more thoughtful than that. Our notions, permutations, and cogitations originate in our animal brains. The animal self always seeks patterns, makes inferences, and draws conclusions. It's our animal brain that makes the world legible. And as long as we can find predictable patterns, our animal brains will reward us with a sense of satisfaction; if we can't, we feel distressed.

Predictability is also behind the feeling of "I." As we'll see in later chapters, much of our conscious experience, this feeling of what it's like to be us, arises from our brains creating maps of the world and placing us within them. Consciousness itself is something of an animalistic prediction game.

Connection

One of the most rewarding things a person can do is to sing and dance with other people. Music and dancing increase our feelings of well-being, decrease our pain, and connect us to something larger than ourselves. And, unlike so many other modern temptations, they don't make you fat, clog your arteries, or isolate you behind a screen. Instead, they are a genuinely guilt-free pleasure.

Playing music and dancing also highlight another crucial feature of the animal self: It works best with others. Just as an orchestra needs many players to make a symphony, we animals also need other animals to thrive. Of course, this is not unique to the animal kingdom; interdependence exists in all branches of the tree of life. Life is constantly interacting with itself, and no self is truly an island.

But among all the creatures on Earth, none can rival the social prowess of mammals. Insects may form colonies, and fish may school together, but these interactions are laughably simple compared to the complicated ways we mammals engage with each other. And our hypersociability arises from another factor that sets us mammals apart: We've got big brains.

Sociability and brain size go hand in hand (or brain in skull, more accurately). The more social the mammal, the bigger its relative brain size tends to be. This connection isn't just correlation; it's a full-blown evolutionary tango. Social species need greater processing power to juggle the demanding intricacies of living in bigger groups. If you are going to keep track of who is an ally, who is an enemy, and where you sit in the ever-shifting pecking order, you need some serious cognitive capacity, and this requires a bigger brain.

But large brains also come with a hefty price tag. Neurons are some of the most energy-hungry cells in the body, and maintaining a big brain requires a lot of food. Large brains also take more time to develop, so big-brained youngsters need extended care and nurturance. If you want to raise a brainy kid, you've got to invest a lot in them. You've not only got to keep them fed and warm for a long time, you've got to tune in to their emotions, read their needs, and respond accordingly.

Enter empathy. Empathy is the ability to share in the emotional experiences of another creature. It's how we mammals mimic each other, setting our emotional and cognitive processes to be in sync. It's feeling what another feels or seeing things from their perspective.

Empathy is crucial for being an effective parent or a successful member of any social group.

In mammals, empathy arises from several hormonal and neural structures. One of the most notable is oxytocin. Often called the "love hormone," oxytocin is nature's way of prepping the mammalian brain for child-rearing. When a mammalian mother gives birth, her brain is flooded with it, creating an instant, powerful bond, a kind of emotional superglue.

Oxytocin is also incredibly potent and powerful in humans, and we've even turned it into a recreational pastime. MDMA, the active ingredient in the drug ecstasy, works by flooding the brain with oxytocin. It allows ravers to tap into the same feelings of connection and bliss that help mothers bond with their newborns, only with a thumping techno beat added to the mix.

Another powerful syncing mechanism is mirror neurons. These are neurons that fire both when we do something (like moving our leg) and when we watch someone else doing the same action (like moving their leg). If we wince when we see someone fall hard, it is because the same reflexes that fire when we fall are activated when we witness others falling.

Mirror neurons are crucial for helping animals learn from and care for one another. They are especially prevalent in humans and work in hyperdrive when we're young. Toddlers and children learn everything from observing and copying others. Our early hominid ancestors learned how to make fire, create tools, hunt, and build shelters, all through first-hand observation. Theirs was a mimetic culture. Like many of our primate cousins (monkey see, monkey do), we are a mimicking species.

Oxytocin and mirror neurons also reveal an essential fact about the self: Our very being is contingent upon our relationships with others. It's not simply that we need others for basic survival (which we do) or to keep ourselves in emotional balance (which we also do); it goes far deeper. Our whole way of experiencing reality, and ourselves, comes from our accumulated social interactions. From an early age, we learn from our caretakers. We imprint their gestures, words, and styles of nurturance deeply within our psyche. If we experience trauma, neglect, or abuse, then those, too, get stamped on the mental template.

As with most experiences that occur early in life, this imprinting usually operates on an unconscious level. Everything we know as ourselves, our whole feeling of being, is based on an invisible mental framework that others have shaped. In our species, this is most profoundly conveyed through language and culture. We'll explore these ideas more in the chapters ahead, but for now, it's enough to remember that the self is not simply emergent from billions of cellular parts; it also arises from interactions with other selves. At our core, we are not just social animals but social *beings*.

The Animal Within Us

Like the ancient Greeks, we often think of our animal self as an obstacle to overcome, a wild beast that needs to be tamed or transcended, a problem needing a solution. But this view is a bit shortsighted. Our animal self isn't just the sum of our bodily urges and problematic desires, the primal lusts symbolized by the satyr's oversized erection. Yes, these are aspects of our animal self, but they hardly define it.

Instead, our animal self is the intricate web of processes that enable our trillions of cells to work together as coherent beings. It's the source of our unity, perception, and memory. It forms the bedrock of our sentience and lies at the foundation of our conscious minds. Like every part of the self, this orchestration is an ongoing process, constantly renewed with each passing moment. And it's also fundamentally connected with the selves of the people around us.

Now, sometimes, this means generating feelings of hunger, sloth, rage, and lust—those impulses we've been taught to label as sins. But more often, the animal self operates in subtler ways. Most animals live with a keen sensitivity to their internal experience, a vibrant hum that pulses through their being. To live as an animal is to be fully alive in the moment, immersed in this electric charge of existence.

Yet, we humans often miss out on this glorious state of being. Instead, we find ourselves plagued by chronic stress, anxiety, or resentment. And that's curious. All other animals seem perfectly content to live fully within themselves. They don't suffer from continual worry, bitterness, or existential despair. They don't feel the need to denigrate their own nature or craft statues that downplay their anatomical features. Only humans carve heroic depictions of themselves and then beat themselves up for not living up to them. We are the only creatures on Earth who seem uncomfortable in our own skins. To understand why this is the case, we must examine the one thing that sets us apart from all our animal cousins; we'll need to see what transforms us from an "I" into a "me."

7

Language

WHEN WE EMBARK ON THE JOURNEY OF SELF-DISCOVERY, most of us start with that age-old question: "Who am I?" It's a reasonable place to begin. After all, if we can just figure out who we are, we'll unlock the secrets of our true selves, right? But as anyone who's ever stared too long in the mirror can attest, finding a clear answer is often more complicated than it seems.

Consider one of the simplest markers of who we are: our names. Our names may be the most common way we identify ourselves, but they don't necessarily say much about us. Nor are they supposed to. In theory, our names are just tags that distinguish us from the herd. We could be called Toilet, Asphyxiation, or 8675309, and it shouldn't matter as long as others know it is us.

But, of course, that's not how we see them. In practice, names have power. Beyoncé, Pepsi, and Caligula all evoke feelings in us. If your parents had named you Hitler, Shleprock, or Mister Cutie Patootie (something one of my students was saddled with), you'd probably change it (he wisely chose to go by Jason). Our names seem to define us even as they don't.

And it's not just our names that have these ambiguities; all our other identities do as well. Today, we carry many labels that purport to define who we are: Asian, husband, mother, lawyer, Muslim, and so forth.

And often, these identities hold enormous power to influence how others treat us and how we think of ourselves. Yet, despite their weight, such labels don't fully represent us. They ebb and flow across time and place. Sometimes, we may know ourselves as white girls, other times as homeowners or fathers, and occasionally as clumsy dancers. But these terms are all social conventions; they're only relevant in certain circumstances, and none truly define us at our core.

If we want to know both the self and "ourselves," then, at some point, we'll need to navigate through this swirling vortex of names and identities. A helpful way to do this is to consider the source of this whirling pool: language. More than anything else, it is language that makes us who we are. Indeed, none of our names, labels, or identities would exist without it.

Language also makes us unique as a species, for no other animals have true language or the identities and moral complexities accompanying it. Koalas don't give themselves names, zebras don't consider themselves striped, and lions aren't ashamed of killing antelopes. Only we humans use words to understand the world, give ourselves identities, and load our actions with moral weight. More than anything else, it is language that makes us human.

Language also comprises the next layer of being, the third nesting doll of human life, the linguistic self. This is also the place where most of the imbalances in our self-processes begin. In all other animals, the flow of order and vitality has been honed by eons of evolution to be in balance with their environment. They live in a way that is true to their nature.

But when humans started speaking, we freed ourselves from nature's control. We developed sophisticated tools and technologies that changed the ways we survived. We made laws and moral codes that reordered our relationships with each other. We generated ideas about who we were and who we were supposed to be. All of these things altered how the life force within us negotiates with reality and threw us out of balance. Ironically, the root of our problems does not start with our animal selves, the convenient scapegoat of Western thought, but the very thing that separates us from the beasts: language.

Domestication

I'm going to start this part of our tour with an odd question, but bear with me for a moment because it will yield something interesting: What was the first domesticated animal?

If you're like most people, you'd probably guess a dog. And this is a pretty good guess. Fossil records show that dogs have an incredibly long connection to humans, including a fourteen-thousand-year-old skeleton found in an ancient burial site. We can tell that it's a dog and not a wolf because of its physical features. Early dog skeletons are more petite, slender, and juvenile-looking than wolves. Yet these findings also present us with a puzzle: If dogs were first domesticated to be co-hunters and protectors, then why are they less robust than wolves? Shouldn't they be larger and more fierce?

The answer to this canine conundrum comes from some fascinating experiments started in the 1950s by a Russian biologist named Dmitry Belyaev. Belyaev had a problem: He believed genes played a crucial role in shaping animal behavior, but this view wasn't popular with the Soviet government. The Communists in the Politburo were convinced that we're all products of our environment and that, with the proper conditioning, the state could mold us into model proletarians. In the era of Stalinist purges, Belyaev had to tread carefully—his brother had been executed for holding similarly "counterrevolutionary" scientific views. To avoid this grim fate, Belyaev retreated to a research lab in Siberia, where he could pursue his work far away from the Politburo's suspicious eyes.

While in this self-imposed exile, Belyaev explored a question that had haunted him for decades: How did dogs evolve from wolves? Looking for an answer, he decided to test some ideas on the packs of wild silver foxes at an experimental breeding farm. He started his experiment by selectively picking foxes by just one behavioral characteristic—docility. He chose only those foxes that were the least frightened of humans and then bred them with each other.

After only a few generations of this selective breeding, he noticed some significant changes, not just in the foxes' behavior but also in their physical appearance. The selected foxes started becoming friendlier and more communicative. They started barking and following commands. And most interestingly, their bodies also began changing: Their ears became floppy, their tails curved, and their coats got spotty. Overall, they became more slender and youthful in appearance. Not only did the domesticated foxes start *acting* like dogs, but they started looking more like them as well.

What Belyaev had orchestrated was a phenomenon known as domestication syndrome, which occurs in nearly every animal humans have tamed. Domesticated animals—such as dogs, sheep, and cows—tend to be smaller, cuter, and less stressed and sharp-minded than their wild counterparts. It's like they've all been to a genetic spa and come out a little softer around the edges.

These facts force us to reconsider our earlier question, for if we look at the fossil record, it appears that the first "domesticated" animal was not a dog but a human being. Compare us to a typical human ancestor that lived more than three hundred thousand years ago, and you'll find some significant differences. Early *Homo sapiens* were built like Olympic wrestlers—tough, bandy-legged, and thick-limbed—just the type of robust creature you'd picture fighting off lions and cave bears. They had heavy brows and more brutal-looking faces. And, contrary to the myth of caveman stupidity, our early human ancestors had significantly larger brains than us. They were undoubtedly very intelligent and attuned to their natural environment. In short, they were physically and mentally formidable, a lot more badass than your average person today.

But sometime around three hundred thousand years ago, modern *Homo sapiens* start showing up in the fossil record.* We modern humans are generally smaller in stature than our ancestors. We have more delicate faces, a higher forehead, refined noses, cheeks, and chins; we're generally much cuter. We have smaller brains, too. In other words, we

---

* The challenge with all of these assertions is that the hominid fossil record is remarkably sparse. The *Homo sapiens* population was very small during its first three hundred thousand years, and the fossil evidence is very fragmentary. Nevertheless, we do see big differences between our modern skeletons and, say, those of Neanderthals, with whom we shared a common ancestor from about four hundred thousand years ago.

have all the hallmarks of being a domesticated species. And this makes sense. After all, if we domesticated so many other animals, it seems necessary that we would first have to be domesticated ourselves. This, however, raises a curious question: Who or what domesticated *us*?

Although there are lots of popular suspects (trade, settlement, aliens!), the most likely culprit was language. This is a speculative conjecture, but several reasons lead me to believe that language domesticated us. First off, the timing is right. The skeletons of our ancestors look like they were domesticated at roughly the same time that modern human language emerged. Several genetic mutations relating to brain size, language functioning, and sociability also appear around this time in the human genome. It's also important to note that the African *Homo sapiens* population during this period was tiny, perhaps no more than ten thousand in size. When our ancestors first started speaking, they were an endangered species. In short, the fossil record suggests that our bodies began changing at the same time that we started talking with each other in a way we would recognize today as a modern language.

However, the most compelling reason to believe that language domesticated us lies in what language demands. If you and I are going to have a conversation that involves more than just grunts and hand gestures, we need to agree on some basics. We need to decide that the word for *fire* is going to be "fire," and then we need to stick with it—no suddenly changing it to "yazink" or "heegabuff" because one of us has a moment of inspiration. In other words, language requires cooperation, consistency, and a bit of obedience.

This is where language began to "select for" the trait of docility—the same trait that Belyaev used to domesticate his foxes. It brought together the tamest of our early human ancestors and rewarded their ability to get along. In early human tribes, it was the docile individuals who could learn from each other, build vocabularies, and share information. They could make plans, gossip, and even flirt. They could form coalitions and shun those ornery loners who were doing their own thing and undoubtedly insisting on their own annoying word for *fire*. As language emerged, being docile suddenly conferred some great advantages.

But domestication did something even more profound: It harnessed us to culture, making us dependent upon symbolic communication for survival. As with dogs, cows, and chickens, we became subservient to our domesticator. Only in this case, rather than our protector being a herder or a farmer, it was symbols, words, and syntax. And all of this gave rise to a new and distinctly human layer of being, the linguistic self. Language is an intrinsic part of not just who we are but also what we are.

What Is Language?

Now, you might be thinking, "What does he mean we're the only species with language? What about all those complicated prairie dog barks or those mournful whale songs? What about that gorilla who could use sign language?" These are reasonable questions. Most animals (and many plants and fungi, it turns out) communicate. And some forms of animal communication, like a bee's "dances," are astonishingly sophisticated. But while animals communicate, they don't have language, at least not in the way we humans do. No matter how much we want to believe that our dog understands us or that birds are singing the next great duet, that's not quite what's happening.

The differences start with symbols and meaning. When animals communicate, their signals are singular, reflexive gestures. They're not sitting around creating abstract concepts or writing haikus about the sunset. Their grunts, calls, and gestures are tied directly to their immediate environment and are always in the moment—cats aren't meowing about the mouse that got away last Tuesday or the can of tuna they hope to eat tomorrow. And while your dog may bark or whine to express itself, it's not stringing those sounds together to create new, complex ideas.

More importantly, animals aren't out to build a shared understanding with their communication. Their signals are more like car horns—short, one-way gestures aimed at changing something around them. When an animal roars, chirps, or flings its poo, it's not inviting dialogue; it's making a singular gesture.

Human language is fundamentally different. Consider the following distinctive features of how we communicate:

Human language uses abstractions. I can say "fire," and you'll know what I mean even if no fire is present.

Human language has syntax and rules that govern how words are put together, and our capacity to learn this is innate. When children start speaking, they intuitively grasp that they should say "I ate that yummy cookie" rather than "That cookie ate I yummy."

Human language has infinite potential. We can create sentences that go on forever, like: "Sue saw Tom thinking about what Molly might have been feeling when she bought those shoes from handsome Freddy who was . . ."

Human language is about creating a shared understanding of the world. When we talk to each other, we build a uniform way of interpretation. Every time we speak, sign, or read a word, we reinforce a *common* framework for ordering ourselves. In doing this, we become bound to all the other people we communicate with.

The really big puzzle is how this all came to be. As psychologist Michael Corballis says, "Language is the hardest problem in science: Nobody really knows how it works, and nobody knows where it came from." There are few questions with as many theories, vicious fights, and rampant conjecture as with the origin and functioning of language.

Part of the challenge comes from its very complexity. Spoken language involves physical traits distinct to our species, such as the particular shape of our tongues, larynx, and pharynx. Language also involves many inborn psychological traits, such as our ability to think abstractly and intuit basic rules of grammar and syntax. And both the physiology and psychology of language are very complicated. Take the simple example of uttering an ordinary sentence. Because we speak by exhaling, our brains need to time our utterances to our breath; they have to make sure there is enough air in the lungs to get you to the end of your sentence. This means your brain "knows" what you will say well before your conscious mind does.

But even if nobody knows where precisely the capacity for language lies, over the past thirty years, researchers have discovered some bits and parts. For example, we now know that some genes, like FOXP2, are crucial for language. People with abnormal mutations in this gene sequence have a tough time communicating. We also know that a couple of regions in the brain's left hemisphere are essential for language. But our knowledge doesn't go much beyond this.

Nor do we know precisely when these parts of our bodies emerged. Some argue that this has been a slow process taking millions of years, while others believe an evolutionary inflection point critically altered our language capacity. This question is even more challenging because language constantly changes and takes on new forms. For example, Americans now use newer words like *selfie* and *emoji*, while older words like *scrumping* and *grundy* have vanished from our vocabulary. While we have a pretty clear idea of what our early human ancestors looked like, we don't really know what their speech sounded like.

What we do know, however, is that between two hundred thousand and seventy thousand years ago, something extraordinary happened—modern human language took shape, and with it, the human self was forever transformed. We invented tools and weapons that catapulted us to the top of the food chain. We began to reshape our surroundings, transforming wild landscapes into farms, building towns and roads, and constructing cozy homes from which we look out and complain about the weather. Within a relatively short period of time, we came to dominate the planet.

But language didn't just change what we did; it also changed who we were. We reorganized our social hierarchies, gave ourselves names and titles, and, in doing so, altered our very consciousness. The "self" became a product of cultural and linguistic invention, a dynamic interplay of words, ideas, and social expectations. And if you're searching for a great example of how deeply language shapes our sense of self, there is no better place to look than your pronouns.

Me, Myself, and I

This is an excellent moment to address one of the biggest questions that comes up when exploring the self: What is the difference between my self (or the self) and myself? It's easy to confuse these terms, but there is an essential distinction between them. The first term, the *self*, has been the subject of this book so far. As we've seen, the self is not what people usually think of when they think of themselves. So far, the self has been mainly about the things that operate well below the surface of our conscious awareness, like our energies, cells, and neural networks. The "self" is all the processes that help perpetuate me as an energy system.

Myself, by contrast, is a reflexive pronoun. As with all pronouns, it is about one's social identity. Individuals in isolation don't need pronouns; only those in groups do. But even the pronouns we use for ourselves arise in relationship to others. *Me* is a social concept. It is the part of the self that I, myself, am normally most conscious of, and it only exists because of language.

This was the insight of one of the founders of modern psychology, William James. James realized that the part of us we commonly know as our "self" comes from our language, for language allows us to comprehend ourselves as objects. In James's view, a creature without language can't reflect on itself because it cannot perceive itself outside of its own subjective experience. And this makes a lot of sense. Try to think objectively about yourself without words; it's impossible. You may be able to see your limbs or feel your body, but you'll still be very much stuck in a first-person frame of reference. Language allows us to generate a self-concept and, in doing so, create an identity.

For James, this was crystalized in the difference between the words *I* and *me*. *I* refers to a primordial being. The "I" is the by-product of our animal self, something active only in the moment. "Me," by contrast, is the idea of ourselves that we use to negotiate among all the people around us. This distinction is evident when we look in the mirror. When we glance at our reflection, we never say "I see I" or even "I see a self." Instead, we see a "me" or a "myself." James's insight was that language creates this "me." Like a mirror, language is a tool through which we can reflect on ourselves and, in doing so, it transforms the "self" into "myself."

In the many decades since James first came up with this notion, developmental psychologists have validated his claims. Our sense of self starts in childhood and arises in lockstep with language. When we're born, we come into the world without any sense of identity. We are merely a "blooming, buzzing confusion," as James aptly described it. Human babies are essentially born premature, nature's tradeoff between our species being both large-brained and bipedal. Newborns don't understand themselves as distinct from the world. They don't differentiate between their bodies, their mothers, toys, or anything else. They can't even recognize themselves in a mirror. Babies perceive reality as just one immense feeling of "I."

But by eighteen months of age, this begins to change. As children begin learning how to speak, they also become self-conscious. A little girl starts saying the word "me" and knowing it refers to herself. She begins to know her name, identifies herself in pictures, and can recognize her reflection in the mirror. In short, she begins to understand herself as a "myself."

The big question is whether this self-awareness is *caused* by language or enabled by it. There is a robust scientific debate on this question. Some researchers believe that self-consciousness can exist without language. They often point to the "mirror test," a famous experiment developed by psychologist Gordon Gallup in the late 1960s.

In the experiment, either a young child or an animal is presented with a mirror. At first, many animals and children don't recognize the image they see as themselves; some will even see their reflection as a threat and try to attack it or run away from it. However, over time, the subjects eventually acclimate to the image in the mirror and many start interacting with it in a familiar way. But do the toddlers and animals looking in the mirror understand the reflection as themselves?

To answer this question, the experimenters remove the mirror and then surreptitiously mark the subjects' faces with red dye. The newly red-faced animals and children are then placed in front of the mirror again. Some animals, such as chimpanzees and elephants, respond to the mark in the mirror by touching or gesturing toward it on their own face. Human children over two years old also seem to recognize the mark, although this varies a lot by culture. Either way, when they connect the red-faced image in the mirror to their own bodies, the subjects seem to show self-awareness. They seem to know that the image in the mirror is them. For some scientists, these findings indicate that self-awareness doesn't require language.

The problem is that all of these conclusions are drawn from a distinctly human vantage point. Mirrors, after all, don't naturally occur in the wild (and no, a fleeting reflection in a pond doesn't quite cut it). When an animal confronts its mirrored image, it's not engaging in existential exploration; it's more like it's stumbling into the strange, reflective hall of human culture. It's akin to handing a chimpanzee a Rubik's Cube—it might twist it around, but that doesn't mean it's solving it, at least not in the way we would. And even if some animals possess a latent capacity for self-awareness, it's likely dormant in their natural habitats because nothing in their world is nudging it awake.

When humans started speaking, we didn't just invent a new tool for communication; we forged a portal to a whole new realm of consciousness. However, this self-awareness was highly dependent on the linguistic tools at hand. Our earliest human ancestors probably weren't self-aware like we are because they didn't have the same vocabulary. They didn't even have pronouns, at least not the ones we use today—and some languages, like Japanese, still play fast and loose with them. In other words, self-awareness isn't a binary switch you flip on or off; it's a spectrum that evolves alongside language and culture.

This point was well-illustrated in another famous experiment taking place around the same time Gordon Gallup was secretly marking the faces of children and chimpanzees. In the late 1960s, anthropologist Edmund Carpenter became intrigued with the Biami people of Papua New Guinea. At this time, the Biami still existed in very primitive conditions, isolated from the modern world. They had neither writing nor advanced tools. As far as Carpenter knew, none of them had seen their own images before, and he was curious about how they might react to mirrors and Polaroid photos. So, with a gross insensitivity to how he might be warping their culture, Carpenter packed up a bunch of mirrors and cameras, marched deep into the jungle, and confronted the Biami with pictures of themselves.

At first sight, the Biami were horrified by their reflections. They knew who they were, but they hadn't had any experience of seeing pictures of themselves before. The mirrors and photographs forced them to reconcile a self-image they carried in their heads with an image that now existed outside them. And this was unsettling. It was like when we hear a recording of our voice—the self suddenly becomes both more familiar and alien. They were also confronted with seeing themselves as others saw them. Carpenter believed this vulnerability, this inability to control their self-image, was terrifying, for the photos made them strangers to themselves.

But here's where the story takes a curious turn. After the initial shock wore off, the Biami didn't just overcome their fear of their reflections; they became fascinated by them. They started using the mirrors to groom themselves, and their preoccupation with their appearance grew. By introducing a new tool of self-reflection, Carpenter unwittingly altered the way the Biami understood themselves, similar to what social media is doing to us today. And, in doing this, Carpenter changed Biami culture forever.

This was precisely William James's point. Much like a mirror, language is a human invention that doesn't just allow us to reflect on ourselves, it also transforms us in the process. Once we start using words, we change how we perceive ourselves. We become the objects of our observation, like characters in a story we're both writing and reading simultaneously. Once you've seen yourself in a mirror, you can't unsee it; your awareness of your appearance is forever altered. Language does the same thing for our identities; it makes them sticky.

Language doesn't merely describe things; it also *ascribes* qualities. When we label something, we inevitably judge it. As Plato recognized long ago, we tend to think of the perfect apple when we think of an apple. We then evaluate every other apple by how far it deviates from this ideal. And this applies to all the labels that describe us as well. With labels, I'm not just a father; I'm a good or a bad father. I'm not just a friend; I'm a loyal or an unreliable friend. No matter how we think of ourselves, all our attributes inevitably reference some standard. And this leads us to another meaningful way in which language shapes the self: rules and morality.

8

Morality

LIKE MOST PEOPLE, I WAS RAISED TO BE A "GOOD" PERSON. I grew up on a steady diet of stories about noble heroes and dastardly villains, each designed to teach clear lessons. Heroes helped those in need. They were not selfish or destructive. They lived by values and principles and sometimes sacrificed themselves for the good of others. Villains were the opposite. They were mean and greedy. They bullied, murdered, and stole things, or just drove on the shoulder to cut ahead of merging traffic. These propositions were so ingrained as to seem as natural as gravity.

But as I got older, I felt more and more that I was not hero material. Maybe not an outright villain, but definitely a flawed person. Perhaps it was my Catholic guilt. Or maybe it was the chaos of my family life. My mother was struggling with mental illness, alcoholism, and drug addiction. My father was distant and withdrawn, lost in his own world. Like many kids from dysfunctional families, I assumed that these problems were somehow my fault. By the time I hit adolescence, I was miserable, and I felt like all this was because I was somehow, inside, a bad person.

But where did these ideas come from? It certainly wasn't from my animal self. Looking around the animal kingdom, you won't find other creatures worrying about their goodness. In fact, the rest of nature is ruthlessly amoral. What often looks like goodness to our human eyes, such as when an animal acts altruistically, is usually the result of instinct toward kin survival. Like scented candles and polyester slacks, morality is a distinctly human invention.

Morality is also where our animal selves start to stumble, tripped up by our linguistic traps. The alienation we humans feel from our true selves isn't just because we learned to speak but because of what we did with this new capacity. We started making rules and crafting moral codes and then found creative ways to punish others (and ourselves) for not living up to them. We invented remorse, shame, and New Year's resolutions. Morality became a cornerstone of our domestication, turning our natural impulses into sources of guilt and our anger into a weapon against anyone who dared break the rules, including ourselves. In the process, we laid the groundwork for a lifetime of suffering, all in the name of being "good."

This is a counterintuitive idea, and one that is easy to misinterpret. After all, we often pride ourselves on our goodness, and we want to think of ourselves as morally upstanding. But morality is also where our chronic misalignment begins, especially if we're living by rules we didn't choose for ourselves. If we want to optimize ourselves, we'll need to see where our morality comes from and ask whether it is helping us live better. To aid us in this quest, let's start with one of history's most provocative and misunderstood thinkers, a nineteenth-century philosopher with glaring eyes and an impossibly bushy mustache by the name of Friedrich Nietzsche.

The Provocateur

Nietzsche's life reads like a Victorian novel about a tortured genius. He was born in 1844 in Saxony, a German region that borders the modern-day Czech Republic. His father was a rural pastor, and his early death left young Friedrich in the care of a stern and overbearing mother and grandmother who raised him for the clergy. But Nietzsche had an exceptional and independent mind. He tore through school, dazzling teachers and peers alike with his penetrating intellect and voracious curiosity. Shunning his mother's oppressive demands, he rejected theology and instead chose philology. And it was in the study of language where he truly shined. By the time he was twenty-four, Nietzsche had won a professorship at the University of Basel, a meteoric rise that would be the envy of any academic.

But Nietzsche's story did not end happily ever after. He was plagued by migraines, stomach ailments, and near-blindness, likely the result of either syphilis or a brain tumor. These afflictions became so severe that by age thirty, he was forced to resign his professorship and retreat into the life of an unsuccessful freelance philosopher, the nineteenth-century version of being a Substack author with only twenty followers. Yet, despite his physical misery and aching loneliness, Nietzsche penned some of the most provocative works of philosophy the world has ever known. And his most lasting legacy was a controversial takedown of morality itself.

In Nietzsche's day, most thinkers were confident that morality was either handed down by God or evolved naturally within us. Few seemed eager to question the substance of their moral codes, and almost no one considered whether those beliefs were beneficial. Good was just *good*, and bad was just *bad*.

Nietzsche, however, viewed things differently. He said that morality was not a beacon of some eternal truth but a tool people used to exert power over others. Nietzsche's most provocative claim was that our modern notion of goodness wasn't a natural inclination, nor was it particularly wise. Instead, it was a recent development born out of power struggles within Western Christendom.

To illustrate this, Nietzsche traced the evolution of terms like *good* and *bad* through history. In the early days of human civilization, the ruling classes used the word *good* to describe themselves. It meant noble, well-functioning, and powerful. It was the kind of "good" you might use to describe a well-bred horse or a particularly sharp sword. *Bad*, by contrast, was the term for everything the ruling class wasn't—common, weak, incapable, like the customer service from your health insurance company.

But then something curious happened. Over time, the definitions of *good* and *bad* flipped. Traits that were once seen as "bad"—meekness, selflessness, humility—became the new "good," while traits that had been considered "good"—power, dominance, and the ability to impose one's will on others—were rebranded as immoral, evil, and "bad."

An excellent illustration of this can be found in comparing a pre-Christian story, the *Iliad*, with the New Testament. The heroes of the *Iliad*, Achilles, Hector, and Odysseus, are brutal killers. They have few scruples about murder, rape, and theft, particularly when it comes to their enemies. They are "good" simply by virtue of their martial prowess, craftiness, and strength. Jesus of Nazareth, by contrast, is heroic in his gentleness. In the Gospels, Jesus reveals his greatness by forgiving his enemies and willingly going to the cross. Noble strength was replaced by noble sacrifice, and righteous dominance with saintly humility.

Nietzsche argued that this semantic shift was no accident. It was a political maneuver by the "priestly classes," those who had knowledge but lacked power (kind of like modern academics). Because these priests couldn't compete with the physical strength of their warrior overlords, they did the next best thing: They demonized the very traits that made their rulers powerful (here again, a lot like modern academics).

In Nietzsche's view, these priests replaced a "noble morality," where goodness was synonymous with strength and superiority, with a "slave morality," where goodness meant meekness, humility, and self-subjugation. In Europe, this took the form of Christian ethics. Early Christians, lacking the military might to challenge the Roman Empire directly, fought back with moral imperatives like "Humble yourself before God" and "The meek shall inherit the Earth." Before the Roman emperors appropriated it, Christian morality was initially a weapon of the weak, and a very effective one at that.

We also see this shapeshifting in today's politics, where groups from every ideological camp scramble to seize the moral high ground, with their victimhood paraded as their most ennobling trait. The weaker side in any fight knows the game: Expand the conflict, recruit sympathizers, and even the odds by wrapping yourself in the blanket of moral righteousness. You do this by redefining your weakness as a strength, a symbol of your integrity, as if an empty wallet or losing any fight turns you into a saint. And in today's world, where narratives of victimhood hold as much sway as facts, it's one of the most potent tactics in the political playbook.

Nietzsche saw this moral rebranding as corrosive to our true potential. He argued that by embracing this "slave morality" as an absolute truth, we end up stifling the very qualities that could make us great. We define ourselves by our weakness and victimization rather than by our true strength. In other words, many of the values we hold dear are, in fact, treacherously self-abnegating.

This is an uncomfortable claim, and it's easy to misinterpret. It doesn't help that reactionary propagandists invoke Nietzsche to justify their racism. Thus it's not surprising that people often scorn him as an apologist for sociopaths and incels. Nietzsche, however, was neither a Nazi nor a monster. His writings are far more subtle and complicated than that. In tracing the genealogy of words like *good* and *bad*, Nietzsche was one of the first thinkers to consider how language shapes us.

Yet, for all this, Nietzsche got his timing wrong. It wasn't just the early Christian priests who first used morality to tilt the political playing field; instead, this has been going on for a much longer time. In fact, it probably began soon after we first started talking to each other. To see this, let's go back and briefly look at how morality arose in the first place.

The Evolution of Morals

Your earliest human ancestors were a fearsome lot. They were undomesticated, robust creatures who lived by a simple code: The stronger get more of what they want. As with other great apes, the *alphas* led these early human troops. They were the mightiest or most cunning, and they bullied everyone to get first dibs on food, sex, or whatever else they wanted.

The rest of the troop consisted of the *betas*. They jockeyed among each other for ever-diminishing scraps, which got smaller the further they fell down the hierarchy. Sometimes they'd suck up to the alphas by grooming them or supporting them in alliances. Sometimes, they'd support the efforts of a rival beta to overthrow an alpha. And all of this was done through episodic violence or reciprocal trading of food and grooming. Their politics were in constant flux. There were no morals to regulate their actions, no standards of behavior to restrain them.

Like any other animal, our early ancestors behaved as the moment allowed, their lives "nasty, brutish, and short," as Thomas Hobbes famously quipped.

But then something extraordinary happened: They began to speak. With the advent of language, the power dynamics within these groups began to shift. Language wasn't just a new way to communicate but a disruptive force that upended the natural order. Suddenly, information could be traded, secrets could be shared, and reputations could be built or destroyed—all through the power of words. Our ancestors could gossip, recount tales of heroism or betrayal, and assign labels like "trustworthy" or "deceitful." Such tales became vital, allowing group members to make informed decisions about potential allies or enemies.

This new power also came with a darker side: the ability to spread lies, misinformation, and slander. With language, human politics graduated from pure brute force to something more Machiavellian. The strong were no longer just those who could physically dominate; they were those who could wield words like weapons, shaping reputations and perceptions of power with the cunning of a Renaissance diplomat. Language became the new battleground, where a sharp tongue could be as lethal as a honed spear. Fake news is probably as old as the news itself.

And the changes didn't stop there. Language also brought about a seismic shift in how we learned about the world. Before the dawn of spoken communication, our ancestors had to absorb everything from fire-starting to toolmaking based on first-hand observation. You watched, mimicked, and—if lucky—survived long enough to pass on your hard-earned wisdom to the next person, all through first-hand instruction. Language upended this. It allowed individual experiences to be shared without direct observation and particular lessons to become codified.

Say someone in the tribe ate a handful of holly berries and got violently ill. Thanks to language, they could now warn all the others: "Hey, watch out for those red berries." Someone else might deduce, "Hmm, maybe we should stay away from all red fruits." Eventually, this deduction might solidify into a rule: "Thou shalt not touch red fruits!" Generations later, people in the tribe would avoid red fruits without knowing why. It's just something they did until some curious freethinker came along and wondered, "But what about those yummy-looking apples over there?"

Our ancestors then took it a step further. Their new moral codes weren't simply instructions on how to make a better fire or avoid getting sick from eating holly berries; they were ways of reorganizing the group's politics. And this is what Nietzsche was referring to when he talked about weapons of the weak. Rules and morality rearranged the human social order.

Much of this revolved around sex. For apes like us, sex is one of the most valuable and complicated resources we possess—think of it as the stock market of the animal kingdom, only with fewer brokers and more bananas. And, as with any scarce resource, there are significant imbalances in who gets what. While in theory, males could potentially impregnate hundreds of partners (assuming they're as ruthless as Genghis Khan or as charming as Mick Jagger), most females can only have about ten to fifteen full-term pregnancies over the span of their lives. Female reproduction is thus a scarce resource, and like any scarce resource, it has high value. The competition among simian males for sex is fierce, and simian females are incentivized to be picky in their choice of mates.

Our primate cousins usually regulate this "reproductive economy" through status and violence. The alpha males in a troop of chimpanzees are like the Wall Street moguls of the jungle, fiercely guarding their mating rights as if they were the last tradable shares of Amazon. They patrol their territories, ensuring no subordinate dares encroach on their reproductive portfolios. And our early human ancestors likely had a similar setup.

But then, along came language, and the sexual market became regulated. Imagine a scenario where the beta males finally got fed up with the alpha hogging all the action and decided to team up. Using their newfound language skills, they plot and scheme, banding together to depose the alpha. Once he's gone, however, they've got a new problem: Who will be in charge? They could pick a new alpha, but that's just trading one tyrant for another. Instead they had to devise a new arrangement that everyone could agree on, a prehistoric social contract.

Enter sexual morality. Instead of letting the mighty monopolize all the sex, the betas created rules that allocated it more equitably. They invented marriage, established rules about premarital sex, and made laws against adultery that often came with severe punishments. This ended up being a huge win for all the betas. Sexual morality leveled the reproductive playing field, giving them all a better shot at passing on their genes. The rules also gave them a shared identity; they were now different from all the other groups in how they kept the peace. Morals and regulations, in short, transformed the troop into a tribe.

And this is where religion comes into play. Religion has never been solely about deciphering the stars or offering comfort in the face of mortality; instead, it has always been about regulating the "reproductive economy." Until quite recently, it was religion that dictated who could marry, when and how sex was permissible, and what acts were taboo. In most cases, these burdens are placed most heavily on females, and most traditional religions put them in a subservient place and strictly regulate their behaviors. These sexual codes are not merely moral guidelines—they are rules for managing a society's capacity to reproduce.

Of course, sexual morality is not a uniform phenomenon. It varies enormously across cultures. In some places, there are severe punishments for breaking rules; in other places, there are not. Much of this depends on the local ecology. For example, the cultures with the strictest sexual rules are often the pastoral ones. It's usually in herding societies where you find the greatest limitations on female mobility, the harshest punishments for adultery, and the most grotesque forms of genital mutilation.

Why? In these tribes, everything depends on the male herders, who are often away from their wives for long stretches of time. If they don't feel confident that their kids are theirs, no one will tend the flocks, and the whole tribe will perish. So they came up with some rather extreme measures to keep everyone in line—like stoning adulterers and pouring molten iron down the throats of deviants. Life in a pastoral culture, it turns out, isn't always pastoral.

What Rules Do to Us

Living according to morals may be essential for helping a tribe survive, but it comes with a price. And it's our psyche that bears most of the cost. This stems from a simple fact: Laws alone aren't enough to keep everyone in line; they need enforcers. If we want to live by rules, we all must become part-time moral vigilantes. And we seem to have evolved some psychological tendencies that make us so.

Many of these innate proclivities concern other people. Consider gossip. Who doesn't relish a juicy tale of someone else's misdeeds, especially if they are a celebrity or someone we know? This appetite for gossip seems innate, nature's way of getting us to keep tabs on who's been naughty and nice. Indignation is another favorite pastime. A passionate hunger for justice seems hardwired into us. Few things grind my gears more than when someone cuts in line—even lines I'm not in—and I will usually confront them (much to Thea's mortification).

Beyond watching our neighbors, laws need us to do something more: They need us to police ourselves. If human civilization was to stay ordered by rules, it required its members to keep themselves in line. They could no longer crap wherever they wanted or punch someone simply because they didn't like their face. They had to control their impulses, even if no one else was around. They had to fashion a psychological chastity belt and put it on themselves.

This is also the point where the human self becomes misaligned, and once again, it goes back to language. Language not only allows us to make rules, laws, and commandments, but it forces us to devise ways of following these strictures, usually through feelings of guilt, anxiety, and shame.

Here again, this is because of what language does—it creates an object out of ourselves, allowing us to view and judge ourselves from a distance. These views and judgments, in turn, are filtered through the lens of our morality. Moral rules not only tell me that stealing is wrong or sex is a sin but also that I'm bad for even wanting these things. The "me," which feels the urge to sneak that donut or sleep with my roommate's girlfriend, is now a "bad" person for even having such desires. And, as with anything bad, these sinful parts of "me" become the subject of scorn and disgust. Language thus gives us the means to hate and punish ourselves.

And it doesn't stop there, for language does something else to our moral sentiments—it extends us in time. Animals always exist in the present moment. They feel fear or excitement only about what is around them. They don't worry about the future or anything beyond a one or two-minute horizon. Similarly, they don't feel bad about the past. Like a New Age guru, animals live in the now.

We humans, however, spend much of our mental lives in the past or the future. And language makes this time travel possible. One minute, we're reliving past glories—like when we hit the winning shot in a middle school basketball game—and the next, we're berating ourselves for last night's pint of ice cream. Or we live in the future, fretting over our next dentist appointment or daydreaming about winning the lottery. Language thus transports us to distant emotional worlds, but this time traveling is an entirely imaginary journey; it doesn't exist outside our heads.

I'll share a personal example of this. When I was ten years old, I was terribly jealous that my friend Carl received an electronic football game for Christmas. It was a ridiculously crude device by today's standards (kind of like a garage door opener with lights), but we were obsessed with it. And, like any ten-year-old, I was extremely jealous. So, one day, after playing at his house, I did the unthinkable . . . I stole it.

Once I got home, I was crushed with guilt. I felt so terrible about what I had done that I threw the game away. I never even played with it. Carl never confronted me about this, nor did I ever confess, but our friendship was never the same. Fast forward five decades, and I'm still haunted by my impulsive theft. Here I am, a middle-aged man, and yet a big part of me still feels horrible about the theft of a long-gone electronic toy. Rosebud, anyone?

And this, dear reader, is how language domesticates us. It wasn't simply that language selected the most docile members of our species; it tamed the most feral parts of the self. When our hominid ancestors lived without language, their world was dominated by coercion and chaos, but they were true to their nature. Theirs was a purely natural animal self. Then along came language, breaking us like a horse to the saddle. Sure, it may have freed us from the arbitrary violence of the alphas and given us the tools to dominate the planet. But it didn't necessarily make our existence any better. It required us to fabricate a synthetic layer of self, and over time, this artificial self took us further and further away from our true natures.

Identity Crisis

"I am a lesbian trapped in a man's body."

I first heard this odd line from a young college professor of mine back in 1986. At the time, I remember cynically thinking, "That's quite the pickup line." And maybe it was. Or perhaps it was the sincere expression of some inner turmoil—with this person, it was tough to know. But I never would have guessed that statements like this, once the material for a Monty Python sketch, would someday be central to American politics. Today, social media is filled with phrases like "Liberals think men can get pregnant" or "I am neither a man nor a woman." Online conversations that trade in phrases like these have become as familiar as cat videos, and with even more heated debate.

I'm raising this point not to wade into the treacherous waters of contemporary gender politics but because it illustrates some more profound ambiguities about our linguistic self. As I've already mentioned, language fundamentally changed us as a species. It gave us the means to reflect on ourselves and to categorize everything from our least favorite coffee to the seven habits of highly effective people. It allowed us to develop laws and morality. But language did something more, for it melded all of these elements together and stamped them upon the self with the powerful imprint of identities.

Identities are the ultimate markers of our domestication. Wild creatures don't have them because they are too busy doing what comes naturally—eating, mating, and avoiding becoming someone else's dinner. But once you start living in a culture, you can't just run around doing whatever you want. You have to play by the rules, and your identities are the labels that tell everyone which game you're playing. To call yourself (or be called) a "lesbian" or a "man" is to be confronted with certain norms and expectations, and, of course, stereotypes: Lesbians only have sex with women, drive Subarus, and usually stay in long-term relationships; men like books about history and war, don't ask for directions, and only cry in the dark. In other words, identities are the most visible ways culture gets woven into the self.

For most of human history, identities were like tattoos—they indelibly marked you. In traditional societies, there is very little choice about who you are. You are born as a man or woman, a hunter or a gatherer, a Brahmin or a Dalit, and that is that. These identities also come with stringent rules and obligations: hunters only hunt, gatherers only gather. The point was always the same—subsume your desires to the demands of your social role, which are then encapsulated within your identities. In short, identities are the linguistic self in full flower but with some sharp thorns.

But the times, they are a-changing. Today, our identities are more numerous and fluid than ever before. What it means to be a woman, Latino, American, or even old depends on wherever you are (for example, I may be fifty-eight years old, but I jokingly identify as twenty-six). Even more confusing is the fact that the definition of these identities is now debatable. For some, it's not simply that they have the liberty to choose whether they call themselves a man or a lesbian or whatever; it's that they have the right to do this, and this is a right that everyone else must respect. Others push back and say that identities, like all of our words, need to have firm boundaries; otherwise, they will lose their utility.

Which takes us back to the question of "Who am I?" At the heart of this question is the uncertainty many of us feel about our very being. This is because the function of identity has become less clear. In the past, your identity was essential for your survival. It was an intrinsic part of your culture that was tightly adapted to your local ecology. It tied you to the tribe, giving you a sense of security and belonging. Back then, the question "Who am I?" would have been met with a confused look because the answer was as obvious as the nose on your face. Once again, "know thyself" usually meant "know thy place."

However, over the past two hundred years, our technology has evolved so quickly that our linguistic self hasn't fully caught up. Some identities (alchemist, serf, Hun) are as obsolete as rotary phones. Some identities are new inventions (nonbinary, influencer, computer programmer), and we don't know if they will stand the test of time. And some identities, like man and lesbian, are being contested.

This shifting swirl is symptomatic of a bigger crisis, namely the loss of a coherent meaning for our lives. Like a stray Pomeranian, here we are, a hyperdomesticated animal, no longer sure who our master is supposed to be and terrified at being caught in the wild. We desperately want a sense of belonging but are uncertain about where we belong. We grope about for identities, picking them up and discarding them like so many used clothes, trying to find the one that fits, but never feeling fully satisfied or comfortable in our own skins.

How then can we get out of this mess? The answer lies in revisiting order and vitality. Remember, the self exists to keep the life force going, and an optimized self does this as efficiently as possible. Language introduced new ways that we humans made order and expressed our vitality. The economic, political, and cultural systems that arose from language became as much a part of the self as our biology.

To live better, we must ask ourselves some tough questions about our culture and politics. Do our rules and morals help us flourish, or are they simply adding more layers to the mess? Is our technology self-affirming or self-destructive? How do our lifestyles work with our animal and cellular selves? These questions have no simple answers. Philosophers and politicians have been debating them for centuries, and they have yet to devise a perfect system. What's more, we live in a time of rapid technological change where our prior models of social order are often out of sync with our current realities.

And here is where we come to a big fork in our tour. While I'd love to map out the ideal social and political system for human flourishing, that's a project for another book, and I'm not even sure I could come up with a satisfying answer. So, instead, I'm going to take us inward—toward the individual self. After all, if we want to build an optimal culture, we'll first need to get a better sense of how we flourish as individuals. And that journey starts with understanding the next layer of our being: the egoistic self.

9

Ego

LIKE MANY PEOPLE, I SPENT A LOT OF MY YOUTH WISHING I was cool. Although I wasn't quite sure what, exactly, cool was, I knew that cool people were different than me. For one, cool people were weirdly confident in their own judgment. They had style and loped about with a laconic nonchalance. They didn't worry about grades or freeze up when talking to cute girls. Cool people floated above their circumstances yet were always intensely engaged. Most importantly, cool people seemed completely content in themselves.

This, however, was not me. No matter how much I wanted to carry myself with the easy grace of a Sam Shepard, Steve McQueen, or Jimi Hendrix, I could never shed my insecurities, at least not for long. In fact, these insecurities usually defined me. I spent much of my early life always trying to fit in or eager to make other people like me. And this went for most people I knew as well.

But why is this the case? Why is being cool something that is so elusive? The answer to these questions can be found in the next layer of being, the egoistic self.

Now, it may seem like we are finally getting to the real heart of this book, for the ego is usually what we think of when we think of ourselves. It's the nesting doll that we believe looks most like us. But, if you've read this far, you can appreciate why your ego is not the full doll, only a part of it. Our ego is more like the surface layer of cheese on a piping hot dinner of energy, body, psychology, and culture. Because it's most visible, we usually believe that it's the whole enchilada, but it's not.

Instead, the ego has a more specific function: It's the part of the self that helps us find our way in society. It's normally a brittle little creature, desperately trying to feel good but often doing the opposite. It craves respect, admiration, and love but spirals into paroxysms of self-loathing and misery. The ego is also the heaviest part of the honey wagon, and if we want to live better, we'll need to figure out how to lighten its burden.

The ego is also where the quest for self-optimization gets especially challenging. It starts with the fact that the ego is something of a nebulous concept. You can't point to it on an MRI scan or neatly define it in a few sentences. Ask ten people what the ego is, and you'll get ten different answers. These can range from Freudian models of the psyche to the more common idea of being a self-aggrandizing jerk to the illusion of separateness that appears in many Eastern traditions. None of these ideas, however, are exactly what I mean here.

When I talk about the egoistic self, I'm referring to the psychological processes that help us navigate our social worlds. It's our sense of status, rights, and entitlement, the things that help us get what we want from other people. The ego also operates all the alarm bells that keep us from doing things that we'd later regret. While it may be inconvenient or sometimes problematic, an ego is essential for making our way in society, polite or not.

The ego also takes us to the murkiest part of our journey. Thus far, our self-exploration has been guided by observable facts. DNA, metabolism, language, and culture are all things we can discern. But the ego? It's opaque. We don't know precisely where it resides in the brain or the neurochemistry of its parts. We don't even know if the ego, as such, exists. It's more like dark matter—we can't see, touch, or directly measure it, but we know it's there by how it bends the light of our experience.

To truly understand our egoistic selves, we need to leave the world of science and enter the world of stories. Our egos live and breathe in the dramas of our lives. They are shaped by the compliments that make us glow, the insults that make us fume, and the endless micro-dramas that weave themselves into the larger narrative of our existence. These personal stories are then intertwined with the narratives that shape how we see ourselves and our place in the universe.

If we really want to know ourselves, we'll need to learn how to decode these stories. We'll need to understand how our ego takes our experiences, filters them through its own narrative prism, and creates this person we most commonly think of as "me." This dive into our own stories, however, is not just about finding the ego; it's about seeing beyond it. Our goal isn't to destroy our egos or pretend they don't exist. It's to understand the ego's part in this symphony of self and maybe get it to start playing its discordant notes a little more softly.

The Evolution of the Ego

The term *ego* is a relatively recent addition to the English language. Before the twentieth century, you wouldn't hear it much, and there's a good reason for this. *Ego* is a Latin word that translates as "I." Unless you were one of the educated elite who read Cicero or Ovid for fun, you probably didn't come across it very much. So, how then did this little Latin expression become the buzzword it is today?

To correctly answer this question, we'll need to go back about three hundred thousand years. Here, we'll find an early human ancestor roaming the plains of East Africa. Let's call her Ava. Like her Neanderthal cousins, Ava was a robust, intelligent creature, but Ava did not have a very refined sense of herself. Although it's impossible to say precisely what her self-conception was like, it was undoubtedly very different from ours.

This was because Ava lived without language. Since Ava did not speak, she had no way to self-reflect, no way of projecting herself into the future or ruminating on her past. Ava's consciousness was always bound to the moment, and her ego depended on who she was with. If she was next to someone with more power, she felt submissive and meek. If she was with someone weaker, she would feel aggressive and domineering. In this way, her sense of self was like a running tally of her position in the troop. Ava's ego was a simple and crude instrument, much like her other Stone Age technologies.

Fast forward to about twenty thousand years ago, and we'll meet Boola, another distant ancestor. Boola had language, which meant she was a domesticated creature, a *modern* human being. She looked like us and spoke, more or less, like we do today. And Boola did some remarkable things. She wore well-tailored clothes, lived in finely crafted huts, sang and danced, and made beautiful art. Most importantly, Boola told stories.

Modern humans are natural storytellers. Indeed, it would be more accurate to call our species *Homo narrans* (storytelling human) than *Homo sapiens* (wise human), given our strong appetite for tawdry gossip and wondrous fable. And our fondness for stories goes back to the evolution of language, information, and the brain. Our species dominates the planet because of one simple fact: We can store and share information across generations. And stories have been the primary way we've done this over time. Our epic myths and sagas were not just about entertainment; they also told us when to plant crops, follow the herds, go to war, and so on.

Boola's stories didn't simply organize data; they also shaped her ego. Unlike Ava, Boola's sense of herself was intertwined with her role in the tribe, a role defined by tradition and custom. She wasn't just someone who cooked the meat or mothered the children; she *was* "Cook" or "Mother." These identities defined her place, and the tribe's myths and rituals continually reinforced them. Boola's stories explained what it meant to be a cook, a mother, or anything else. Her place in the world was crystal clear.

This, however, is not our world today. Unlike Boola, we have enormous freedom to decide who we are and how we want to live. In the vast arc of human history, our epoch is something of an extreme outlier. Anthropologist Joseph Henrich has developed a catchy acronym to describe this cultural oddity we inhabit: WEIRD. It stands for Western, Educated, Industrialized, Rich, and Democratic. Our WEIRD values, ideas, and customs are very peculiar compared to other cultures. In traditional societies, the emphasis is always on the group. The tribal elders have unquestioned authority. The truth is something like a family recipe, carefully tended and passed down from one generation to the next. Your friendships and family relations are tightly bound, and you always consider yourself relative to the group.

We WEIRDos, by contrast, are all about the individual. We believe that each of us is distinct and special. This individualism is everywhere—it's in our economy, where we exist as isolated consumers and workers; it's in romance, where we find love through swipes and roses; and it's in our general expectation that we should each be recognized first and foremost as citizens with particular rights and liberties. In short, to be WEIRD is to have a hyperindividualized ego.

One way to see this is in the evolution of Western art, especially painting. Before the 1900s, most portraits were simply meant to capture what someone looked like. Usually, these folks were high-status aristocrats, priests, or merchants. People were depicted in their social roles or maybe as characters in some mythic story. By the start of the twentieth century, however, art radically changed. Pablo Picasso, Francis Bacon, and Lucian Freud painted their subjects as complex and often distorted figures, lonely persons often at odds with themselves. Modern art shows a conflicted and lonely individual behind the image.

It also highlights an uncomfortable truth about our condition: WEIRDos like us are psychologically insecure. We often don't know who we are or what our place in the world should be. We are beset with chronic anxiety about our purpose and have nagging worries about our worthiness to feel happy, almost as if life were some ongoing, cosmic audition. And much of this comes from the paradoxes of our modern lives.

Consider just a few examples. We all want to be respected as equals, yet we also want to stand out as special individuals. We crave deeper meaning for our existence but remain preoccupied with personal success and appearances. We often feel anxious and lonely, yet we might spend much of our time self-promoting on social media. Our culture demands that we exercise vast amounts of individual self-control yet floods us with a sea of consumeristic temptations.

The modern ego is maintained through a life of lonely self-subjugation. This is not a natural way to be, and, not surprisingly, few people can achieve success in this with any measure of happiness or self-assurance. It's why being cool is such a rare phenomenon.

How then do we resolve this dilemma? For much of human history, the answer was religion. Until about two hundred years ago, it was religious beliefs that told us how to act and what our place should be. But today, religion has come undone; most WEIRDos no longer rely on it as their primary guide to living. Instead, we have been forced to find new, secular ways of knowing our place. And among all of these new techniques, there is one that stands out as the defining way to understand yourself today. It is a modern method, less than 150 years old. It offers a bespoke way of knowing our individualized ego, and it is the ultimate expression of our WEIRD culture. I'm talking about therapy.

Therapy

I went to a therapist for the first time in 1981. I was fifteen and very depressed. My parents had recently divorced after many years of unhappiness, substance abuse, and infidelity. Wanting nothing to do with either of them, I moped about in lonely isolation. I was doing poorly in school, getting into lots of trouble with the police, and didn't care that much about living. The bright, secure, and happy child I had once been was long gone. My self was clearly not functioning well.

A school counselor noticed this, and the next thing I knew, my dad started driving me to this office every week, where a nice man with a beard asked me gentle questions about why I was sad. I don't remember much about the first couple of sessions beyond the fact that I ended up sobbing in his office, letting out a lot of misery that I had been carrying around for a long time. After four sessions, however, I decided to quit. I found out how much therapy was costing, and it shocked me. My parents didn't have much money, and spending fifty dollars every week to cry in the nice man's office seemed wildly extravagant.

Instead, I decided to solve my problems on my own—I would DIY my way through my depression. It occurred to me that if I wanted to be happier, it was up to me alone to make this happen. No magic fairy would come along and, poof, make everything better. So I took it upon myself to improve my own life. Happiness was going to be something I would earn, and I would do this by constructing a new ego. And, funnily enough, this actually worked for a while.

It started with achievements. I began working harder in school, got into a good college, and imagined a life filled with fame and external validation. I also went out of my way to make friends and find community; I yearned for a place where I felt I belonged. Of course, it was not all great. I was still emotionally unsteady, often arrogant, boastful, and generally self-centered. I was perpetually hungry for acclaim. I would fluctuate between feelings of excessive self-confidence and waves of thick self-loathing; sometimes, I was the world's best person and worst person at the same time.

Nevertheless, my new self-construction took me pretty far. I made terrific friends, finished a PhD, and got my first job at Princeton. Everything was going great . . . until it wasn't.

It started with a phone call in the middle of the night. It was from my girlfriend, who was then backpacking through India. We had been dating on and off for five years and were thinking of getting married. But she was really bored living in Princeton, New Jersey, and still had the itch to travel, while I was super busy climbing the tenure ladder. So, in a moment of generosity or naivete or something else entirely, I bought her a plane ticket to India. I was hoping it would help her find whatever she was looking for. And, ultimately, it did. Just not in the way I expected.

She called to tell me that she had met someone else and "wanted to explore" what a relationship with him would be like. Confused, I begged her to return, but she demurred and quickly hung up. I wanted to find her, but I had no idea where she was, nor did anyone else. India is quite a large place. After two agonizing weeks, she finally called me back and said she wanted to keep traveling with this new guy. Facing the grim truth that she didn't love me, I hung up the phone and never spoke to her again.

And then I came undone. I had just moved to New Jersey and hardly knew anyone. Heartbroken and isolated, I couldn't eat, couldn't sleep, and could barely function in front of my classes. I was lost and bewildered, and it seemed I was back to where I had been at age fifteen, only worse. The absolute low point came a few weeks later. I was standing at a busy intersection, and it occurred to me that all my pain would go away if I just stepped in front of an oncoming truck. That impulse scared the shit out of me, if only because getting run over by a garbage truck in New Jersey seemed a truly humiliating way to go. So, instead of ending it all, I decided to see a therapist.

Once again, I started having weekly meetings with a nice, bearded man who asked me gentle questions about why I was sad. But luckily, this time, I didn't worry about the cost. I finally had a decent job and health insurance, and I wanted to find an answer. My adolescent attempt to fashion a workable ego may have gotten me through my twenties, but, clearly, my new ego wasn't built for the long haul. In fact, it turned out to be pretty brittle. To make it through the rest of my life, I would need a different approach.

Rebuilding my ego started with my stories. One of the first things my terrific new therapist did was to get me to reinterpret the woeful tale I had been telling about myself. He told me upfront that his job wasn't to validate my feelings of hurt and victimization. He didn't want to indulge my self-pity. Instead, he wanted me to rethink my role in my life's dramas. How did I contribute to the breakup? What was I papering over about my past? How was I the source of my miseries? I spent the next five years in therapy looking for answers.

Therapy is mostly about rehashing your stories. Typically, these are the fables of your childhood. In trying to figure out the miseries of your present, your therapist will inevitably suggest you look to your past. But you also have to grapple with the stories of the moment, which usually revolve around your relationships or feelings about yourself. Going to therapy is like having a personalized critic for the epic novel of your life, and much like literary criticism, it is ultimately about interpretation.

Any story can be viewed from many different angles, and this is especially the case with our own. We usually tell our stories in ways that validate our feelings about ourselves. For example, is the story I just related a tale of a brave boy trying to find happiness in life? Or is it about a status-hungry achiever so focused on work that he wasn't attuned to people around him? Or is it something else entirely? Much of my time in therapy was spent trying to figure this out. And what I eventually realized was that my ego wasn't defined by any one story, but by many stories that were often in conflict with one another.

All of this is really WEIRD. In traditional cultures, there is usually just one way to interpret your story—the orthodoxy of your tribe's beliefs. Traditional people don't try to figure out their problems by crafting a bespoke interpretation of their childhoods. They don't contemplate the depths of their own interior lives. And they certainly don't share their most intimate details every week with a nice bearded man who charges over $200 an hour. Therapy today is a uniquely WEIRD practice.

However, if you are uncoupled from traditional myth and culture, therapy is probably your best option. And millions of people are turning to it as a way to live better. Yet therapy still comes with a real challenge: How should you interpret your own stories? How can you make sense of the dramas of your own life? To start answering these questions, let's visit the two men who both pioneered therapy and the modern idea of an ego—Sigmund Freud and Carl Jung.

10

Psyche

AT THE END OF THE EIGHTEENTH CENTURY, MOST EUROpean thinkers were riding high on a wave of rationalism. The Enlightenment had triumphed, and the new "civilized man" prided himself on being in control of his thoughts and impulses, a trait that made him superior to all other animals and those other non-European peoples he so arrogantly colonized. He believed his self was entirely visible to his conscious mind—what you thought was what you were. If you happened to think something unsavory or do something regrettable, it was because you were flawed, weak, or depraved, and thus worthy of subjugation.

By the late 1800s, however, this tidy little notion began to crumble, with the biggest cracks appearing in middle-class women. Out of nowhere, they suddenly started crying uncontrollably, clawing at their hair and skin, and withdrawing into catatonic stupors. Doctors didn't know what to make of this, so they lumped these symptoms together under the catchall diagnosis of "hysteria." The prevailing theory was that hysteria came from a "wandering uterus" that needed to be coaxed back into place with smelling salts or clitoral stimulation. Doctors in the nineteenth century were often quacks.

That is, except for one. His name was Jean-Martin Charcot. Largely unknown today, Charcot was one of the most famous doctors of his time. He was a pathbreaking scientist who helped found the modern field of neurology and discovered many diseases that still bear his name today (the curious way that medical researchers get immortalized in history). In the case of hysteria, he believed the problem was not in the body but in the mind. Women with hysteria did not suffer from a wandering uterus but from an unsettled psyche. Charcot thought the best way to treat women was not with smelling salts or vibrators, but with hypnosis.

Charcot's ideas were revolutionary. For starters, he legitimized the idea that simply talking about one's problems could have a therapeutic effect. In this, he unwittingly planted the seeds of what would become psychotherapy. Even more importantly, Charcot's hypnosis suggested something more: a shadowy figure lurking behind our conscious thoughts and behaviors, a hidden puppeteer pulling the strings of our actions. This notion would influence Charcot's most famous student, a young Viennese doctor who would fundamentally change how WEIRD people like us understand the self and interpret our own life stories.

The Birth of the Ego

If we really want to understand Sigmund Freud's theories, it's essential to know something about his life. Freud was born in 1856 in a small Moravian town within the Austrian Empire. His father, Jacob, was an unsuccessful wool merchant and a widower with two grown sons when he met and married a pretty teenager named Amalia Nathansohn. Soon after, Amalia gave birth to her first child, Sigmund, but family life was a tumult of sexual and financial tension—evidently, Amalia and her two grown "stepsons" had some frisson. By the time Sigmund was eight, his hapless father went bankrupt and moved the family to the Jewish ghetto in Vienna, where he drifted from one implausible scheme to another. Young Sigmund thus spent his childhood in poverty, the family getting by mostly from the generosity of relatives.

Sigmund, however, was a brilliant boy and the vessel of his adoring mother's dreams. Amalia doted on him, smothering him with affection and drive. Buoyed by a voracious curiosity and a formidable intellect (he was, among other things, proficient in eight languages), Sigmund catapulted through grammar school and university. While he yearned to be a scientist, he also craved the comforts of a middle-class lifestyle, so he chose the more lucrative career of a doctor, embodying the old Jewish joke that "it's nice to be smart, but it's nicer to pay the rent."

But the science bug would not relinquish its hold and, even as he practiced medicine, he continued to write papers on everything from the benefits of cocaine, which he enthusiastically used, to the complexities of eel genitalia, which to this day remain a scientific mystery. Then came a pivotal moment. When Freud was twenty-nine, he won a prestigious fellowship to spend four months studying with Charcot in Paris. It was there that he learned about Charcot's methods of treating hysterical patients with hypnosis. Seeing an intriguing and potentially lucrative opportunity, Freud quit the hospital and set up a private psychiatric practice in Vienna. He also began a fifty-year exploration into the unconscious mind that would dramatically change Western culture in the twentieth century.

As he began treating hysterical patients, Freud noticed a striking pattern. After probing into their life stories, most of them reported early sexual abuse, although this trauma was typically buried in the recesses of their memories. Normally, it took a lot of effort to unearth these deep, dark secrets. This discovery led him to two further insights.

First, Freud realized that there weren't just conscious and unconscious parts of the mind. Somewhere, shrouded within the psyche, lurked an invisible mental censor that keeps disturbing facts out of conscious view. In other words, there are hidden parts of our minds that control our ordinary thoughts.

Second, much of this censorship was preoccupied with sexual feelings. It was sexual impulses that wreaked the greatest havoc on the minds of his patients. Their feelings of erotic desire often thrust them into fits of paralysis or physical spasms. What's more, they were mostly unaware of the potent sexual urges that were churning within. In short, Freud realized there was much more to us than what appears on the surface.

He soon concluded that in order to understand what was happening in his patients' minds, he would first have to untangle the knots in his own. What unseen forces were steering his actions? Why did he feel both compelled and horrified by his sexual desires? And more important, why was so much shame baked into his mental cake?

To answer these questions, Freud began probing into his psyche, starting a conversation with himself and recording his findings. There he was, notebook in hand, digging into his dreams and impulses like Sherlock Holmes on a cocaine bender, except the only suspect in this investigation was himself. This is important to consider. Psychoanalysis wasn't just a clinical breakthrough; it was the product of one man's relentless, neurotic, and oddly impressive compulsion to talk to himself. Freud didn't just create a new method of treatment; he gave birth to a whole new way of thinking about one's being. In a way, psychoanalysis is the ultimate act of intellectual, WEIRD self-obsession: Freud, analyzing Freud, discovering Freud, and finally diagnosing Freud.

After all this self-investigation, Freud came to some startling conclusions: Repression and neurosis weren't just afflictions tormenting his patients; they were alive and well within his psyche, too. Like a seasoned detective who suddenly finds his own fingerprints at a crime scene, Freud uncovered innumerable compulsions, neuroses, and stymied sexual feelings lurking beneath the polished surface of his consciousness.

The deeper he ventured, the more discoveries he unearthed. His dreams? Not just the whimsical wanderings of a weary mind but instead elaborate narratives crafted to fulfill his unconscious wishes. His verbal hiccups, the infamous "Freudian slips"? Nothing less than repressed impulses bursting forth like uncaged animals. And jokes? Well, Freud realized they were funny because they let loose all those pent-up desires that societal norms had told us to keep under wraps. Armed with these insights, Freud embarked on a staggeringly ambitious project: He would draw a map of the unconscious mind.

Freud's Theory of the Ego

According to Freud, there are three parts of the mind. The first is one we are born with. Writing in German, Freud called this part *das es* (literally "the it"), but his English translator, James Strachey, chose to translate it as "the id." The id is our animal self—those raw, unfiltered urges that seek immediate satisfaction. It's the source of our basic desires for food, pleasure, sex, security, and domination. The id doesn't care about social niceties or the feelings of others; it just wants what it wants, and it wants it now; and it will often fight anything that gets in its way.

The id was also Freud's frontal assault on nineteenth-century European notions of the self. Rather than describing the mind as built upon the Enlightenment foundation of reason and rationality, Freud says that we are, at our core, creatures of passion and violence. The id is a hypersexual and highly aggressive beast, the undomesticated animal that lies within us. Although we don't normally see it or even want to acknowledge it, the savage id is at the center of human life. It's also telling that Freud called this primal part of ourselves an "it," almost as if the id were some impersonal, alien force that had infected our minds. In doing so, Freud inadvertently echoed the classical Greek's disdain of the animal self as an almost nonhuman force within us.

Then, we have the second part of the psyche: the ego. Freud originally called this *das Ich*, which means "the I." But Strachey, perhaps fearing that "I" would be confusing and that *Ich* would make English readers feel like they had something stuck in their throats, opted for the more refined Latin term, "ego." But either way, *das Ich* or "the ego" is the sense of self we identify with most powerfully, the "me" that fills our heads with endless chatter about our likes, dislikes, aspirations, and anxieties. It is the part of us that stands at the helm of our conscious experience—the self-proclaimed captain of our psychological ship. Freud's ego is the part that proudly wears our name tag and mistakenly believes it's in charge.

Here's where Freud dropped one of his more provocative insights: The ego, this rational "me" that we hold dear, is not some inborn essence or even something intrinsic to us. Instead, it's the by-product of our upbringing. It is also the primary compass that we use to navigate the often treacherous waters of society. The person we know as ourselves results from a delicate negotiation between our primal urges (the id) and the demands of our families and societies. Essentially, our egos are forged in the crucible where biology meets culture, emerging as the somewhat beleaguered diplomat trying to keep both sides happy.

Childhood forges this "me" out of our animal self and turns it into the person we know as ourselves.

Although these ideas were unconventional for their time, they were also pretty straightforward. Where Freud plunged into scandal was in how he said the ego develops. According to Freud, when we're born, we're little more than id-driven creatures, entirely focused on satisfying our erotic desires. Our early months are a blissful haze of groping for the comfort of our mother's breast and embrace, with nary a thought for anyone else's needs or wants. But as we toddle into early childhood, we realize there's more to life than gratifying our every whim. We begin to recognize ourselves as distinct individuals, and with this new identity comes a new revelation: We must learn to control all the animalistic eros and aggression within the id.

Our first lesson is with the toilet. Freud believed that our egos are initially shaped when we learn to control our bowels, typically around eighteen months. This moment of holding in our shit until we find a toilet not only teaches us self-control, it marks the beginning of our understanding that we are separate from the world around us. Of course, this is also when we start learning to speak. Had Freud lived a few decades later and benefited from advances in developmental psychology, he might have placed more emphasis on language rather than bowel control as the cornerstone of ego development. But then again, maybe not—Freud was famously stubborn about his theories.

Either way, language, self-control, and the ego progress together in lockstep. As Freud saw it, a stronger feeling of self arises with each clash between the child's infantile, pleasure-seeking impulses and a world that demands such impulses be kept in check. With every reward for being good and every admonishment for being naughty, the child adds more coherence to their sense of self.

Take young Sigmund, for instance. As he learns his name, he learns what's expected of him. Some behaviors—like following the rules or obeying his parents—are rewarded, while others—like throwing food or playing with his penis—are not. Over time, these lessons fuse with his growing sense of "me," shaping his self-awareness. Freud's famous dictum, "Where id was, the ego shall be," captures this process perfectly: As we learn to regulate the self, we begin to create *ourselves*.

This ego, however, is more than it appears. At a surface level, we define ourselves with the obvious markers. Young Sigmund learns he's a boy, a student, a son, and so forth. But these labels don't simply tell him how to think about himself; they also tell him how to feel. In order to win his parents' love and avoid their condemnation, Sigmund wants to be a good boy, an excellent student, and a dutiful son, aspirations that promise emotional payoffs. And this holds for all of us. Our ego navigates the world using social rewards as its beacons.

Freud argued that these ego processes operate primarily in the unconscious depths of our minds. To really know ourselves, Freud says we needed to pull back the curtain of mental life and discover the mechanisms beneath. One of his early ideas was that the mind uses certain kinds of emotions to counteract others, especially ones that are socially unacceptable. In other words, we train the self to use our feelings against each other. For example, we use our aggression to repress our sexual desires, and this aggression reveals itself to us as punishing feelings of guilt and shame.

However, all this training leaves a heavy mark on our psyche, imprinting it with stifling emotional habits. Freud called these habits neuroses. A neurosis is an inappropriate emotional reaction—a mental state misaligned with present circumstances. It's the anxiety that gnaws at you when there's no real danger, the resentment you feel despite no actual harm, the self-loathing that lingers even when you've done nothing wrong. These neurotic feelings stem from those early childhood experiences that have slipped out of our everyday awareness, and yet they dominate our waking lives.

To illustrate how this all occurs, Freud turned to classical mythology and the story of Oedipus. In Greek legend, Oedipus is a tragic figure who unknowingly kills his father and marries his mother, ultimately ascending to the throne of Thebes. When he discovers the horrifying truth of his actions, Oedipus blinds himself and spends his remaining days stumbling about in an anguished lament. Freud saw this tale as emblematic of the central drama that animates all of our childhoods—the desire to destroy our fathers as obstacles to the sexual conquest of our mothers and the punishing feelings of guilt that plague us ever after.

This is the famous (or infamous) Oedipal complex. In this myth,

Freud saw the origin story of all our neuroses, and considering his childhood—being raised by a beautiful young mother and a hapless father—it clearly reflected his own experiences. But Freud generalized this to all of us. He believed that our juvenile sexual impulses are so strong and the fear of their destructive consequences is so great that our fragile egos simply can't cope. They are unable to contain the ferocious power of our animalistic desire to sexually dominate our mothers and wreak violence against our fathers. The ego's inability to restrain these impulses is terrifying because its weakness could lead to our destruction.

To prevent this mental train wreck, the mind employs a bit of psychic jujitsu. It takes all that pent-up aggression and frustration from being sexually thwarted and redirects it inward. It uses our own animalistic impulses against each other. Over time, this tactic becomes a well-worn habit. For instance, whenever a child experiences sexual feelings, instead of acting on them or even seeing them for what they are, those feelings get smothered in waves of anxiety or guilt. Eventually, this self-punishment becomes a habit and any sexual impulse triggers an almost reflexive spasm of self-recrimination.

Freud called this inner enforcer the *über-Ich* or "over-I," which Strachey translated as "the superego." This is the third pillar of the mind. According to Freud, the superego is the iron-fisted authority figure within us, operating mainly out of sight. The reason we don't go around constantly raping, pillaging, or just generally acting like rock stars on a bender is because our civilized personality is kept in check by this internal policeman.

The superego keeps us in our place, imposing feelings of anxiety, guilt, and discontentment whenever we stray too far from socially acceptable behavior. In this way, civilization functions thanks to the invisible cop that patrols the minds of all its members, ever vigilant against the chaos lurking within. Here again, language domesticates us by getting us to incorporate society's rules into our own psychic processes.

And this takes us back to the ego. Freud says this sense of "me" we all carry around is just a thin veneer, a delicate mask barely concealing the tumultuous struggle between our primal desires and our fears of their terrifying consequences. Sometimes, our raw instincts win out, and, sometimes, our superego smacks them down, but caught in the middle is the fragile ego, the stage where our conscious self resides. This ego is constantly buffeted, always looking for something to hold it all together. But more often than not, it buckles under the pressure, leading to a cascade of neuroses bubbling up from the unconscious. Freud believed that this is why we spend much of our time wrapped up in our psychodramas—the visible expressions of the endless battles waged in the hidden depths of our minds.

What Freud Tells Us About Ourselves

Despite the many problems with Freud's theories, he was a true pioneer of the self. He gave modernity its first detailed theory about what underlies our sense of being and a framework for interpreting our life stories. This strong sense of "me" we carry around is the by-product of our upbringing. Our consciousness is molded by lessons dictated by our language, family values, and the broader culture. We are, fundamentally, the sum of our nature, childhood experiences, and the society we were born into. Most important, Freud revealed to us that there is much more to our minds than what is consciously visible; that most of our actions are driven by unconscious processes.

We may take this idea for granted today, but it was revolutionary for its time, and Freud deserves great credit for it. But Freud didn't stop there. He also emphasized that each of us has a unique, individual ego that emerges from our particular life history. This idea truly marks him as a modern thinker. In Freud's view, we are each distinct as individuals; each of us has peculiar stories and personal pathologies. The psychological dramas defining us are unique, even if they follow the same Oedipal storyline. This was a profoundly WEIRD idea, and, as far as big ideas go, it was huge. And Western civilization has never been the same since.

But what, then, should we do with all of this? Freud didn't say. Indeed, he was pessimistic about our prospects for a happy, flourishing life. It goes back to the demands of living in civilization, which require us to become neurotic in order to control our inner, antisocial desires. Freud says that if we want to coexist in peace and harmony, we need to weigh ourselves down with loads of chronic guilt and anxiety.

Our limited consciousness is also where our suffering begins. Freud says that we rarely see our emotional sufferings as inappropriate. Instead, we take them as gospel truth. We end up rationalizing our negative feelings and seldom questioning their validity. If I feel anxious, it must be because I'm in danger. If I feel guilty, it must be because of my depravity. If I'm resentful, it's because of some awful wrong that someone else has done. The ego, ever the industrious little storyteller, churns out these narratives to paper over the inner turmoil of the mind.

Thus, we spend our days caught up in various psychic dramas, starring in tragedies penned by the unseen hands of our past—more like unwitting actors than conscious authors. The best we can hope for, according to Freud, is to recognize our neuroses and try to keep them from totally running the show. Orthodox Freudian analysts suggest this requires years, if not decades, of therapy. And even then, all that hard work might only scratch the surface, giving us just enough relief to limp along under the harsh oversight of our superego's brutal regime.

And that's pretty depressing. It's hard to read Freud and not come away with a feeling of despondency. For here is one of modernity's greatest thinkers telling us our domestication curses us to a life of discontentment. He said that we could only partially alleviate this suffering by focusing on "work and love," a very Germanic idea, and one we'll reevaluate later on. But before we get too depressed, it's important to remember that Freud wasn't hosting the only psychoanalytic game in town. At the same time Freud was speculating about the id and superego, another explorer was trailblazing a much different and more hopeful pathway into the unconscious with a vision of true transcendence. His name was Carl Jung.

11

Archetypes

ONCE UPON A TIME, THERE WAS A YOUNG CARPENTER WHO lived in a small, quiet village. Like his father before him, he spent his days building doors, tables, and anything else people needed. But the carpenter wanted more than this humdrum life. There was an itch within him, a niggling craving for something better. One day, he heard of a wandering mystic who could reveal profound truths to worthy people. Curious, the young carpenter packed up his things and went to find him.

The mystic was a wild-eyed and daunting man. He wore a camel hair shirt, ate nothing but bugs and honey, and told harrowing stories of an imminent, burning apocalypse. Undeterred, the carpenter approached the mystic and asked to be blessed. The mystic, seeing something special in the young man—possibly the fact that he wasn't moving back slowly in the opposite direction—agreed to baptize him in a nearby river.

When the carpenter arose from the water, he was filled with a celestial vision, commanding him to go into the desert and find his truth. Following this inspiration, the carpenter ventured forth, fasting and praying for forty days and nights. Soon, he was visited by a spirit who tried to seduce him with visions of power and pleasure. The young carpenter resisted these sordid temptations, and eventually, he was filled with visions of divine transcendence. With this newfound wisdom, he returned to his people, telling them about how they, too, could find eternal peace.

This is the story of Jesus Christ as related in the Gospels of Matthew, Mark, and Luke. It describes his encounter with John the Baptist and his awakening to his spiritual purpose. It is one of the foundational stories of Christianity. And, like most of the Bible, it is subject to many interpretations.

Take, for example, the term *spirit*. Some Christians interpret the Greek word Σατανάς (pronounced Sata-nas) as meaning a literal devil, Satan, an infernal demon trying to derail Jesus in his mission to save humanity. Others read the story differently. Maybe the spirit represents Jesus's mind, tempting him with his animal nature. By this reading, Jesus isn't overcoming a demon; he is overcoming his weaker self. Which is the correct interpretation? We'll never know. The Bible is a poetic collection of stories. What we see in them depends on what we're looking for.

And the same goes for our egos. To know ourselves, we must reflect on our stories, but it's not always clear which version of our story is the truth. As I mentioned earlier, traditional people like Boola decipher their stories through orthodox readings of collective myths. We WEIRDos, however, are not constrained. We're left to our own interpretive devices, and it's not always clear which one will be the most illuminating.

The first modern person to offer a nonreligious, authoritative system for interpreting our life stories was the guy we just met, Sigmund Freud. His vision of superegos, repression, and unconscious motives became the dominant lens by which secular Westerners began deciphering their own life narratives in the first decades of the twentieth century. But like any great prophet, Freud inspired other visionaries who took his ideas in new directions.

Of all his acolytes, the most significant was Carl Jung. Jung not only created an entirely different mode of psychotherapy, he launched a more spiritual approach to understanding the self. In contrast to Freud, Jung thought therapy could be a pathway to the greater spiritual forces of the universe. In our grand tour of the self, Jung is another can't-miss stop. So, let's see what the great Swiss psychoanalyst can tell us about ourselves.

The Modern Mystic

Carl Jung was born in 1875 and grew up in a small Swiss village, the son of a rural pastor and a homemaker. Like Freud, Jung initially chose a medical career and worked at a hospital until he, too, came under the influence of an older physician; only in Jung's case, it was Freud himself. After reading Freud's early works, Jung reached out, and the two immediately hit it off; evidently, their first conversation went on for thirteen straight hours. Freud was so smitten with Jung that he soon anointed him as his successor, making him the first president of the International Psychoanalytic Association. It also helped that Jung, as a Christian, could alleviate the stigma of psychoanalysis as a "Jewish science." If Freud was the high prophet of the modern psyche, Jung was his number one disciple.

But, as with many great romances, the honeymoon didn't last. Their falling out started with Jung, who began to chafe under Freud's insistence that the unconscious mind was nothing more than a seething cauldron of sexual repression and unresolved Oedipal conflicts. Jung, instead, saw the unconscious as something far grander. For him, it was a vast reservoir of creative potential, a portal to the collective wisdom of the ages, not just a battleground of suppressed desires. Where Freud saw a grim struggle to keep our baser impulses in check, Jung envisioned a journey toward wholeness, a path to transcendence.

Not surprisingly, these growing differences strained their relationship. Freud, ever the disciplinarian, wanted Jung to stay in line with his psychoanalytic orthodoxy, while Jung, ever the free spirit, wanted to follow his own visions. By 1913, the break was official: Freud essentially excommunicated Jung, who, in response, tumbled into a deep existential crisis. Jung dealt with his situation by doing what any self-respecting psychoanalyst would do—he analyzed himself. Emerging from this long period of introspection with his illustrated Red Book in hand, Jung had drawn a distinct and highly mystical portrait of the psyche.

Like Freud, Jung's impact on Western culture is enormous. Jungian analysis remains one of the most robust fields in modern therapy. His ideas pop up everywhere, from movies to corporate self-improvement. Have you ever called yourself an introvert or talked about your shadow self? That's all due to Carl Jung.

But Jung is not a straightforward thinker to pin down. Unlike Freud, who was obsessed with creating a unified, specific theory of the mind, Jung was on more of a spiritual quest. His prose is famously twisted, a maze of metaphors and arcane references that can leave even the most dedicated readers scratching their heads. Nor was Jung particularly concerned with being scientific. Where Freud craved the validation of his establishment peers, Jung was perfectly content to draw inspiration from the supernatural and the occult. His theories are informed more by intuitive conceptions of spirit and soul and less by empirical ideas of brain and body. Nevertheless, I'll try to summarize them here briefly.

Jung, like Freud, believed that we all have an ego, a handy compass for navigating our social worlds. But unlike Freud, Jung says that our ego is not forged in the single crucible of early sexual repression; instead, it comes from a wider array of sources. Forget the universal Oedipal drama—Jung saw childhood as a smorgasbord of complexes that define our later selves.

Let me illustrate Jung's approach with the example of Sofia. She is a thirty-eight-year-old television producer in Los Angeles. She's intelligent and charismatic and seems to have it all. But underneath this polished veneer, her reality is messier. Sofia is chronically insecure, lonely, and stressed. She has trouble maintaining intimate connections and feels she has no real friends. She fights a lot with her husband because he "fails to understand" the constant pressure she's under. Sofia often loses her temper with her young daughter, Ella, if she makes a mess or cries. And she rarely feels comfortable in her skin. In short, Sofia has an ego that is useful in some ways but problematic in others.

Freud would probably locate Sofia's struggles in some latent sexual energy, perhaps over her frustrated attempts to possess her father or because her ego got arrested during her anal stage of psychological development. Jung, however, would take a broader view. He would look at Sofia's entire life story—her erratic, critical mother; her distant father—and see how all of these figures shaped her whole mind, not just her feelings of sexual repression. He'd notice that, at an early age,

Sofia learned that the best way to get her parents' love was by acting precociously and charmingly, and that this is how she continues to engage with the world. In other words, adult Sofia still follows a rulebook written as a young child.

Sofia, however, is not regularly conscious of this. All she typically experiences is low-level, chronic anxiety, which is a mask for an even greater infantile terror that was stamped on her psyche at an early age. Her ego is brittle, partly because of the erratic and emotionally impoverished upbringing that forged it, but also because all our egos naturally have some fragility.

Notice that there is nothing here about sexual tension or instinctual repression. Yes, young Sofia wanted her parents' love and was terrified she would lose it, but her ego was not shaped by the desire to possess them sexually, as Freud might have insisted. Nor was Sofia afraid of her father's wrath; if anything, it was the opposite—she desperately longed for recognition from him. In Jung's account, our complexes arise from many sources and typically involve more general longings for security, love, and acceptance.

These complexes are visible in the many expressions of our ego. Jung believed that our egos are not fixed in one form but comprise many different *personae*. Jung's use of this term is artful. *Persona* was the Latin word for the mask that Etruscan mimes wore in the early days of the Roman Republic, and it is the root of the English word *person*. It means the face we present to the world. In Jung's view, our egos take the form of different personae (or masks) depending on our situation. At work, we may put on the mask of the competent achiever; among friends, we may act the jovial clown; with our parents, we may perform as the dutiful child. Our experience of the moment is shaped by whichever persona comes to the fore. In the case of Sofia, much of her ego consists of the persona she fashioned as a child: the mask of the intelligent, overeager-to-please angel who is also hypersensitive to being ignored.

Our reliance on these personae is why Jung believed we would never find our authentic being in our egos. Again, the ego is a part of the self, but only a part. Jung says that as long as we identify our whole selves with our egos, we will be frustrated because we will only identify with a temporary vehicle for a particular moment. And because the ego constantly shifts among personae, there will never be one identity that represents our true self. In other words, I may identify as a loyal friend, a competent father, or a genial professor, but none of these masks represent me at my core.

Complexes and personae, however, are not the only parts of the self. Lurking in the unconscious is another element that Jung calls the shadow self. This hidden part of our psyche is often incompatible with our conscious egos. Remember, the ego exists to bring us social rewards. We want to feel good about ourselves, win acclaim or approval, and get what we want from others, and our collection of personae makes this happen. Our shadow self is the part of us that is incompatible with these ego demands. It holds the masks that we dare not wear in public, the parts of us that might cause others to condemn or hate us.

The shadow self often takes the form of antisocial impulses or immoral desires. It is the part of us that secretly wants to have an affair with our sexy neighbor, abandon our screaming children, or steal our friend's video game. These parts are primarily hidden in the unconscious, but the shadow self occasionally surfaces in our fantasies, dreams, or moments of weakness. And while the shadow self is often seen as dark or immoral, it isn't always evil. For example, I'm usually cheery, but, as I mentioned before, I frequently play mournful, sappy songs on the piano. Perhaps this is because these songs are easier to play, but Jung might see this as an expression of my shadow self, the sad parts of my mind that I don't want to acknowledge consciously.

Taking this together, Jung offers us a version of psychoanalysis unencumbered by the problems of Freud's Oedipal psychodrama. Jung's portrait of the ego is more nuanced and personalized. If Jung had stopped there, his psychological theories might have been more widely accepted. But Jung took his ideas in a further direction, which, depending on who you ask, either made him a pioneering visionary or a deluded crackpot.

The Collective Unconscious

To appreciate the controversies surrounding Jung, we'll need to wade back into the murky waters of the unconscious. Jung, ever the imaginative thinker, believed that the unconscious mind was like a well-stocked basement composed of two distinct levels. First, there's the personal unconscious—a cozy storage unit filled with all our unique complexes, life experiences, and the dusty costumes of our personae. It's the part of the psyche that belongs just to us.

But that's not the only room in the basement. Jung believed there was also a more mysterious layer to our psyche: the collective unconscious, a mental template shared by the entire human species. Picture it as a vast ancestral warehouse cluttered with the primordial instincts and timeless keepsakes from humanity's past. And Jung had a particular word for all of its contents: archetypes.

Jung defined archetypes as recurring "patterns" that echo across all human cultures, manifesting in common images, symbols, and stories. As a Jungian therapist once put it to me, "An archetype isn't a thing or an image; it's the potential for one." Imagine it as a cosmic mold, just waiting for the right moment to stamp out another monster, lover, or father figure. Or, as Jung himself said,

> An archetype is like an old watercourse along which the water of life flowed for centuries, digging a deeper channel for itself. The longer it has flowed in this channel, the more likely it is that, sooner or later, the water will return to its old bed.*

In other words, archetypes are sneaky, invisible forces flowing through humanity's collective unconscious, shaped by the shared experiences of countless generations that have come before us. They're like the ultimate rerun—popping back into existence when the narrative demands it, reminding us that we're all part of a much bigger story, whether we realize it or not.

The most common way these archetypes make themselves visible is through dreams, art, and myth. In dreams, we don't just get a replay of that embarrassing thing we did in high school; we also see images and symbols that have been making cameos in human minds for mil-

---

* From Jung, C. G. (1936). "Wotan." In *The Collected Works of C. G. Jung* (Vol. 10).

lennia: the monster chasing us, the blocked pathway, the descent into the labyrinth. Jung believed that it was no coincidence that the same images kept popping up repeatedly in ancient myths and stories across different cultures. They all draw from the same well. It's like humanity's collective unconscious is stuck, replaying the same dramas over and over again.

Jung says these archetypes aren't just casual influencers; they're more like full-blown puppet masters, pulling the strings on our personalities, desires, and life choices. Many of our personae, like the stern father, the nurturing mother, and the playful child, come straight out of the archetypal warehouse. Since these archetypes emerge from the collective unconscious, they also tie us to the rest of humanity, like a psychological network we didn't even know we were connected to.

If we're seeking transcendence, Jung says we'll need to peek behind the curtain and see which archetypes are pulling the strings. This intense dive into your unconscious to meet your archetypal master is a process Jung calls individuation. It's like going on a spiritual road trip where you discover who you are by facing down all the uninvited guests steering the van. This individuation process is itself an archetype, one commonly called the hero's journey.

According to mythologist and Jung devotee Joseph Campbell, all the world's cultures share a "monomyth," or a universal hero's adventure, the blockbuster hit of human storytelling. In this epic, the hero starts living a mundane life—maybe stuck in a dead-end job or endlessly scrolling through social media—until she realizes she has some untapped potential, like a hidden superpower. Then, something shakes her life: a mysterious message, a betrayal, or the breaking point of unceasing boredom. This moment becomes her call to action, pushing her out of her comfort zone and into the wild unknown. And so, off she goes, ready to face whatever adventures await.

For all its mystery, the journey usually follows a familiar script. First, our hero meets a wise, older mentor—Gandalf, Yoda, John the Baptist. Then she receives an empowering gift: a magical sword, a powerful wand, or some ruby slippers. Along the way, she finds some loyal sidekicks, friends who will aid her in the quest. She faces a few more minor challenges that allow her to improve her skills before her ultimate showdown with her true nemesis.

This epic battle usually goes down in some dark, creepy underworld, like the dragon's lair, the witch's castle, or Christmas at the in-laws'. In this climactic struggle, our hero has a brush with her metaphorical death, a moment where she sheds all the shadowy baggage weighing her down. Then, like a phoenix rising from the ashes, she emerges from this trial reborn, not quite the same person who set out on the adventure. She's found a new way of being, discovered transcendence, and has the metaphorical battle scars to prove it. By the tale's end, the hero returns to her ordinary life, but now she's been upgraded.

If this story sounds familiar, it's because it's woven into the fabric of our most enduring sacred and secular myths. It's the tale of Jesus, Muhammad, and the Buddha. It's also the plotline of everything from *The Wizard of Oz* to *The Lion King* to *The Matrix*. George Lucas had the good sense to use it as a blueprint for *Star Wars*, ensuring a permanent place in the cultural zeitgeist and an empire built on merchandise. If you dream of writing the next blockbuster novel or screenplay, the hero's journey is the narrative equivalent of a foolproof recipe—just add characters and stir.

According to Campbell, the monomyth is popular because it taps into our unconscious, collective yearnings. The hero's journey speaks to a universal desire for self-actualization and transcendence. To truly discover who we are, we must all, at some point, heed the call to adventure, leave the safety of the familiar behind, and confront our greatest fears. In Campbell's framework, the dark underworld represents our unconscious mind, where we must wrestle with our shadow selves and the parts of our psyche that hold us back from realizing our full potential. Transcendence is the reward for shedding old patterns, finding empowering tools and allies, and, ultimately, locating our true selves.

The appeal of the hero's journey as a narrative trope is undeniable. After all, who among us doesn't feel they have some untapped power just waiting to come out? Who doesn't want to go beyond the ordinary and find a way of overcoming their inner malaise? The real question is not why the monomyth is popular but whether it draws its power from a timeless archetype, as Campbell claims, or if it's simply a brilliant storytelling device that reflects a common aspiration for living better.

I bring this up because there's no shortage of people who take Jung's archetypes as literal truths. Step into any New Age bookstore, and you'll find walls lined with posters and shelves packed with hefty tomes that link Jung's archetypes to everything from tarot cards to the Greek pantheon. The Myers-Briggs Type Indicator is the most famous example of how people have tried to turn Jung's fluid ideas into something more concrete, neatly packaging our personalities into types like INTJ or ESFP. Some enthusiasts mix and match these systems so that an INTP might be dubbed "the sage," while an ESFJ gets the label "the lover."

It's easy to see why these systems are enticing. Our brains, still wired for survival in the wilderness, crave certainty, and there's something undeniably comforting about a system that promises to tell us precisely who we are. But there's a vast difference between seeing yourself in a tarot card labeled the sage, because you fancy yourself wise and thoughtful, and claiming that card represents an immutable aspect of a collective unconscious that links all humanity in an eternal web. And this is where Jung's theories start to get a little murky.

For starters, Jung had a knack for being maddeningly vague about where these archetypes come from or how they appear in our conscious minds. He once described the collective unconscious as "inherited knowledge" derived from human history, which sounds profound until you realize it's as helpful as saying your lost car keys are "somewhere in the house." Sometimes these archetypes make an appearance, and sometimes they don't. There's no reliable way to know when they're on stage, because our interpretations are the only way to recognize them. Essentially, figuring out which archetype is relevant to us is like reading tea leaves—what you see often says more about your imagination than any universal truth.

Moreover, Jung wasn't exactly a model of clarity when explaining the workings of the mind. He sidestepped strict categorizations, nibbling occasionally without committing to a full plate. And this came from his nonscientific orientation. Jung's ideas were more about spiritual exploration than creating a neat, coherent description of human psychology. This makes his writings both fascinating and utterly ripe for misinterpretation. While his notions might be catnip for those with a mystical bent, they can feel like a long stretch for those not already inclined to see the cosmos as a spiritual kaleidoscope. For the former group, Jung offers an intriguing lens through which to interpret their favorite myths or life stories. However, for the latter, many of Jung's ideas don't play well with basic scientific empiricism.

So where does this leave the rest of us wandering through the tangled woods of our psyches with a flashlight that often loses power? Allow me to offer a personal observation from my journey. When I turned fifty, I decided it was time for a psychological tune-up—not because my life was veering off course, but because I had this nagging sense that there was more to explore. So I started working with a Jungian therapist. I wasn't in a crisis—no midlife meltdown, no red sports car or affair with my personal trainer. Life was rolling along quite nicely. But that didn't mean the trip was over. I felt like a lot that needed further investigation was going on with me.

Thankfully, my therapist wasn't fixated on archetypes or the collective unconscious like some modern-day oracle. He was a well-rounded MD with one foot firmly planted in the real world and the other prodding through the murky waters of the psyche. He knew that shoehorning me into some mythical framework would be unproductive. Instead, he guided me through a thorough exploration of my mental habits, borrowing wisdom from Freud and Jung without being shackled to either.

For instance, we spent a lot of time dissecting how a bright, eager-to-please boy like me might have navigated life with a mother who was, let's say, psychologically unpredictable and a father who was as emotionally accessible as Antarctica. We delved into my Catholic upbringing, especially in the resonance of Jesus, who was also a "special" son suffering from an absent father and smothering mother. With this knowledge, we examined how much of my adult life was still informed by these early lessons. We unraveled how my self-worth got so tightly bound up with career achievements and my identity as an A student, which, while good for grades, was not great for romantic relationships or inner peace. We dug into the dynamics of my marriage and why I often felt like catastrophe was imminent, rather than recognizing Thea as the extremely loyal partner she is.

And this has been helpful. Recognizing my old complexes and mental habits didn't make them vanish, but it lessened their power over me. Instead of getting entirely swept up in a compulsive thought like "I'll only be happy if I write an amazing book" or "Thea doesn't really love me," I can now see these notions for what they are—echoes of some early noises first heard long ago. And while these demons still occasionally wreak havoc on my mental landscape, they don't entirely dominate me.

For all their quirks and shortcomings, both Freud and Jung have something valuable to offer those of us trying to make sense of the stories we live by. But, at this point, neither Freud nor Jung provides a clear path to transcendence. They are more like psychological Ginsu knives, suitable for slicing and dicing certain things but inadequate for preparing the whole meal. If we want to go beyond our egos, we will need a better map. And the best one I've come across wasn't drawn by a cigar-smoking Viennese doctor or a Swiss mystic, but by a wandering monk who lived 2,500 years ago in northern India.

12

Transcendence

TRANSCENDENCE IS A PECULIAR CONCEPT. ASK MOST PEOPLE what it is, and they'll probably conjure up an image of something remote and glorious, a place that exists somewhere far beyond our everyday struggles. It's the ecstatic Heaven, the radiant Nirvana, the unattainable Shangri-la. We typically think transcendence is somewhere out there, a hidden garden at the end of a mysterious, arduous journey, usually guarded by some cryptic riddle.

But if you ask most people how they *experience* transcendence, the responses change. Sure, some mention those rare, ecstatic moments—riding the perfect wave or sharing a mind-melding, simultaneous orgasm with your lover. Psychologists call the first a "peak experience," and for the second, let's just say their vocabulary hasn't caught up. But, for most people, transcendence is found through everyday indulgences: a cocktail after a long day, the sweet immersion of a good book, or even zoning out in front of the television for a few hours. In practice, transcendence is anything that takes us away from the reality of the moment, even if that reality is nothing more consequential than folding the laundry.

Yet, regardless of whether it's found in a blessed paradise or another margarita, both notions share one thing in common: Transcendence is something always different from the now. And this makes sense. After all, the word *transcendence* means "to climb" (*scend*), "beyond" (*trans*), so our intuition that transcendence is being somewhere else fits the term.

Ironically, this is also the exact opposite of how real transcendence occurs. Ask anyone who meditates long enough, and they'll tell you the same thing: Transcendence isn't about escape, because there is no place we can ever truly escape to. Sex, surfing, and margaritas may elevate the moment, but, inevitably, we always end up back where we started, sometimes with a hangover. As the Buddhist teacher Jon Kabat-Zinn likes to say, "Wherever you go, there you are," and yes, your baggage is always with you.

Rather than being some esoteric state of enlightenment, transcendence comes from realigning order and vitality among our other layers of being. We've already seen a little of this in our exploration of the cellular and animal selves. Keeping our cells healthy and staying in touch with the harmonious nature of our animal being is crucial to self-optimization. A big part of transcendence is simply eating right, taking care of our bodies, and maybe laying off some of the ordinary ways we typically experience transcendence (for example, margaritas).

But this isn't the whole picture, for transcendence isn't just about mastering your physical body. The real challenge lies in dealing with the more complicated parts of our being, the linguistic and egoistic selves. These layers are the breeding grounds for our neuroses, insecurities, and all those personal dramas that keep us locked in loops of frustration and self-doubt. The practice of transcendence comes in untangling the knotty stories and illusions. If you want to be liberated, you must figure out both what's throwing you off balance and how to regain your footing. And we'll start with the very first person to offer a guide on how to do this: the Buddha.

The One Who Woke Up

Buddhism looms large in the Western imagination, and it is often misunderstood. There are many reasons for this. For starters, Buddhism defies easy categorization. It exists somewhere between religion, philosophy, and psychology, yet it is also distinct in itself. Buddhism also has a wide array of traditions, ranging from the austere Zen practices of Japan to the elaborate rituals of Tibet, and it appears to us in a wide variety of iterations.

Buddhism is also ancient in origin and has accumulated many myths and mysteries. To Westerners, it can seem exotic, tinged with a romantic allure that makes it irresistible to those who want something more from life. When I was young, I was convinced that powerful secrets lurked within some esoteric Buddhist texts, pristine recipes for gaining superpowers that could only be mastered through the deepest study, a notion I probably got from watching too many kung fu movies.

However, the biggest reason we misunderstand Buddhism comes from our frame of reference. We want to compare it to the West's philosophies and religions, which are based on straightforward deductions and rules. The problem with this approach is that Buddhism is ultimately a *practice.* Yes, it has precepts and theories, and as in many traditions, it carries myths and dogmas, but the heart of Buddhism is in the meditative experience. Buddhist truths are understood ultimately through a living application, not as a text. In other words, reading about Buddhism is like reading about sex, eating, or music—words alone don't convey its true essence. If you want to understand Buddhism, then at some point, you've got to sit down and meditate.

Nevertheless, here we are, bound together in the words of this book. So let me briefly summarize Buddhism and how it explains our thoughts and consciousness, even if I can't convey all its glorious subtleties.

Like all other religions, Buddhism starts with a story. Around 2,500 years ago, a prince named Siddhārtha Gautama was born in a prosperous kingdom north of the Ganges River. According to legend, Gautama spent his early years without care or concern. His adoring parents doted on him, and his every need was met with splendid indulgence.

Yet, despite this cosseted luxury, eventually, he encountered sights that shook him to the core. One day he came upon a diseased person, another day he met someone who was crippled, and finally, he encountered someone who was dying. This parade of suffering prompted an existential crisis. Gautama realized there was more to life than the sensual pleasures of his royal cocoon. Hearing the call to adventure, he decided to renounce his palatial decadence and search for a way to transcend this worldly misery. His hero's journey had begun.

At this time, India was populated by bands of wandering ascetics known as sramana (the term is pronounced "shra-man-ah" and is not officially related to the word *shaman*, but still close enough to make you wonder). Sramana were spiritual seekers who had renounced their worldly attachments to pursue enlightenment. The theory behind most sramanic practices was simple: To eradicate human suffering, one must tackle its source, the self. Typically, this involved stringent regimes of extreme self-mortification, including fasting, celibacy, and living without shelter or protection.

Soon after leaving the palace, Gautama joined one of these movements and became its star practitioner. He spent years living outside in deep meditation, surviving on one grain of rice daily. Yet, even after starving himself into near oblivion, he was still not finding the great insight he sought. So one fateful day, he decided on an alternative, a "middle path." Instead of denying his emaciated body, he nourished himself with a small cup of food. This left many of his fellow monks aghast, for Gautama seemed to be abandoning his ascetic devotion. But he had an inkling this might be a better way.

Buttressed by his new energy, Gautama made a final, determined effort to realize the ultimate truth. Placing himself under a bodhi tree, he began to meditate. Eventually, after overcoming a series of titanic struggles and temptations involving his inner demons whispering all manner of seductive, sweet, and threatening nothings, he was able to let go of his attachments to this life and enter a state of enlightenment. He spent his remaining years teaching others the path he had discovered. His journey was complete, and his followers gave him the title of Buddha, which means "one who is awake."

Despite their apparent simplicity, the Buddha's teachings are anything but. As I mentioned before, partly this is because they are based on experiential practices and not abstract theories, and partly this is because they are interwoven with foreign concepts like karma and reincarnation. So, as I go through the Buddha's teachings, please note that I'm not giving them the full explanation they deserve. It's more like flipping through some postcards rather than looking at the complete vacation album. But for now, let me briefly explain the Buddha's central ideas, particularly as they relate to the general themes of self-optimization and transcendence.

The Four Noble Truths

The heart of the Buddha's teachings is the Four Noble Truths. Purportedly, these are the ideas he first communicated after his enlightenment, and they are common in all Buddhist traditions. They go as follows:

1. All existence is *dukkha*.
2. Dukkha is caused by negative mental and bodily habits.
3. Dukkha can be eliminated.
4. The elimination of dukkha comes from redressing these negative habits through following the Eightfold Path, a program of healthy living and meditation.

Okay, that sounds simple enough, but what exactly is dukkha? This word is notoriously difficult to interpret. In English, it is commonly translated as "suffering," but this is like calling a symphony a bunch of musical notes—it misses the larger picture. Dukkha is not simply pain, physical discomfort, or even emotional turmoil, although these are expressions of it. Instead, dukkha is the existential unease of living in a world that never quite fits right. It is like a wheel that wobbles instead of spinning smoothly.

Another way of translating dukkha is with this book's themes—the chronic imbalance between order and vitality within the self. Our self-processes exist to sustain our life force, the energies within us that are resisting entropy. Ideally, we want to have the right mix of order and vitality. But somewhere along the way, we humans became domesticated by language, and our natural processes of order and vitality fell hopelessly out of sync. Our thoughts became constrained by language, our psyches bound by rules, and our minds situated in time. Our egos and identities came to seem like all that define us. This is dukkha ensnaring us in constant waves of discomfort, an endless game of neurotic Whac-A-Mole.

Dukkha is not simply about pain or any other sensation. It's about our habitual response patterns, the cravings and aversions that dominate our living moments. These habits ossify our minds, giving us a distorted view of reality and keeping us from realizing the true nature of our essence: that we are beings of continual flow and change, not the static, stressed-out creatures we often assume ourselves to be.

The path to transcendence is found through unlearning these mental habits. The end of dukkha comes from the cessation of our recurring cycles of craving and aversion. But, in Buddhism, these negative mental habits go far beyond our mere thoughts; they penetrate to the deepest levels of our very being. To see what exactly is at the core of what we are, we'll need to explore what Buddhism says about thinking, consciousness, and the self.

Self or Non-self?

One of the most common questions I hear about Buddhism is, "Doesn't Buddhism say there is no such thing as the self?" Well, yes, and also no. To explain this odd paradox, we need to place Buddhism in its proper context. Buddhism didn't just spring up out of nowhere. Like all philosophies and religions, Buddhism evolved from predecessors; in this case, the same Vedic traditions that gave rise to Hinduism and Jainism. That's why Buddhism shares many concepts like karma and reincarnation with these other great faiths. But what set Buddhism apart was its stance on a significant spiritual question of the time: What is the self?

On one side were the Brahmin, India's highest social caste and the guardians of its ancient spiritual wisdom. Like their classical Greek counterparts, the Brahmin held a dualist view of the self. They saw the self as existing in the body and in the form of a higher spiritual consciousness, the *atman*. While the body would eventually degenerate, the early Brahmin believed the atman would persist throughout time and across the universe. Their yogic spiritual practice aimed to realize the atman's true nature and reconcile it with ultimate reality, or Brahman, thus finding a path to cosmic reintegration.

On the other side of this debate was the Buddha. He said there is no such thing as the self, at least as the Brahmin commonly understood it. His doctrine was *anatman*, which translates as "non-self" or "no-self." According to the Buddha, the self that we commonly perceive is a mental construct, a psychological sleight of hand. The Buddha claimed that the atman does not exist outside the mind—our feeling of self is just a mental projection. This schism over the self is one reason Buddhism broke away from Hinduism and became a separate religion.

But the Buddha was not saying that the self, at least as I'm describing it, does not exist. Instead, he said that this egoistic self that we understand as ourselves, this atman or feeling of "me," is an ephemeral illusion. To understand this claim, let's explore what the Buddha says about our being.

According to the earliest Buddhist texts, this existence we are currently muddling through is brought to us by the five aggregates of Being.* They are:

1. physicality, the whole realm of matter that comprises us;
2. sensation, the range of organs that give us information about the world;
3. perception, the ways we organize the information that our senses provide;
4. volition, the thoughts and intentions we make about the world;
5. consciousness, our awareness of all the layers of being, that spooky sense of "I" that ties it all together.

Each of these elements is composed of yet other parts, and each, weirdly enough, has its distinct consciousness. I won't go into all the details, but I would like to point out two things about this list. First, the Buddha's take is strikingly consistent with scientific models of cognition, which we'll dive into later. He describes thinking as the aggregation of physical and neural data. This was quite the visionary move for a guy who lived a couple of millennia before MRI machines. Back then, most people were convinced that the mind floated around like some ethereal cloud, detached from the messy business of the body. Bud-

* As you might have noticed, the Buddha really liked to enumerate things and there is a reason for this: Because Buddhism was largely an oral tradition for its first several hundred years, numbering the truths and pathways was a helpful way to remember them. So if you read through early Buddhist texts, you find lots and lots of numbered lists.

dhism, however, firmly places our conscious minds within our physical selves, not in some eternal, floating soul.

Second, this list is analogous to our model of the self. It arises from physicality (cellular self) to sensation (animal self) to perception (linguistic self) to volition (egoistic self) and finally consciousness (transcendent self). Just as all layers of the self work in concert, so do the five aggregates. The Buddha says that the essence of our being is an emergent phenomenon that builds up from our bodies through our minds. To my way of thinking, the same goes for our different layers of self.

But here's the rub: the five aggregates are also the source of all our problems. According to the Buddha, the quiet disquiet of ordinary life stems from our pesky habit of clinging to the five aggregates as if they were our permanent selves. We reflexively see them as fixed parts of us rather than the transient, bubble-on-the-surface-of-the-ocean phenomena they are. In other words, dukkha arises because we mistakenly believe that our bodies and minds are stable foundations of a self that is equally stable and permanent. We get attached to these aggregates, and in doing so, we lose sight of the ultimate truth: Everything is impermanent, including our cherished sense of self.

One reason we get so caught up in these illusory attachments is karma. Karma has many definitions, but I prefer the one that describes it as the collective residue of our past experiences. The idea of karma is both simple and profound: As we live from moment to moment, we also live from reaction to reaction, and these reactions leave traces that calcify in our psyche as habits of mind. Karma is the accumulation of all our past thoughts and actions within us.

Say, for example, you wake up one day feeling vaguely off. You stumble to the bathroom, look in the mirror, and zero in on some part of your body you're not particularly fond of, like your nose. The five aggregates, ever helpful, start connecting the dots between your bad mood and your nose. Soon, your nose becomes the scapegoat for your malaise, and you're stuck in the mental loop of "If only my nose were different, I'd be happier," or worse, "Maybe I should get a nose job." Over time, this becomes a fixation. Before you know it, every glance in the mirror triggers a wave of self-loathing, and you equate your worth with your dissatisfaction about your nose. In this sense, karma is like Pavlovian conditioning—reflexive, consistent, and maddeningly powerful.

This type of neurosis is only the tip of the iceberg. Most of our karmic imbalance builds up well below the surface of our conscious awareness, like existential barnacles on a ship's hull. You might occasionally be aware that you hate your nose, but lurking behind this thought is a complex web of mental habits you're unaware of. Yet every time you look in the mirror, you reinforce this pattern, even when you're not consciously thinking about your nose.

This is a crude example of how existence is dukkha. Buddhism says it arises because our minds become habituated to unhelpful ways of thinking, and our consciousness becomes constrained to irrelevant focus points. Our mental life is built upon layers and layers of these thick, karmic bents, most of which operate below our ordinary cognizance. As a result, we spend most of our time in a fog of attachments, fantasies, and thoughtless routines. We don't see reality for what it is; instead, we float in a dreamlike state, tethered to our past like an old balloon stuck in a tree.

The Buddha's solution? Live in a way that unlearns these mental habits, what Buddhists often describe as "waking up." It starts with living in an honest, egoless, and compassionate way. This is the Eightfold Path, and it is specified in the fourth Noble Truth. It includes the following ideas (with my rough translations):

1. Right View: recognizing that all our actions have karmic consequences;
2. Right Intention: making spiritual growth the center of life;
3. Right Speech: not lying or speaking harmful words;
4. Right Action: not stealing, harming others, indulging our sensual appetites, or taking intoxicating drugs;
5. Right Livelihood: not earning your keep from harmful means or by exploiting others;
6. Right Effort: letting go of unproductive emotional states like lust, anger, sloth, anxiety, and doubt;

7. Right Mindfulness: cultivating self-awareness and working to be present in the moment;
8. Right Contemplation: engaging in a meditative practice.

The Eightfold Path is not a list of commandments. These aren't "thou shalt not" types of demands. In Buddhism, there is no hell awaiting sinners in the afterlife, no fiery pits or sulfuric wastes waiting to consume evil souls (although, in many Buddhist traditions, there are recurring afterlives). Even though each one begins with the prefix "right" (at least in most English translations of the Pali term *samma*), they are not hard and fast rules. Instead, they are a guide for reducing our karmic imbalances. So it may be helpful to replace the word *right* with something softer, like *wise* or *useful*. Either way, the goal is the same: removing unhelpful tendencies that keep us trapped in our imbalanced way of being.

Consider, for example, right speech. Lying is harmful not simply because of what it does to others but because of what it does to us. When we lie, we are trying to deceive other people. We lie so that others will not see us as who we are but as an image we are trying to project. Lying, however, ultimately bolsters a false sense of self. It reinforces our attachment to illusions. When we lie, we are not just manipulating others, we are manipulating ourselves, and this has negative consequences for everyone.

Although the Eightfold Path can help correct our thoughts and actions, true liberation is found through contemplative practice. Meditation is a way of retraining the mind. But this retraining is not just a way of suppressing our intrusive thoughts or quelling our anxiety. It is doing something more fundamental: disassembling the deeply ingrained mental patterns that define our self-experience. Meditation trains us to let go of our reflexive attachments to our egos, identities, and neuroses. What's even more remarkable is that most of this work occurs unconsciously. When you sit and meditate, focusing on your breath or some mantra, you are reorganizing the hidden layers of your psyche.

The Experience of Meditating

A common misunderstanding I often hear about Buddhism is that it's a form of escapism, as though sitting on a cushion and meditating lets you dodge life's messy bits. To many, the Buddha's ideas of detachment sound like a polite way of saying, "Let's just pretend those difficult feelings don't exist." In this view, meditation is like a spiritual version of sticking your fingers in your ears and humming loudly.

But that's not what meditation is. In fact, it's the opposite. Far from numbing you, meditation sharpens your senses, making you hyperaware of what's happening inside. Several meditation teachers have explained this to me with an excellent analogy: Most of us experience our feelings like hair running across a fingernail—barely noticeable unless we focus on it. For meditators, our experiences feel more like hair running across the palm; it is more precise and distinct. And for advanced practitioners like monks and yogis, sensory experience is even more intense, like a hair dragged across the surface of an eyeball.

In other words, meditation amplifies your feelings rather than suppressing them. It trains your mind not to knee-jerk at every passing impulse. Instead of reacting to every itch or fleeting frustration, you let them be and this gives you the freedom to explore deeper layers of awareness. This openness applies not only to discomfort but also to joy and pleasure. The serene, radiant Buddha you see in statues isn't someone numbing themselves; it's the image of a person fully embracing their existence, riding the highs and lows with equanimous grace.

And here's the wild part: Meditation does all of this unconsciously. When you limit your focus to the breath or any other point of concentration and refuse to indulge in your usual mental habits, you begin rewiring the circuitry of your brain. Neuroimaging studies of experienced meditators reveal fascinating differences in their brain function, and their patterns of consciousness are notably different from those of non-meditators. I'll explain the neuroscience behind this in later chapters, but suffice it to say that meditation doesn't just change your mind; it reshapes your neural networks.

Some practitioners dive so deeply into meditation that they dissolve the boundaries of the self entirely, reaching states of ego dissolution and extreme sensitivity. But even casual practitioners can experience enormous benefits. Many report feeling calmer, more transparent, and more grounded—qualities that ripple out into everyday life. I, too, can vouch for meditation's transformative power. Over the years, it has helped me unravel the tangled knots of my mind, allowing me to move through life with more equanimity and lightness. It's not always easy. There have been moments when sitting with my thoughts felt like wrangling a tornado of emotions. But the journey has been worth it. To give you a glimpse of how this path has unfolded for me, let me share a bit about my own experience.

When I was twenty-nine, I signed up for my first ten-day silent meditation retreat. At the time, I was nervous. While I had long been intrigued by Buddhism, all my prior attempts at meditating had been failures. Typically, I would sit down and try to focus on my breath or say some odd mantra, and within ten minutes, I'd be up and pacing, my mind buzzing like a swarm of neural bees. This alarmed me. If I couldn't meditate for even an hour, how would I make it through one day, much less ten?

My fear was not unwarranted. Sustained meditation is one of the hardest things I've ever tried, and thirty years later, I'm still not particularly good at it. Meditation requires a willingness to sit with intense pain or agitation in a highly amplified state without resorting to our usual distractions. It's about opening yourself up to all the jagged edges and sticking points that lurk beneath your conscious awareness and then patiently staying there. It's grueling work.

I often illustrate this to my students with the joke: "Why are Buddhist monks always smiling in photos? Because they are so happy not to be meditating!" Okay, maybe the joke isn't funny, but it conveys my point—meditation is tough.

But with the proper guidance, meditation can be revelatory, and one of my most profound insights was about the life force itself. Let me explain. I practice a form of meditation called Vipassana, which comes from the Theravāda Buddhist tradition of Southeast Asia. For the first three days of my course, I was instructed to focus only on my breath, keeping my attention on the natural flow of inhalation and exhalation.

Every time my mind wandered, I gently guided it back to focusing on my breath.

Then, something remarkable happened: The noise in my head started to settle. The chatter that usually ran my life faded to background static, and I started finding little pockets of quiet stillness between the relentless thoughts. By day three, my mind was finally calm enough to move on to the next step: body scanning.

This was where things got interesting. Using my newfound concentration skills, I was instructed to observe my body, slowly scanning it from head to toe and noticing any sensation that arose. At first, this was weird. How often do you observe the backs of your wrists or the space between your toes? But with time, I began to sense these hidden parts of my body with surprising clarity. I could feel the length of my esophagus, the quiet hum of my stomach, and even the twists and turns of my intestines. It was like someone had handed me a special camera to see my body.

And then, somewhere around day seven, my experience shifted further. My body no longer felt like a solid block of flesh and bone. It was more like a field of energy—a shimmering, ever-changing flow of sensations. Pleasure felt like a warm current, effortless and expansive. Pain appeared as thick and dense blockages, like knots in a garden hose, interrupting the flow. It was as if I had stumbled upon the hidden circuitry of my being. Everything, from joy to frustration, was energy moving through me differently.

The deeper I went into this process, the more I realized that my thoughts and emotions were another part of this energy field. They weren't permanent fixtures or defining truths. They were passing states, rising and falling like waves on the ocean. Even the discomfort I initially dreaded became more manageable once I stopped resisting it. Pain, I discovered, wasn't the problem; it was my aversion to it that caused real suffering. And when I let go of that resistance, I found myself opening up to pleasure and joy in ways I hadn't before.

This ability to let go, I realized, is the real power of meditation. It teaches you to observe your being as it is—without the mental noise, without the stories we tell ourselves about what we should or shouldn't be. It shows you that energy isn't just some abstract idea; it's something you can feel directly. In those moments of stillness, when the mind quiets and the body hums with awareness, you begin to experience the life force in its purest form.

It's no wonder so many religious traditions, whether they call it qi, prana, or the Holy Spirit, point to this type of experience as a glimpse of the divine. When you're in tune with these subtle flows of energy, it feels like you're tapping into something vast and sacred, as if you've stumbled upon the underlying rhythm of existence. Some might call it Nirvana, others Brahman, or even God's grace. Whatever label you give it, the experience remains the same: a deep-seated connection to something greater than yourself.

Now, I'd love to tell you that after that retreat (or the many retreats that have come since), I emerged fully enlightened, levitating my way through this life. But that's not how it went. Meditation is an ongoing practice, not a one-time epiphany. Even now, decades later, I still struggle with restlessness and frustration on the cushion. But that's part of the beauty of the practice. It's not about achieving some perfect state; it's about learning to be present with whatever arises, whether joy or pain, triumph or failure, effervescence or flatness.

For me, that first retreat was a turning point. It gave me a new lens through which to view my mind and body, a way to navigate the highs and lows of life with greater ease. I learned that transcendence isn't about escaping to some distant paradise—it's about fully inhabiting the moment, regardless of how it appears. And that, I think, is the natural gift of meditation: It teaches us that we don't need to run from life's challenges. Instead, we can sit with them, breathe through them, and sometimes find a little lightness along the way.

What Buddhism Can Tell Us About Ourselves

Over the past four decades, Buddhist meditation has become increasingly popular in the West. Books on meditation pour off the shelves, and the waitlist for retreat spots can be months long. And this makes sense. Who wouldn't want a taste of glorious effervescence in exchange for a few hours of mindful sitting?

However, we should also approach Buddhism with a bit of caution.

Much like the historical Jesus, the historical Buddha is a bit of a mystery wrapped in myth. We know about him primarily through stories passed down like a centuries-old game of telephone. Along the way, plenty of scribes and scholars likely sprinkled in their interpretations, much like I'm doing here. For example, my explanation about the Four Noble Truths will undoubtedly trample on somebody's toes. But that's how these things go.

What's more, it's perfectly understandable if those who aren't Buddhists raise an eyebrow at some of its claims. After all, the Buddha lived in a time long before modern science, and many Buddhist traditions embrace ideas like reincarnation, which defy science's natural laws and can seem downright odd to those of us who think of life as a one-way ticket rather than a perpetual round-trip ride.

So, with these caveats in mind, allow me to summarize what Buddhism tells us about the self. It all starts with the simple claim that your brain gives you a skewed impression of your existence. To a Buddhist, the mind isn't just a factory churning out thoughts on a 24/7 assembly line; it's a complex interplay of physical and psychological processes that concocts ideas, and first among those ideas is the very sense of self that thinks it's in charge. Yet the Buddha says there's no separate "me" standing apart from the thinking—the conscious mind is as shackled by mental habits and ingrained patterns as the thoughts themselves. Not only are our thoughts shaped by our past experiences, but our life as a "thinker" has been molded and tweaked along the way, too.

This last insight is the most profound one. My intuition is that I'm somehow the same person I've always been. There's this comforting idea that a single thread of self links me back to my childhood. Sure, my thoughts have changed over time, but the "thinker" making them? Well, that's been a constant. It's the part of me that feels solid and permanent, the reliable generator of my thoughts and their ever-present witness. This is what most people refer to as the soul.

Buddhism, however, pulls the rug out from under that cozy notion, suggesting it's all an illusion, a clever trick our minds play on themselves. The conscious experience of self is a projection that gets remade every moment like an ever-shifting sandcastle. It's born from our past actions and current circumstances. It's constantly reshaped with each passing thought and emotion. But here's the silver lining: This illusion isn't set in stone (or even sand, for that matter). We can reshape our conscious experience, expand our sense of being, and lighten the load of our past mental habits.

But we shouldn't just take the Buddha's word for it. Indeed, that was his advice. If we want to find the truth, he said we'd need to discover it for ourselves. Rather than spending years testing his hypothesis in deep meditation, we can take a shortcut and examine these ideas from a scientific perspective. So let's return to the present and see what modern neuroscience says about our thoughts, consciousness, and living well.

13

Thinking

"I THINK, THEREFORE I AM." WITH THIS SIMPLE EXPRESSION, René Descartes translated a common-sense impression into a foundational idea within Western culture: Because we are thinking, we know that we exist. However, the power of this phrase goes beyond mere philosophical deduction, for Descartes was also expressing an even more profound intuition: that the way we know ourselves is through our thoughts. In other words, thinking is what defines our very being.

Yet what exactly is thinking?

Oddly enough, most of us don't really know. When I think of thinking, I typically imagine it as a deliberate act of reasoning, like when I'm trying to divide 548 by 37 or when I'm figuring out what to get Thea for her birthday. It's the deep pondering embodied in Auguste Rodin's iconic sculpture, *The Thinker.*

Lurking behind this idea are three powerful (and erroneous) assumptions. The first is that thinking only happens in the visible, conscious part of the mind. In this view, "thinking" consists entirely of those thoughts, and only those thoughts, that are apparent to us. And this makes perfect sense; after all, how else can we know our thoughts except through those we perceive?

Second, there is a thinker, an "I," that is somehow separate from the thoughts it generates. In other words, our thoughts come from some "thinking machine" in our skulls, and that same machine is part of us but also distinct from the person observing its output. By this reckoning, our thoughts are the result of a deliberate will, a will that somehow exists before the creation of the very thoughts that are the same expression of this will, a will that is an intrinsic part of this feeling of being me.

Third, we commonly assume that our thoughts are accurate reflections of reality. Embedded in Descartes's famous sentence was an unquestioned faith in his thinking process, that whatever story he told himself about the moment must be correct, a pristine refraction of what was happening. We typically revere our thoughts as unfiltered expressions of the truth.

None of these assumptions, however, is correct. Thinking is an incredibly complex set of neural processes that have yet to be fully understood. Most of our "thinking" happens in the hidden recesses of our psyche, far beyond the reach of our conscious attention. Thinking also involves the simultaneous creation of a thinker, a thought, and an observer of the thought. The conscious mind, the "I" that observes the thought, is as much a mental fabrication as the thought itself. So, if we want to understand what's happening with both our thoughts and our consciousness, we need to explore not just what makes our thoughts but what makes us *thinkers*.

The Foundations of Thought

Thinking starts with neurons, the eighty-billion-plus cells spread throughout our brains and bodies. No thoughts are possible without them. Neurons are the foundation of all cognition, the unsung heroes of our mental existence, transferring electrical signals from one part of the body to another like tiny messengers zipping around with urgent, invisible notes. Other neurons then use these data to do something else, usually directing the body to move somehow, like when you pull your hand away from a hot stove or wave enthusiastically at someone you're trying to impress. The neurons in our brains further elaborate on these processes, generating ideas or storing memories, perhaps even the idea that waving with such enthusiasm might not have been the smoothest move.

Thinking is the way these neural signals get processed and configured.* Although we typically associate thinking with thoughts in our conscious minds, it goes much deeper and includes the following functions:

- Registering information from the environment and body (sensation);
- Organizing this sensory information (perception);
- Storing and retrieving information (memory);
- Intentionally reordering mental concepts (reasoning);
- Generating a specific focus of attention to enable deliberate action (consciousness).

A couple of things are noteworthy about this list. First, thinking is something that any animal with a nervous system does. For simple animals like jellyfish, "thinking" is mostly a series of crude reflexes.† It starts with sensation, a neuron taking one particular information signal and transferring it to another body part, something like the movement of messages in an internal post office.

Perception is the aggregation of neural information into what psychologists call concepts, the arrangement of many sensory bytes into a larger whole. If sensation is like individual letters, say D, G, and O, then perception is like grouping these letters into particular words (dog, god, good). Just as we form terms by arranging letters into different orders, your brain generates its mental concepts by arranging neural bits into particular configurations.

This last point is critical to understanding thinking. All the images, thoughts, and sensations in your head, from the softness of a cash-

---

* This definition is consistent with the etymology of the term "cognition" from its Greek/Latin roots of *cognosco* (*con* "with" and *gnosco* "knowing").

† Admittedly, I don't know much about jellyfish psychology, so I might be doing them a great disservice. If anything, recent discoveries in biology suggest that even simple animals have a more complicated cognition than we commonly realize. Once again, writing about biology is really hard because any generalization one makes always seems to find a contradiction.

mere sweater to the deepest rumination in philosophy, are based on compilations of concepts and images assembled from even smaller bits of neural data. Everything in cognition apparent to our conscious minds, and even our conscious minds themselves, are built upon many tiny neural parts.

An excellent example of this is our vision. It's intuitive to believe that we see the world by simply opening our eyes and having it present itself to our brain, something akin to a movie projector casting images onto a screen. But this isn't how vision works. Instead, we see the world through a process of breakdown and reaggregation. Each optic receptor in our eyes is attuned to a distinct type of shape or color signal, those rods and cones we often hear about. When light reflects off specific shapes and colors, particular optic nerves activate and send individual messages to the brain. Your visual cortex then reassembles these distinct signals into a coherent whole and generates a unified visual field. Vision, in short, is a process of discrimination and reaggregation. It's more like assembling a jigsaw puzzle than watching a movie.

The same thing happens with all our cognition. All our senses and thoughts are collections of individual bits of neural data, assembled into "concepts," which are then woven into a larger whole. Thinking is a lot like an improvisational symphony, a singular noise from each of many different instruments all playing together and in constant motion.

Another critical fact about thinking is that it is always happening. We often understand our thoughts as static things, like snapshots in an album. But thoughts are just temporary energy signals. Like traces in the sand, they are only sustained by repetition. When we think, we are making a map of reality that begins to fade immediately after it is drawn, so it must be continually remade and remade, slightly altered in each iteration. Your whole experience of being is a dynamic mental process, always humming along and constantly regenerating itself.

The next crucial element of thinking is memory. As I mentioned before, memory is the way our bodies store information. Most of our memories are short-lived and exist for only milliseconds before the next wave of sensory inputs displaces them. But some of these perceptions stay with us, leaving more lasting neural impressions, especially if they are unusual or distinct. This sounds straightforward, but why then do we store the memories we do? For example, why do I remember some random song from my childhood but can't remember the name of someone I just met? To answer these common questions, let's examine memory a little more closely.

For something so crucial to our being, we remain remarkably ignorant about how it works. When I was young, I naively believed that my memories were stored within specific neurons in my head. In other words, I thought there was a neuron that held the image of my dog and another one that housed the opening riff to Jimi Hendrix's "Purple Haze" and so on. In college, my friends used to joke that by drinking lots of tequila, they were trying to destroy all the neurons that held the traumatic memories of their childhoods. And while this approach might have been an effective strategy for the night, it didn't last past the following day.

One reason (among many) that the tequila technique didn't work is that whole memories aren't stored within neurons; instead, they exist primarily in the synaptic space between them. Your brain's cells hold tiny bits of information, but these are only the parts of a memory, not the complete picture. Memories get stored by reinforcing the connections among neurons that hold the relevant bits. When you memorize a fact or learn a skill, you reinforce a particular set of synaptic linkages, like repeatedly walking across the same bit of underbrush: it flattens all the resistance, making it easy to walk through the next time.

Let me illustrate this with an example: Picture a box of Cheerios. It's not just any box; it's that iconic, bold, and sunny yellow box you've seen innumerable times in the cereal aisle. It's designed to be instantly recognizable, the box that practically waves at you as you pass by. In your brain, that box is not stored as a whole image but as a series of distinct elements. All those little details (the shape, volume, color, and so forth) are held within thousands of different neurons, each responsible for a tiny puzzle piece. Even if you destroyed a lot of neurons with tequila, you'd still have enough of the original ones in place to generate a memory, albeit a less precise one.

When the image of the Cheerios box pops into your head, your visual cortex is essentially firing up the original connections among the neurons that hold those parts. It's like your brain hitting the "replay" button, reactivating many of the same neurons that fired when you first laid eyes on it. When you picture the Cheerios box, you're not just seeing it but reliving the moment you last encountered it. In this sense, memory is your brain mimicking its activity during the original perception or thought.

When we store memories, we strengthen the connections among all those component neurons. And, indeed, this is how we learn everything, whether it's mastering a new language or perfecting your basketball shot. Learning is all about reinforcing synaptic links.

Learning happens every time you recall a specific memory. No matter if it's your first pet, your grandmother's face, or that box of Cheerios, every time you think of these things, you're retracing those neural pathways and deepening their imprints, albeit imperfectly, like redrawing a map that's already been drawn a hundred times before.

These imprints, in turn, shape our later thinking. A great example of this is the image here. At first glance, it seems like a garbled collection of smudges, the kind of abstract painting that makes you scratch your head at a modern art gallery. But look a little closer and you'll see it's an image of a cow. If you're struggling to see it, here's a hint: The cow looks at us with her head turned slightly to the left. Her face is in the center-left part of the picture, starting from her dark snout at the bottom, leading up to two black eyes, with her ears flaring out on either side. The right side of her face is shaded, and her slightly spotted body runs along the right side of the image. Still can't see the cow? Look at the end of the chapter, and you'll see a clue.

Once you see the cow, however, you can never view the image the same way again. The formerly chaotic scribblings are now unavoidably a cow. If you put this book down and come back and look at this page, you will always see a cow.

Involuntarily seeing cows is how our brains organize information. Our inner animal wants to make sense of the world by finding patterns. Whenever it encounters uncertainty, it naturally tries to impose some order. But here's the catch: Once we've created a concept, we become very attached to it. Our perception of the world starts to follow preset routines, and often, these routines are impossible to break out of, like that cow you now can't unsee. The only time we transcend these routines is when we encounter a situation that forces us to reason.

Reasoning is when the brain takes existing concepts and starts rearranging them in novel ways; reasoning is basically how we teach ourselves new ways of thinking. Before humans had language, they reasoned with objects they could touch and see, what psychologists call concrete reasoning. These early humans had to think with sticks and stones because they had no other way of holding concepts in their heads. It's also why our hominid ancestors' culture stagnated for so long; they could only reason with what was right in front of them, and this made innovation quite difficult.

Language changed all of this. Remember, words are just another way of perceiving the world, an alternative method of bundling information into concepts. When we assign words to things, we forge new neural patterns in our brains. And like any form of perception, these words shape our later thinking. Just as with the image of the cow, once we learn a word for something, our thinking about it becomes centered around that word.

Consider, for example, three simple words: *tree*, *bird*, and *flight*. If I say these words to you, they generate expectations in your mind about what these things both are and should be. A tree should have branches, a bird should have wings, and flight means soaring through the sky. These concepts also have distinct relationships with each other. We connect trees and birds and birds and flight, but not trees and flight. Words and reasoning thus help us better classify and understand our surroundings. If thinking is about making maps of reality, words give these maps labels; when thinking is about making predictions, reasoning helps us calculate probabilities.

Language then takes our thinking a step further. It allows us the ability to reason with abstract ideas, rearranging our mental concepts in ways that would never naturally occur. For example, with words, we can imagine a flying tree. We can then elaborate on these fanciful ideas—like a flying tree that flaps its branches. We can create metaphors and allegories, such as a flying tree that soars like an eagle. And we can invent entirely new rules of reality, like a flying tree that travels back in time. Language frees our minds from the constraints of circumstance and enables a distinctly human form of thinking: imagination.

Imagination is yet another way that language changes us. As I mentioned before, other animals can see their bodies and differentiate themselves from what they touch, but their sense of self is limited to a first-person perspective, an "I." Language, by contrast, not only allows us to think of ourselves as a "me," it enables us to imagine who we want this "me" to be. We can give ourselves names and identities or fantasize about an image of ourselves divorced from reality, such as identifying as twenty-six when, in fact, you're fifty-eight.

Language also shapes our self-perception in another subtle way: It makes our thoughts visible as conversations. When we think with words, we generate an internal dialogue, basically mimicking speaking to another person. Much of our thinking is self-talk. For example, as you're reading this book, your brain is essentially playing a one-man show, imitating what it would be like if I were reading these words aloud to you. One part of your brain is busy activating concepts, while another part sits back, munches on metaphorical popcorn, and enjoys the show. In short, when you think with words, your mind pulls double duty, creating both a speaker and an audience. This is why you sometimes might feel like your thoughts are coming from someone else: because, in a way, they are. You're the one doing the talking but also the one doing the listening.

This little mental trick also raises a question that has haunted humanity throughout recorded history: How do we know that our thoughts are indeed our own? The answer, it turns out, isn't straightforward. In fact, the idea that we are the author of our thoughts might be a relatively recent development in human history. According to a controversial hypothesis from psychologist Julian Jaynes, ancient peoples didn't realize that the "voices" in their heads were their own thoughts. Instead, they believed these voices were messages from gods, spirits, or other supernatural beings. Jaynes suggests that it was only when people started engaging in the revolutionary acts of reading and writing that they began to catch on to the idea that they were running the cognitive show.

Jaynes points to evidence of this in ancient texts like the Hebrew Bible and Homer's *Iliad*. These works began as oral tales, passed down by generations of storytellers long before anyone thought to jot them down. In these preliterate myths, the gods are forever chiming in with their two cents, constantly chatting with humans. Think of Abraham and Moses believing they were hearing the voice of God or His angels. The people in these stories don't have inner monologues; instead, they credit their thoughts and motivations to otherworldly beings.

It wasn't until the development of widespread literacy, Jaynes argues, that humans started seeing themselves as the captains of their own mental ships. The breakdown of the bicameral mind is why God stops directly talking to people in the later parts of the Bible—once they had a written religion, they realized they were the authors of their own mental dialogues. Eventually, they came to believe that, as with René Descartes, this dialogue was proof that they even existed. But even this deduction didn't settle everything. Once we started reasoning, we started reasoning *about* our reasoning, and this led to another perplexing question: Do we have free will?

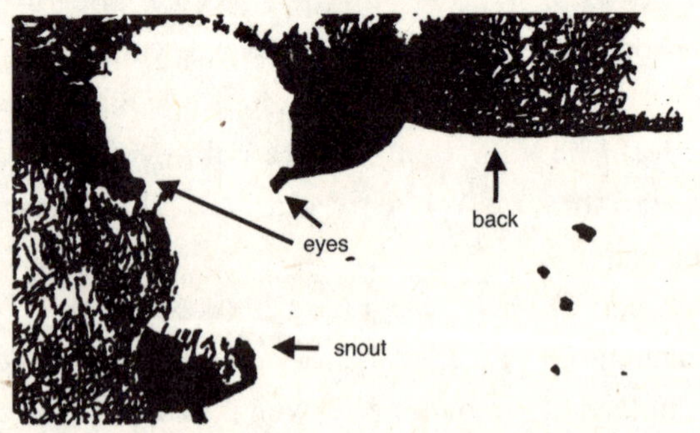

14

Intention

OF ALL MY MANY VICES, NONE HAS ITS HOOKS IN ME QUITE like sugar. Despite my fondness for alcohol, drugs, sex, and even the internet, none of these temptations put up much of a fight when I resist their tremendous allure. But sugar? It has me wrapped around its little crystalline finger. I'm fully aware that it's terrible for me, and I can clearly see how it throws my mood into chaos, yet I can't seem to help myself; I always want more. The worst is late at night when the ice cream cravings hit like a freight train. Too often, I find myself "taking the dog for a walk," only to end up in the neighborhood bodega, grabbing yet another pint. In short, I feel about Ben & Jerry's the way Frederick the Great felt about tall, Prussian soldiers . . . they are my *veakness*.

My ice cream compulsion raises a question that has pestered humanity since the time of the ancient Greeks: Do we have free will? On some level, we'd all like to think we do. Aristotle, for one, was convinced that reasoning allows us to control our actions, which is why he believed we're morally responsible for our choices. Later Christian theologians took this idea and ran with it, adding concepts of sin and divine judgment. Free will even underpins Western law, where people are held accountable not just for their actions, but for their intentions.

But our thoughts are far more complicated than this. Our intentions are simply the final step in a long chain of unconsciously learned routines, and most of these are not under our deliberate control. While we're not mindless robots, we don't think with pristine clarity, either. And because our thinking is inevitably skewed, it also means that our will is far less free than we commonly believe.

I bring all this up because our intentions are crucial in our quest for transcendence. Our suffering often comes from the obsessions, preoccupations, and mental loops that grip us so tightly. At some point, self-optimization means changing our thoughts. But our thinking is never as free as we'd like to believe. Our mental habits run far more deeply than what's on the surface of our ordinary consciousness. We all have our vulnerabilities, whether they're ice cream or tall Prussian soldiers, and these vulnerabilities are deeply woven into the fabric of our minds. Self-optimization will never be as simple as saying, "I'm going to exercise my free will and become enlightened." To truly understand how hard it is to change ourselves, we'll need to appreciate what is behind the deliberate parts of our minds.

Thinking Is (Mostly) Misperceiving

I normally believe that I've got a pretty good handle on reality. I assume that the things in front of me—this room, this book, and this body—exist exactly as I perceive them. But if there's one thing life likes to remind us, it's that we can't always trust our assumptions. We never perceive the world as it is. Instead, we're perpetually caught up in an amateur translation of reality, with our brains playing the role of a semireliable interpreter. And, as with all interpretations, we often get a distorted view.

Take the example of an optical illusion, the Kanizsa triangle. There's no triangle in the image, but our brain conjures one up anyway. It sees

a few corners, infers, "Ah, yes, a triangle!" and then generates an image of one in our visual field. This kind of creative problem-solving extends to all our thinking. Whether we're smelling a rose or penning an epic poem, our brains constantly pick up tiny scraps of neural data and then fill in the gaps. But instead of getting a precise reproduction of reality, what we conjure is more of a Picasso—a subjective, interpretive picture that is often a little off-kilter. We never see the world as it is, only as our minds choose to imagine it.

The culprit is our biology. Remember, neurons are super-expensive cells. They demand much more energy than the other parts of our body. So evolution has pruned their function. Animal brains do not generate a complete picture of the world because it is unnecessary. Instead, our brains just try to fabricate a *good enough* approximation of what is happening around us so that we can find food, get sex, and avoid death. To achieve these goals, the brain doesn't need to obsess over every grain of sand on the beach; it just needs to process enough information to figure out what to do next. Like those readers who always skip to the last page of a book, our brains are more interested in predicting the ending than savoring every detail.

How does the brain pull off this act of mental efficiency? By relying on prior routines. Most of your "thinking" happens well below the level of conscious awareness. At this moment, your brain is processing tens of millions of bits of data, but it's doing so by falling back on tried-and-true procedures. It's like a well-oiled machine, humming along based on what it's learned from past experiences, all without you ever needing to lift a mental finger, so to speak.

We already saw an example of this with the picture of the cow. Once your brain cracked the code, it had an efficient way of handling the incoming visual data. And that's why, after you've managed to see the cow once, you will always see a cow whenever you look at that formerly garbled image. The rest of our thinking usually works this way, shuffling information through preexisting channels. But because it all happens so quickly, we rarely appreciate how automatic this process is or how much our thinking is based on our prior assumptions.

Now, if the world were a static place, this routine-based thinking would be a dream come true. We'd figure out how things work, lock everything down, and be done with it. We could even shrink our brains down a size or two and stop stressing so much about the future, for we'd all know how the story ends. But, alas, the world is in constant flux, and our brains have to adapt to an endless parade of surprises. It's in this variance that we see the foundations of free will.

The best way to illustrate the possibility of free will is with the example of Ben & Jerry's. I love their ice cream, but I also want to be thin and healthy; Chubby Hubby and toned abs are two concepts that don't go together. When I'm in the bodega, I experience a lot of conflict, pushed and pulled by different impulses.

Psychologists have a scheme for describing this battle: System 1 and System 2 thinking. System 1 thinking is our everyday thinking. It is fast, automatic, and intuitive. It's the thinking we do without trying, like knowing that one plus one equals two or seeing a bird in flight. System 1 thinking is about the familiar; it's the mental path of least resistance, like what happens when I mindlessly eat ice cream.

System 2, conversely, is the slow, deliberate thought processes that kick in when we are faced with something new or perplexing. It happens when we're solving a puzzle, making a big decision, or trying to resist buying another pint. System 2 is what we do when we're thinking hard and our well-worn routines won't cut it.

System 2 thinking can be exhilarating—it's why we enjoy games, mysteries, and fantasy stories—but it's also stressful, and for good reason. Our ancestors needed to be able to predict their surroundings if they didn't want to perish. When the world presented them with something new, their ability to make accurate predictions dropped, and with it, their chances of survival. That's why when animals hear something unfamiliar, they tend to freeze and become hyperalert. They're trying to figure out how to fit this new information into their prior understanding of the world. The same thing happens to us. We deploy System 2 thinking until we can redraw our mental maps or smooth out the bumps in our standard operating procedures.

System 1 and System 2 thinking are also essential for understanding the problem of free will. Free will is just an elegant synonym for System 2 thinking. We naturally equate our free will with those moments of deliberate, ponderous cogitation, where we imagine ourselves as rational beings, thoughtfully steering the ship of our lives. When I resist Ben & Jerry's siren call, I think I'm exercising my free will, rising above my base impulses, and asserting my autonomy. I imagine myself as a liberated thinker, a veritable philosopher-king of the dairy aisle, and all this rational glory is courtesy of my System 2 processes.

But there is a big problem with these vainglorious notions: System 2 thinking isn't built to be our default state. It's more like a temporary backup plan we are forced to adopt when things don't go as planned. Most of the time, we happily coast along the well-worn tracks of System 1, content to let our established habits do the driving. Our sense of self, expectations about the world, and even our consciousness are all shaped by neural habits cemented during our formative years. Most of what we call "thinking" is just a mental reflex. This means we're in far less control of our minds than we'd like to admit. We spend most of our waking hours on autopilot, processing information and generating perceptions based on those deeply ingrained, unconscious habits.

Psychologists have a fancy word to describe all of this: heuristics. Heuristics are mental shortcuts, the quick routines our brains rely on when making everyday decisions. Some of these heuristics are learned, the little tricks we pick up through our prior experiences. I've got loads of these. For instance, when I'm buying a bottle of wine from the liquor store, I usually pick the one from the emptiest rack. After all, if everyone else is buying it, it must be good, right? And most of the time, that's a pretty safe bet, although I sometimes wonder if wine shops secretly thin the racks of the stuff they're trying to offload.

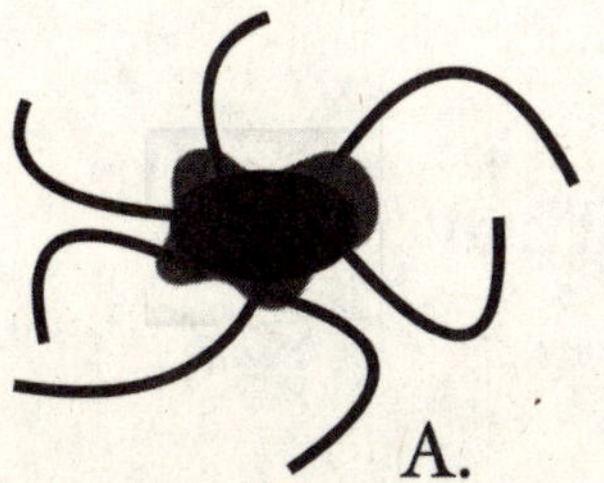

A.

B.

But many of our heuristics are inborn, hardwired into us like the factory settings on a smartphone. They're the decision strategies that make up the grammar of our intuitions, guiding us with gut feelings rather than careful analysis. We've got loads of these innate heuristics, and they permeate our thinking. We can see an example of this in the illustration above. Here are two nonsensical shapes that don't seem to be anything in particular. But if I asked you which one was the most dangerous, you'd probably choose A. In numerous surveys I've conducted, this is the overwhelming choice. Why? Animals like us evolved to be wary of spiders, and shape A looks somewhat "spider-like," whereas shape B may be generously interpreted as a sliced open coconut. The irony is that more people die every year from falling coconuts than from spider bites, which goes to show that you can't always trust your intuitions. Nevertheless, our brains, ever the creatures of habit, tell us that shape A is the most dangerous.

This echoes what the Buddha was getting at when discussing the five aggregates of Being. Buddhism teaches us that most everyday thinking is shaped by habitual tendencies—those mental grooves carved by our past experiences. Because these grooves are deeply entrenched, we usually cruise along without noticing them. Yet, together, they form a totality that feels very real, even though it's more of a mental magic trick than an accurate reflection of reality.

As a result, we spend a good chunk of our lives in a dreamlike state. We think we're inhabiting the real world, but we're more like unwitting participants in a mental projection, a mashup of our innate tendencies and learned habits. We'll dig deeper into this idea in the chapters ahead, but since we're on the topic of thinking, now seems like a good time to hit the pause button and ponder how we might wrestle back some control over the thoughts bouncing around in our heads.

Willful Thinking

"You have power over your mind, not outside events. Realize this, and you will find strength."

"When you get up in the morning, remember what a privilege it is to be alive."

"Our life is what our thoughts make of it."

These are the kinds of quotes that you used to find on those motivational posters advertised in airline magazines, back when there was such a thing as airline magazines. And you might assume these nuggets of wisdom were penned by some self-help guru, someone like Deepak Chopra. But despite their contemporary flair, these words are not modern bon mots. In fact, they are nearly two thousand years old.

Their author was Marcus Aurelius. He was one of Rome's last "good emperors," recognizable to most people today as the character played by Richard Harris in the movie *Gladiator.* He was noteworthy because of his *Meditations*, journals filled with commandments to himself. Marcus Aurelius was a student of Stoicism, an ancient Greek philosophy that suggested that a flourishing life comes through self-mastery, reason, and virtue. His journals were not meant for publication; they were simply pep talks he gave himself. Nevertheless, they have survived through the ages and are considered one of the foremost examples of Stoicism in the Western canon, if not the earliest self-help book.

Psychologists today also have another term for what Aurelius was trying to do: self-efficacy. Self-efficacy is the idea that we can live better if we adopt a proper mindset. It starts with a simple but often overlooked observation: We're our own worst enemies when it comes to getting what we want—a better job, a nurturing relationship, a more fulfilling life—because we tend to drown ourselves in a flood of negative beliefs.

The theory of self-efficacy suggests we have the power to change all that. We can give ourselves a much-needed mental makeover by deliberately confronting our self-doubts and replacing them with positive, affirming statements. Or, as I like to put it, we can reorder the self by reordering our thinking, an idea consistent with Stoicism.

This concept appears in modern psychology in two primary ways. One is cognitive behavioral therapy (CBT). CBT emerged from the groundbreaking work of American psychologist Aaron Beck in the 1960s, though there are now several variations. Beck's idea was straightforward: Much of our mental suffering stems from our thoughts getting trapped in distorted cycles.

Imagine, for example, that you're passed over for a promotion at work. You feel lousy and start thinking, "Maybe I'm just not good enough." As a result, you put in less effort, your performance drops, and you don't even bother trying for the next promotion. Your negative thoughts become a self-fulfilling prophecy.

Beck believed we could break these negative thought patterns through deliberate and mindful actions. This is quite similar to the Buddha's concept of "right intention." By redrawing our mental maps of reality, say by engaging in CBT, we can reshape ourselves and lead better lives. In practice, CBT is often used to help people with obsessive-compulsive disorder, chronic anxiety, or intrusive thoughts. A therapist guides the patient, helping them recognize when they're spiraling into obsession, and encouraging them to develop strategies to derail their runaway mental train.

Another way self-efficacy appears to us is in scores of popular self-help books. From Norman Vincent Peale's *The Power of Positive Thinking* to Gary John Bishop's *Unf*ck Yourself*, the basic message across these books is the same: You have the power to intentionally reorder yourself and your relationship with others. And this promises remarkable results. As the best-selling author and therapist Wayne Dyer writes in *You'll See It When You Believe It*, "You can make your most impossible dreams come true, turn obstacles into opportunity, rid yourself of guilt and inner turmoil, and spend every day doing things you love."

The key lies in changing the way we think. Adopting new storylines about ourselves can disrupt the patterns that keep us in those negative emotional states. In CBT, this is done with the assistance of a therapist; with self-help books, it's usually accomplished through a mix of peppy aphorisms, inspirational anecdotes, and self-guided exercises. The promise is simple: Figure out who you want to be, and presto, your thoughts will pave the way to your best self.

Or at least, that's the theory. In practice, realigning our thinking is rarely that easy. Part of the problem is the sheer scale of the task. Many of our thoughts are like ancient buildings constructed upon foundations laid long ago. Our self-conceptions are deeply baked into us, rising from habits acquired back when we were still figuring out that "LEGO" and "banana" were separate things and not interchangeable snack options. These patterns are so familiar and ingrained that we slip into them without realizing we've just stepped into a mental trap. Just as we don't remember when we first learned to say "LEGO" or "banana," we probably don't recall when we first decided we were a "bad person" or believed that "no one will like me as long as my nose looks this way."

The power of habit is also why self-help books and our New Year's resolutions tend to work for only a short time. Sure, you can devour an inspiring book, feel ready to conquer the world, and maybe even pick up a couple of better habits. But holding on to that shiny, new, positive self-image? That's the tricky part. It's like trying to keep a sandcastle intact when the tide's coming in.

Inevitably, most of us find ourselves sliding back into the comfortable, well-worn patterns we were trying to escape in the first place. Like dieting, self-efficacy isn't something you can achieve once and then check off your to-do list; it's a disciplined practice and hard to keep up. It's also why Marcus Aurelius kept writing those little pep talks to himself—he had to keep reminding himself that he was good enough, smart enough, and that, doggone it, people liked him.

This is also why self-efficacy is much more effective when you've got a therapist in your corner. It's a bit like trying to lose weight. Sure, you can go it alone, but if you're serious about shedding those pounds, it's much easier with someone there to push you beyond your usual limits and maybe pry that pint of ice cream from your hand. You can read all the self-help books you want, which might be helpful, but if you want to tackle those stubborn, unhealthy habits, having someone else guide you through them can make all the difference.

But even the best therapist, coach, or mentor can't do everything for you. Self-efficacy only works if you've got some self-awareness to start with. To change your mind, you first need to be able to step back from your thoughts and get a clear, objective look at what's going on. And that's no small feat. Seeing ourselves objectively is exceptionally challenging. Moreover, all the positive reinforcement in the world won't do us any good if we're not addressing the real source of our problems. If we want to change our minds, we'll need to tackle the big kahuna of cognition: consciousness.

15

Consciousness

AT THIS MOMENT, TWO REMARKABLE AND MYSTERIOUS events are going on. First, you are having an experience of your own being—you are conscious. Second, nobody knows precisely how this is happening. Science can map the genome, send robots to Mars, and even clone sheep, but when it comes to understanding what's happening inside our heads? Well, that's where our shoulders begin to shrug. Psychologists are not exactly sure what consciousness is, where it comes from, or how it operates. As something in itself, it's also quite baffling. How does the vast collection of proteins and molecules that make up our bodies generate this feeling of themselves as one? How is living tissue capable of being sentient?

For thousands of years, prophets and philosophers have conjured answers ranging from the divine to the downright strange. The most popular idea is one we've already encountered: dualism. It suggests that consciousness comes from a source separate from our bodies, often referred to as a "soul" or the "atman." According to this view, consciousness is like a tenant renting space in our bodies and moving out after the lease ends. Where it lands next—be it an eternally blissful afterlife or getting reborn as a dairy cow—depends on your faith and possibly your karma.

Then there are the more cosmic theories, which appeal to those who pride themselves on thinking outside the box or maybe outside the galaxy.

For example, some mystics argue that consciousness pervades the entire universe. According to a theory known as panpsychism, consciousness isn't just a human thing; it's everything. By this reckoning, stars, planets, and even your living room couch are conscious somehow (so you might want to think twice before getting it reupholstered). Some thinkers take it even further, speculating that consciousness predates space-time and that the universe is just consciousness trying to express itself.

For this leg of our exploration, however, I will steer us in a different direction, one that stays closer to home. For the past few years, I've taught a seminar at the University of Chicago on consciousness. With the help of some brilliant students, I've pored through the vast literature on consciousness, ranging from philosophy to neuroscience. And from all this reading, I've come up with a simple conclusion. Instead of being something intrinsic to our soul or a force pervading the universe, consciousness is simply a process that living beings perform. In other words, consciousness isn't something we *have*; it's something we *do*.

And this brings us back to self-optimization. Living better ultimately means experiencing reality in new ways, freeing ourselves from the ordinary routines that usually define our perception of the world. According to almost every spiritual and philosophical tradition, this is done by "expanding" or altering our consciousness in one way or another. Once we're unshackled from our mental chains, we'll be more in sync with our natural rhythms. In other words, self-optimization inevitably requires us to change the ways we perform consciousness. Sounds fantastic, but before we dash off to that ayahuasca retreat in some remote Peruvian jungle, it might be wise to understand what exactly is making these consciousness processes happen in the first place. So let's explore the purple haze of being you.

What Exactly Is Consciousness?

One reason consciousness remains such an elusive subject is that we can't seem to agree on what it is. It's like getting a group of partiers to confess what happened when the police came; everyone has their own version, and none of them makes complete sense. We intuitively think we know what it is. Consciousness is this feeling of existing. It is what it's like to be me. But what is going on as we're having this feeling?

The truth is, nobody knows. There's no definitive handbook on consciousness or even one widely accepted way to describe it. Most of what we think we know is based on a jumble of speculations that often contradict each other. And there are a lot. From the philosopher David Chalmers's "hard problem" to the mathematical Integrated Information Theory, scores of competing schemes purport to describe (or not describe) what's behind this experience of being you.

If this were a book on consciousness, I might lead us through the maze of theories and philosophical debates. But instead, I propose we skip the labyrinth and keep things simple. We'll start with a definition:

Consciousness is how a living entity prioritizes information about its entire being in order to take deliberate actions.

Okay, now, this is a somewhat vague and clunky definition. It doesn't entirely shed light on that nebulous feeling of "being you," but it's a start. So let me break it down further.

First off, consciousness is a series of actions. Recall that it is something we *do*, not something we *have*. To be more specific, consciousness is a process we perform. Like all processes, it needs certain physical preconditions. Just as a fire needs wood, consciousness needs living matter to happen (I'll get to AI in a moment). Yet, contrary to what some philosophers and mystics say, consciousness is not intrinsic to matter any more than fire is intrinsic to wood. Like dancing, laughing, or farting, consciousness is a process that arises from bodies only when the material conditions are right.

I know this view of consciousness is not one everyone shares, but I think it's the most reliable one. Nonmaterial accounts of consciousness depend on things we can't commonly observe, like the soul, quantum superstrings, or someone else's mystical experience. But if you don't share the prophet's belief or the shaman's vision, you must take them on their word, as there is no other way to adjudicate their claim. And this leaves us on shaky ground. Ideally, we want a definition of consciousness that doesn't require a leap of faith or a degree in cryptozoology, and according to our best current science, consciousness springs from the activities of living tissue.

Moreover, consciousness isn't a one-size-fits-all affair. A common misconception is that consciousness is a uniform experience. Panpsychics, for example, assume that the consciousness of a tree or a star is the same as that of a mouse. Yet this is like thinking that flying, leaping, and falling are all the same actions because they all involve moving through the air.

This, however, is clearly not the case. We can see this in our own experience. Consider, for instance, a typical day. After the morning's coffee, we are usually alert and perceptive. As the day wears on, we slip into daydreams or sleepiness. Perhaps we get caught in the downward spiral of a bad mood, or maybe we get lost in a good book. In the early 1980s, my father-in-law was so wrapped up in a novel he was reading that he boarded the wrong connecting flight and didn't realize his mistake until he inexplicably found himself in Des Moines (ah, the good old days of minimal-security air travel). In short, our experience of being varies a lot across time.

Another common trap is our tendency to equate our human experience of consciousness with consciousness itself. We tend to think that our self-awareness and linguistic introspection are the gold standard of what consciousness is. We then rank other beings like they're competing in some consciousness Olympics: chimps and dolphins get the silver, bats get the bronze, and starfish don't even make it to the qualifying rounds.

Yet this, too, is a misleading conceit. Assuming humans perform the ultimate expression of consciousness is akin to declaring your smartphone the end-all of technology because it's more advanced than a kitchen knife. While it's true that our consciousness is more complex than that of other animals, it doesn't necessarily mean it's the best mechanism for every situation. If you need to chop a tomato, your phone isn't very helpful.

The same goes for consciousness. It evolved to help organisms navigate their environments effectively, and it has done so in different forms, each adapted to its specific needs. Take the example of plants. They exhibit a consciousness that's highly specialized for their ecological niche. While they might not grapple with their purpose in life, they do very well in figuring out where to grow, when to pollinate, and when to shed their leaves. Plants represent a minimalist approach to consciousness: efficient, practical, and ideally suited to their environment.

We humans have a far more complex set of tools for negotiating with reality than other creatures, so it makes sense that our consciousness is also more complicated. But that doesn't mean that our form of consciousness is any better or closer to what consciousness is. This takes us back to a central idea: consciousness exists to help an organism thrive. How it does this depends a lot on both the organism and its environment.

We can see this in our own species. Humans have expressed different forms of consciousness over time. Our current experience of being is very different from that of our early African ancestors, who probably didn't realize that the thoughts in their heads came from their own minds. And our experience of being will probably be different from what our later descendants will feel. While we might think we're the pinnacle of consciousness, future generations might look back at us and wonder how we ever got anything done without a fully integrated brain-to-quantum-cloud interface.

I realize these comments may raise some eyebrows, so let me explain them in more detail.

All living creatures, from the most minuscule microbe to the most mammoth mammoth, will better survive if they can sense their environment and respond to it. Bacteria, plants, fungi, and animals have different ways of doing this and their specific biology shapes how they perform consciousness. Like DNA or metabolism, consciousness is another way our life force negotiates with reality. This is also why inanimate objects don't perform consciousness—they don't need it because they are not *doing* anything. Consciousness only arises in beings that act in the world. And, as far as we know, only life forms are doing this. Rocks may be solid, and rivers may flow, but they aren't known for their excellent decision-making skills.

But what about robots or AI? It often seems like my Roomba or ChatGPT has some sentience, but this is a human projection. Current AI systems aren't performing consciousness because they have no incentive to. They are not independently integrating all their information to make decisions; all of their actions inevitably come from a human prompt. In the future, we may program AI systems to act completely autonomously and even to sustain and reproduce themselves (in effect, gain a life force). At this point, they may start performing consciousness, but it will be unlike our consciousness because they will rely on different types of information. But for now, AI systems are not performing consciousness.

What mainly distinguishes consciousness from other forms of thinking, or a computer's information processing, is its scope. Most forms of cognition tend to be very specific to particular types of information. Seeing is about processing data from light waves, taste from chemicals, and so forth. Consciousness, by contrast, is a *meta-process*, something that integrates *all* the information within a living being. In doing this, consciousness always encompasses four essential elements:

1. Awareness: Consciousness begins with taking information in.
2. Perception: Information is then bundled into concepts that give particular signals to the organism.
3. Attention: Some criteria then rank these signals.
4. Deliberation: High-priority signals are compared with each other to choose how to act.

In my class, we call this the APAD model of consciousness (for Awareness, Perception, Attention, and Deliberation). Everything that performs consciousness is doing APAD in some way. The experience we know as consciousness is a very elaborate version of these four APAD processes, which occur at all layers of our being.

Let's start with the cellular self. At first glance, suggesting that our cells perform consciousness may seem peculiar, but even single-celled life forms perform APAD consciousness. We can see this with our cells. They are constantly bombarded with chemical information. Every moment they have to differentiate nutrients, hormonal signals, and viral threats. They sift through this flood of data and "decide" on appropriate responses, like whether to divide or undergo apoptosis, a fancy term for cell suicide. Our cells exhibit a basic form of consciousness, albeit in its most rudimentary stage. Similar analogies exist in bacteria, plants, and fungi, as they, too, perform their version of APAD.

This may not *seem* like consciousness because bacteria, plants, fungi, and cells don't have a mental image of themselves; they aren't sentient. But consciousness isn't just about having a self-concept. Take us, for example. Plenty of times, we get so caught up in the moment that we "lose" ourselves, yet we're still conscious, sometimes even more intensely so. When you reflexively yank your hand away from a hot stove, you're making a decision, but it's happening well before you get a chance to think about it. Consciousness doesn't need introspection or even System 2 thinking.

Where consciousness becomes more recognizable is in the next layer of being, the animal self. As a large, multicellular creature, our animal self faces a challenge: Our brains are absorbing vast amounts of data, and we could potentially focus on millions of pieces of information, yet we only have two legs, two hands, and one body. Consequently, our brains need to figure out which, of all these possibilities, will be acted upon, filtering up only the most essential information for system-wide action.

Most of this filtering process happens well below our cognizance. In other words, most of our consciousness operates in unconscious ways. An excellent example of this comes in how we see. Vision is generated in a part of the brain called the primary visual cortex (PVC), which takes up a large portion of your hindbrain. If this part of the brain gets damaged, such as from an accident or a stroke, it typically leads to blindness. Lose your PVC, and you won't be able to see.

But this doesn't mean you'll lose visual *awareness*. Many people with damaged PVCs can detect objects around them even if they can't see them. For example, they will avoid obstacles when walking across a cluttered room. Even more remarkable is that they aren't consciously aware they are doing this. If you ask them why they are walking in a zigzag pattern, they'll say they are just walking naturally, as if zigzagging is a normal way of moving about.

The ability to have visual awareness without seeing is known as blindsight, and it exemplifies a crucial part of consciousness: Our sense of being is not simply about cognizance; our sense of being is built upon a torrent of information that never garners our attention. What we commonly think of as consciousness, this feeling of self we are currently experiencing, is just a sliver of our mental processes, the final output, as it were. Most of the data that informs our consciousness does not register in our waking minds, but it's still a big part of the process.

So what then makes it to the attention stage of consciousness? The answer is usually variance. Our brains are like drama-hungry TV viewers; we like to tune in when something unusual or unresolved happens. Take your body, for instance. Until I mentioned it, you probably weren't aware of your left knee. It's not that your knee wasn't sending out signals; it's just that those signals were about as exciting as a coffee table. If those signals stay steady and predictable, your brain sees no need to act. But the moment your knee starts to ache, sending a pain signal to your brain, suddenly it's the star of the show. The signals that generally move up to our conscious attention are the ones that break the monotony, like the part of the movie where the plot twist finally happens.

Once these abnormal inputs get elevated to attention, our brains need to hold them in time while we figure out what to do with them. And this is a difficult thing to do. Remember, thoughts are electrical impulses coursing through the brain. They are naturally ephemeral, meant to quickly arise and pass within seconds. This is why keeping an image in your mind is such a challenging thing to do.

We can see this with a simple experiment. Close your eyes and try to picture your mother's face. Usually, we can do this for only a few seconds before another image or thought displaces it. No wonder, then, that it is helpful to write out our ideas when trying to think through an abstract problem; we relieve our brains of the burdens of holding them in working memory.

Together, this sifting, prioritizing, and holding neural information in focus is consciousness at work. It is all these processes coming together: the awareness and fabrication of all our mental concepts *and* the determination of action. It is really about formulating and expressing a will, although, as we've seen, this will is less free than we normally believe.

It sounds simple, but one reason consciousness is such an elusive phenomenon is that all these processes are in constant flux. Our minds are like the kitchen in a bustling restaurant, always dealing with a torrent of conflicting signals—orders flying in, pans sizzling, and someone yelling about a missing ingredient. Moreover, there's no standardized recipe for creating perceptions, attention, or decisions. Instead, there are countless routines. Consciousness is never quite the same from one moment to the next because our minds constantly adjust to whatever the situation demands. This variance is why the psychologist William James first described consciousness as a "stream of thought." If you've ever tried to focus on a single mental image for more than a few minutes, you know exactly what he means.

But this raises the million-dollar question, at least for consciousness studies: If our minds and bodies are in constant flux, why do we feel so solid and permanent? Where does this continual feeling of "I" come from?

The answer is that our mind tricks itself. The way we experience our being is a hallucination, as both modern neuroscientists and the Buddha describe it. Once again, it goes back to our animal selves. Remember, our animal brains evolved to be prediction machines. They want to generate an adequate picture of reality now and in the next moment, like Google Maps, but with better traffic updates.

Consciousness does the same thing, only with *all* of our sense information. This feeling of self we have right now is a prediction that our minds are making about reality. And just as our sight creates a visual tableau, our minds weave together a continual and seamless experience of self from millions of various neural inputs. They do this to have a coherent object (a "me") to compare with the rest of reality (not "me"). The feeling you and I have of ourselves is just a helpful reference device that our brains concoct to make their way through the world, a mental flag saying "you are here."

Much of this hallucination of self is built out of learned neural routines and habits. When we are born, our consciousness is disjointed, and we don't have a coherent sense of self. Our brains exist in a choppy storm of chaotic neural firings. But as we mature, our brains adopt patterns and develop regular ways of channeling these surges. Throughout childhood, as we navigate the world, our consciousness becomes situated around language, values, identities, and ego concerns. We create representations of ourselves and then learn to prioritize these self-concepts.

All of this also has a deeper implication: Consciousness is not simply a process that *is*; it is a process that is *learned*. At its deepest level, life teaches us our experience of being.

This is a somewhat subtle and elusive idea, so let me illustrate it again by returning to the example of vision. We intuitively believe that vision is innate and that we are born simply knowing how to see. But vision is partly learned. If you kept a child locked away in a dark room (which, for the record, would be a horrible idea), they would develop amblyopia (otherwise known as lazy eye) and would not be able to see correctly as adults.

An analogous situation happens with our consciousness. Our very experience of ourselves now is the product of our childhood. If you were brought up in a sensory deprivation tank, in a war zone, or surrounded by social media, you would have a different experience of being than if you were not. Consciousness, it turns out, is a bit like Play-Doh; it's malleable and molded by the hands that work it.

And here is where the linguistic and egoistic selves come into play. As we've already seen, the self is shaped by our language, culture, and life stories. These same factors exert an enormous influence on how our consciousness gets learned and performed. For example, WEIRD people like ourselves not only have a different ego, but we have a different way of experiencing reality from people who are not WEIRD (a reminder: Western, Educated, Industrialized, Rich, and Democratic). We understand the world through distinct concepts, pay attention to different things, and make different choices than non-WEIRDos. Our consciousness is often obsessed with our identities, our continual need for affirmation and validation, and our endless quest for status and love. All of these preoccupations come from living in a large, consumerist, and increasingly online society, where Likes and retweets have somehow become measures of self-worth.

Consider how your average American today performs consciousness. Much of our information comes from social media, cable news, and mass entertainment. We are saturated in these virtual worlds that are vivid and compelling and yet disconnected from our immediate reality. We are seduced into paying attention to abstractions such as global conflicts, outrages in faraway places, and indiscretions of celebrities we'll never meet. Or we become preoccupied with the myth that if we want to be happy, we must get that new car, the bigger house, or more Likes on an Instagram post. We thus end up exerting lots of energy about concerns that have no real bearing on our lives. This further locks us into an imbalanced way of living, with our self-processes spiraling further out of alignment.

If we want to correct this imbalance, then we'll need to readjust our consciousness. We'll need to find ways of focusing on the critical information rather than the ephemera that continually distracts us. We'll need to *unlearn* the habits of mind that keep us preoccupied with dramas that don't matter and illusory goals that are far away. We'll need to reorient our consciousness. I've already mentioned a few ways to do this, like meditation, therapy, or simply adopting a positive mindset. But if we want to really optimize ourselves, we must go deeper. We'll need to see where our brain's consciousness is operating. And one intriguing way to do this is with a hit of LSD.

16

Enlightenment

AT FIRST GLANCE, ALBERT HOFMANN WOULD SEEM AN unlikely candidate to launch a spiritual revolution. A meticulous and mild-mannered Swiss chemist, Hofmann spent most of his days conducting precise experiments with esoteric chemicals. One of these was lysergic acid, a by-product of the fungus ergot. Scientists at Sandoz Labs suspected it might be used as a medical stimulant, but Hofmann was having a hard time testing this idea because lysergic acid tends to disintegrate quickly. Hoping to stabilize it, he added the chemical diethylamide and synthesized a new compound, lysergic acid diethylamide, that he named LSD for short.

Then, one day, Hofmann accidentally absorbed some of it through his fingertips and noticed it gave him some mildly pleasant sensations. He described seeing "fantastic pictures, extraordinary shapes, with intense kaleidoscopic plays of color." This piqued his curiosity and, a few days later, Hofmann decided to take things a step further and impetuously downed 250 micrograms of it (evidently, chemists often do this kind of thing).

This time, the experience wasn't just mildly pleasant but intense. He started feeling dizzy, anxious, and, much to his sober Swiss horror, extremely giggly. Feeling completely out of sorts, he did the unthinkable and left work early. Wobbling home on his bicycle, he spent the rest of the day, well . . . tripping his brains out. That day, April 19, 1943, would later be immortalized as Bicycle Day. It was the first time someone intentionally took LSD, and it marks the moment when Albert Hofmann accidentally launched the psychedelic revolution.

Now, contrary to popular belief, LSD didn't start as a "hippie drug." It was initially embraced as a potential treatment for mental illness, with psychiatrists leading the charge. This roused the interest of government agencies like the CIA and the US military, who thought it might work as either a truth serum or a weapon. But while doctors and government agents were busy dosing lab subjects and soldiers, LSD was also being discovered by spiritual seekers. Counterculture icons like Aldous Huxley, Timothy Leary, and Richard Alpert began to champion its mind-altering potential, proclaiming that LSD was going to spark a great spiritual awakening and accelerate the evolution of human consciousness.

And, to a certain extent, they were right. In the 1960s, psychedelics exploded into Western popular culture. Millions of people started using LSD, psilocybin (magic mushrooms), and other hallucinogens for spiritual enlightenment, psychological healing, and not-so-simple fun. Meanwhile, Richard Nixon's administration, horrified by the sight of all these long-haired hippies spinning around in circles and rejecting their parents' values, classified LSD and psilocybin as Schedule 1 drugs, which declares them to have no medical use and a high potential for harm. And they remain Schedule 1 drugs today.

Despite their criminalization, psychedelics have radically changed how many people experience their self. Millions of users have reported glimpses of ethereal transcendence, tapping into the spiritual insights that Indigenous Americans had been finding for centuries. Psychedelics are also enjoying something of a renaissance today, with lots of new research on their therapeutic benefits. Scientists also believe psychedelics can reveal new insights into how our brains function. So, in our exploration of the self, psychedelics are a worthy place to visit.

But before going any further, let me clarify a few things. I won't spend much time discussing the possible spiritual revelations that can happen when you trip. I generally find other people's firsthand accounts of LSD to be rather tedious, and I won't bore you with my own. Writing about psychedelics is like dancing about architecture, to riff on an old saying, because tripping is simply impossible to describe with words.* The psychedelic experience is so visceral and intense, so discordant and disrupted, that it doesn't easily align with ordinary consciousness.

Nevertheless, there is one psychedelic experience that is worth mentioning because it bears directly on our explorations of self, consciousness, and the brain. It is the feeling of ego dissolution or what is sometimes called ego death.

I've experienced this myself. It's difficult to describe, but ego death feels like being utterly integrated with reality, where the boundaries between self and other dissolve. Your narrative self is shattered. Names, identities, and egoistic attachments no longer hold any relevance and can even appear as distant absurdities. Sometimes, this experience can be ecstatic, and sometimes, it can be terrifying—much of this depends on your mood and circumstance, but either way, ego death radically alters your feeling of being.

Ego death is also interesting because it offers some tantalizing hints about the neuroscience of consciousness and transcendence. Recent advances in magnetic imaging have begun to show us which parts of the brain are active when we perform consciousness, and these observations coincide with the firsthand accounts of psychedelic drug users. In other words, the experience of ego death that many people feel while tripping comes from disruptions to the same neural networks that underlie our ordinary sense of self. Psychedelics can not only help us open our minds, but they can reveal where in our heads we usually reside.

The Connectome

Where exactly in our bodies are we? Philosophers and scientists have debated this question for thousands of years and made some rather creative and often wildly inaccurate guesses. Aristotle, for example, famously said that our conscious mind resided in the heart; the brain,

* This line is often attributed to the comedian Martin Mull, although lots of people have repeated versions of it.

he thought, was there to cool the blood. Two thousand years later, Descartes conclusively rejected Aristotle's absurd claim; consciousness, he said, obviously arose from the pineal gland—that tiny pinecone-shaped organ in the middle of the brain!

It's easy to laugh at these speculations today, but, to be fair, the brain is a very knotty organ. Not only is it extremely complex, it's also very delicate. We can't just crack open people's heads and begin poking around to see what each brain region is doing. It's tough to know which parts are behind all our mental functions. But thanks to some spectacular new technologies, we are now gaining a better picture. And neuroscientists have come to a new idea about where, exactly, in the brain we reside. In a word: everywhere.

Consciousness doesn't stem from any one region; it's a product of many different areas working in harmony. As neuroscientist Anil Seth puts it, consciousness arises from how the "different parts of the brain speak to each other." Psychologists have created a neural map of the brain to describe this: the connectome.

Imagine the brain as a vast metropolis with numerous suburbs, neighborhoods, and business districts. These subunits are all synaptically connected by neural "roads." Our thoughts and feelings are like the pedestrians, cars, and buses that travel along these routes, while neurotransmitters like dopamine and serotonin act as traffic lights, regulating the flow. What we're thinking about at any given time is determined by which "neighborhoods" are linking—this integration is the connectome.

It starts in the reticular activating system, a part of the so-called reptilian brain near the base of your skull that regulates breathing, heart rate, and fight-or-flight responses. If this part of the brain gets damaged, you'll lose consciousness—a fact that informs the trope you see in many action movies where the hero knocks out the bad guys with karate chops to the back of the head.

This area, in turn, connects with other regions. For example, as you read this, the various barrios that make up your visual network, a vast web of neurons in your hindbrain, are busy creating a visual field. Your auditory network is also processing nearby sounds. All of this sensory information is then channeled through the salience network, which streams through the top parts of the brain. This is the same network that lights up when you encounter something unexpected, like a loud crash.

Mediating all of this is the attention network, which acts as a meta-level traffic control. It filters and prioritizes the neural information cascading through your mind, deciding which network gets activated and which takes a back seat. This filtering depends a lot on your environment and internal state. For example, neural traffic in your salience network will subside in a quiet room, making way for your dorsal attention network and allowing you to concentrate, as you may be doing right now. This is also why libraries are as quiet as tombs; monotonous spaces help us engage attention networks.

As a general phenomenon, consciousness is the activity across the various networks that comprise the connectome—the regular hum of neural firing throughout the brain. Your particular experience at any moment depends on how much and where this activity occurs. To continue with our urban metaphor, ordinary waking consciousness is like a city during the day, with steady traffic flowing across many neighborhoods and roadways. Sleep is like the city at night, with far less traffic moving along disparate paths. And being in a coma is like the city on Christmas morning, eerily quiet and subdued.

It all goes back to the idea of the brain as a prediction machine. Because it's constantly anticipating what will happen next, the brain is always scanning our environment and bodies, looking for important information. It does this by comparing new inputs with established routines. If a group of neurons starts firing more intensely or out of sync, your brain will prioritize the unusual information and bump it up to attention. In other words, our brains are wired to pay attention to variance and disruption, the things that trigger System 2 thinking.

This is also why there's no single place in the brain conducting consciousness, because consciousness is never quite the same from one moment to the next. Instead, there are competing networks, each jockeying for the lead position in the ongoing race for our attention. This competition isn't entirely random. Some patterns usually take pole position based on our daily habits. And the more we stick to our physical and mental routines, the more our consciousness ossifies around these recurrent experiences of self.

To see this, let's return to our handy city metaphor. Early in life is when the roads are being laid, a time when our initial neural pathways are under construction. As we develop and learn new skills, we don't just create new neural byways; we "widen" the ones that get the most traffic. Those connections that don't get much use? They're left to wither like old, forgotten side streets. As we age, we get increasingly set in our ways, both in life and our minds. Just as you probably take the same route to and from work every day, your brain also relies on familiar pathways to handle most of your mental traffic.

But, like all routines, these attention patterns can also become calcified. We get used to focusing on particular thoughts—what's wrong with our house? am I about to get fired? do I look fat in these pants?—and can find it challenging to think about much else. As our thoughts become oriented around our habitual concerns, our consciousness gets constrained to certain points of focus. Mental calcification is your karma operating at a neural level.

Imagine, for example, that you're a chess grandmaster. You spend all your time playing chess, and your brain becomes attuned to focusing on abstract sequences of moves. Your attention becomes habituated to living on a chessboard. You might get excellent at chess, but you'll start tuning out other things—like whether you've remembered to feed the cat or that your wife has been talking to you for the last ten minutes.

And it's not just chess masters who fall into this trap; we are all prisoners of habitual distractions. Parents might be overly preoccupied with their children, dieters with food, narcissists with themselves, and so on. What we pay attention to at any moment is primarily shaped by the intersection of our neural routines and the demands of our immediate circumstances. Yet, we're so accustomed to these thoughts that we hardly ever consider alternatives. Instead, we settle into a particularly narrow kind of consciousness that makes us feel solid, regular, and accurate. This steady experience of "being you" is, in truth, mostly a neural habit. And this habit originates in a network that often sits at the center of our conscious minds: the default mode network (DMN).

The Ego in the Brain

The DMN was something of an accidental discovery. In the early 2000s, neuroscientist Marcus Raichle and his colleagues at Washington University in St. Louis were using new brain-scanning equipment to see which parts of the brain "lit up" during various tasks, like looking at interesting pictures or solving tricky math problems. When their subjects weren't doing anything in particular, Raichle assumed that activity in their brains would slow down, much like how traffic on highways eases up during holidays. After all, brains are glucose-guzzlers, and if we're not using them, it only makes sense that they'd conserve energy by shutting down.

But to everyone's surprise, this wasn't the case. Instead, Raichle found that when subjects were not focusing on a specific task, a different network of neurons became more active—the DMN. To see the DMN in action, just stop doing anything in particular and watch your thoughts for about fifteen minutes. You'll likely notice your mind quickly wanders, meandering from one thought to another like a distracted tourist in a foreign city. This mental wandering is the DMN at work. It's where daydreams and fantasies arise. It's also the part of the brain that is engaged when we listen to stories. Most interestingly, it also kicks into high gear when thinking about yourself. Whenever you're wrapped up in some egoistic concern, it's the DMN that is behind it all.

So, if any part of the brain could claim to be the home of your sentient mind, it would likely be the DMN. It's the neural region that connects us with language, generates our egoistic micro-dramas, and pulls us into the past or catapults us into the future. The problem is that the DMN operates like all our other neural networks—it's highly routinized. It follows well-trodden paths, which we often experience as repeating self-absorbed storylines: people at work don't respect me, I look fat in these jeans, and so on.

All of this suggests a straightforward solution: If we want to overcome our negative mental habits, we'll need to rewire our DMN. Rewiring the DMN, however, is not an easy thing to do. It goes back to our brain being a prediction machine. We become accustomed to our mental routines because they seem to work for us. Our normal thoughts end up feeling both right and inevitable. It usually takes a powerful lever, like a great trauma, loss, or some other extraordinary experience, to dislodge us from these ruts.

And here is where psychedelics come into the picture. Psychedelic drugs affect our brains by disrupting serotonin, a critical neurotransmitter. The DMN is particularly sensitive to this disruption. Returning to our road metaphor, psychedelics cause massive roadblocks in the DMN. If you drop acid or take psilocybin, your neural traffic has to find alternative routes. The brain is forced out of its everyday thinking routines and starts generating unusual byways. It's this neural rerouting that makes psychedelic experiences "trippy."

These neural roadblocks also explain why psychedelics can cause feelings of ego dissolution. The DMN is where our ordinary sense of self is typically organized. If this part of the brain stops functioning normally, our self-concept disintegrates. In other words, that extraordinary feeling of oneness with the universe you had on that amazing ayahuasca retreat is not you tapping into an alternative reality; it's just your brain gummed up by a flood of serotonin.

Another activity that suppresses the DMN is meditation. When you are meditating, you are retraining your brain to bypass the DMN. As you meditate, you are taking your ego off center stage. This is why advanced meditators report experiences of ego dissolution similar to those of people who have taken LSD. They have trained their minds to do the same thing as hallucinogenic drugs: to override the DMN. But meditators are doing this without chemical aids.

Although neurological research on psychedelics, meditation, and the DMN is still in its early stages, it raises all sorts of intriguing questions about our brains, egos, and transcendence. For one, it suggests that our default mode of consciousness is ego-centered. When our brains aren't engaged in specific tasks, they inevitably revert to solipsistic melodramas. We daydream, fantasize, or worry about some conflict that always involves our fears, hopes, or unresolved annoyances.

We can see this in our everyday experience. Consider what happens when you're stuck somewhere with nothing to do. Typically, your mind does two things: It focuses on yourself, and it places you either in the past or the future. The brain's default activity is to create a story with you as the lead actor. Often, these egoistic stories are uncomfortable. We rehash our bad memories or obsess over desires or fears about the future. Indeed, the relentless pressure of the egoistic self is why many people find it intolerable to live in the moment. Think about how excruciating it can be to sit in a dull place like your dentist's waiting room. Instead of comfortably relaxing with the full might of our thoughts, we'll grab at anything—phones, televisions, old gossip magazines—to distract ourselves. The DMN is typically not a place of great comfort.

Research on the DMN also supports what psychologists have speculated about early childhood. When we're young, our DMN is incoherent, and its neural firing is not synchronized. This may explain why taking psychedelics can feel like reinhabiting the mind of a toddler. In this disrupted mental state, a blade of grass becomes fascinating, and ordinary items like clothing can seem absurdly silly. But as we age, this playful mental cacophony goes away. Our brains become dependent upon routines that have proven successful. By the time we're adults, our minds are entrenched in well-worn neural pathways that comprise the core of our ordinary consciousness.

Psychedelics can change all of this, at least for a few hours. When taken wisely, psychedelics offer brief glimpses of a different way of thinking and being, and this can be liberating. Many of the imbalances in our egoistic selves stem from neuroses, those anxieties, rages, and depressions that too often consume us. These afflictions arise because we reflexively return to the well-traveled highways within our brains. Anxiety and depression can become chronic when they become the familiar pathways in our minds; in other words, they become the stable traffic patterns of our psyche. Psychedelics disrupt these patterns, showing us brief possibilities for thinking differently. They can reveal creative ways to reorder our cognition and expand our consciousness.

Interestingly, this view of psychedelics may also explain how antidepressants work. Despite their enormous popularity, doctors and psychologists don't exactly know how or why antidepressants alleviate our depression. Like many people, I always assumed that SSRIs work by making us feel better. But it turns out this may be a misconception. According to new thinking, antidepressants might be effective not because of how they make us *feel* but because of how they make us *think*. By gently disrupting habitual thought patterns with mild doses of serotonin, antidepressants do subtly what psychedelics do more dramatically—they help rewire our brain's neural networks and take us out of our calcified mental traffic routes.

Taken together, all of this sounds like fantastic news. If we want to reorganize our minds, we should start gobbling up mushrooms and LSD, right? At least, that's what Timothy Leary would have had us believe. But, of course, there's a big catch with this simple plan: Transcendence never comes cheap. One problem with psychedelics is that, on their own, they're not guaranteed to help you find better ways of rechanneling your mental traffic. In fact, they might send you careening into a multicar pileup.

A lot of this depends on what practitioners call "set and setting." If you're in a great mindset or a beautiful place, then taking LSD or mushrooms can be an effervescently wonderful experience. But if you're feeling depressed, anxious, or stuck in the chaos of a noisy city, the experience can quickly turn into a nightmare. To this day, I'm still haunted by some bad trips I had in my twenties. Most people I know struggle to keep ordinary life from unraveling, and disrupting the fragile balance of the mind can open the door to all sorts of monsters lurking in the shadows. Or, to paraphrase Nietzsche, if you want to gaze into the fertile void, you must be careful about what might gaze back at you.

The other problem with psychedelics is what happens when the trip ends. Sure, a brief psychedelic experience can be inspiring or healing, but eventually, we all come back down to earth and our regular routines. Habits of mind are stubborn things, and you're not guaranteed to build new traffic patterns in your brain with just one trip or even many. Shedding those negative thoughts requires understanding why you're clinging to those self-images in the first place. In other words, to rewire yourself, you must determine the motivation behind your mental habits. And to get a handle on that, we should turn our attention to another crucial part of our psyche: emotions.

17

Emotions

HOW ARE YOU FEELING RIGHT NOW?

If you're like most people, the answer is probably something like, "Oh, I'm fine," which is the emotional code for "I'm not sure what I'm feeling, but I'd rather not get into it." This mask, however, hides a lot. Beneath our ordinarily placid veneers, a cauldron of emotions is always brewing. Emotions are like that—ever-present, even when they're simmering in the background on low heat. Yet, most of the time, we don't see them. We may go through the day feeling okay but inevitably find ourselves scrolling aimlessly on our phones, making another trip to the fridge, or inexplicably reorganizing the closet without recognizing the underlying emotions nudging us along.

Nor do things get much better when we're feeling something distinct. Even if we are angry or sad, we often have difficulty describing our experiences. We may know what pisses us off or when we feel blue, but when pressed to describe how those emotions actually feel, we usually fall back on synonyms like, "Angry is when I'm feeling mad," or "I'm feeling a little down." These aren't really descriptors of our feelings; instead, they're more like vague nods in their direction, the emotional equivalent of giving someone driving directions by saying, "Oh, it's over there somewhere."

The problem with this emotional ignorance is that these unseen masters are often running our lives. Every day, we typically spend hours fretting over something that might occur next week or fuming about something that happened years ago. Rather than recognizing the moment for what it is, our emotions often trap us in some mythical past or catapult us into some imaginary future. And this is not a great way to live.

A big part of self-optimization comes in navigating our emotional waters with more skill. It starts with recognizing the moments when we are stuck in reactive emotional loops, the times when we take a bad feeling and hit replay over and over, trapping ourselves in a neurotic vortex. This recognition allows us to see what's really going on when we're screaming at that "asshole" driving badly in front of us or gripped in the certainty that we are the world's worst person. In labeling our emotions, we create space between our conscious awareness and the feelings swirling through us. When we observe our emotions with compassionate detachment, we lessen their power. And the trick to doing all of this is learning how to recognize what we're feeling in the first place.

What Exactly Are Emotions?

The word *emotion* is a surprisingly recent invention. It only appeared in English in the sixteenth century and didn't catch on until the mid-1800s. Before that, when English speakers wanted to talk about their feelings, they used terms like *passions* or *sentiments*. But even today, psychologists still can't agree on what the word *emotion* means. Some believe that emotions are distinct, encapsulated experiences and that particular parts of our brains are dedicated to generating them. Others disagree. They argue that emotions are just arbitrary points on a broad spectrum of energy and sensation. They also debate whether emotions are the cause of physiological changes within us or the result of them, a classic chicken versus egg question. To make matters even more confusing, there's a significant disagreement about whether our emotions are innate or shaped by our culture.

Let me cut through this confusion with a simple definition: *emotions are motivational processes*. Or, to get a bit more scientific, they are neurophysiological states that prompt and direct our behavior. Emotions are the driving force behind everything we do—every action, no matter how small, is initiated by an emotion. And we are constantly experiencing them. From the moment we groggily roll out of bed to the time when we finally drift off into slumber (and even while we sleep), we're always following an emotional prompt. Feelings, by contrast, are the neural expressions of these motivational processes, the specific signals the emotions are triggering within our brains.

A great way to understand this is by looking at our first animal ancestors. Remember, when our jellyfish grandparents started swimming around, they needed to do two things: map their world and choose the best course of action. Their perceptions were how they created maps, and their emotions were how they figured out where to go. These early emotions took the form of physiological triggers, and these same triggers remain in us. All our emotions contain elements that trace far back in our evolutionary lineage. Whenever we experience joy, sorrow, horror, or intrigue, we use the same ancient neurological circuits that kept our early ancestors alive.

This last statement might sound a bit strange. We often think of emotions as something lofty and refined, like the delicate etching on the windows of human experience. In fact, for most of history, philosophers believed that humans were the only creatures who could experience happiness, anger, or sadness. But this is a misguided conceit. The same biological triggers behind our emotions are in our fellow animals, too, because they all serve the same general purpose—to make us act in specific ways. A reflex makes us instantly pull our hand away from a hot stove, a sharp pain makes us stop walking on an injured leg, and an elevated heart rate pumps up our energy. In the same way, sadness, joy, and anger prompt us to act in their peculiar ways.

Moreover, all of these processes are deeply intertwined. When we "jump in fear" or "melt in love," it's our reflexes doing the jumping and melting; the "heavy heart" of sadness and the "lightness of ecstasy" draw upon ancient neural systems. Emotions encompass many other mental and physical processes that operate below the surface of consciousness and stretch far back in our evolutionary history. In other words, those feeling states we call emotions are the brain's way of combining different physiological triggers.

Or, to use another analogy, emotions are a bit like cocktails. The specific blend and the resulting "flavor" depend on the type. Some emotions are like the classic gin and tonic, simple and straightforward. Surprise, fear, hunger, and lust fall into this category, going way back in our evolutionary lineage and remaining relatively uncomplicated. Guilt, anxiety, resentment, and jealousy, by contrast, are more like those elaborate, multilayered offerings with pretentious names that you find at a fancy bar—recent adaptations and neurologically more intricate. But even these sophisticated emotions still contain many of the same essential ingredients (even if they claim to use that obscure gin). Anxiety, for instance, is whipped up from reflexive tension, guilt comes with a splash of pain, and jealousy spikes our heart rate like an espresso martini.

This is why emotions are not distinct, neatly encapsulated feeling states. Instead, they arise from a neurophysiological swirl, like a whirlpool of various ingredients tossed together in a mental blender. Although we like to think of emotions like happy, sad, and angry as neatly packaged entities, as in the terrific movie *Inside Out*, that's not really how they work. No little brain compartment makes anger or sadness. Instead, *anger* and *sadness* are just handy words we've learned to slap onto complex neural states that occur with some frequency.

We can see this with the following thought experiment: Say you didn't have a word like *anger* in your language. Would you even recognize when you were pissed off or what was driving your actions? There you are, going about your business, and then one day, you find yourself sharpening your spear, ready to skewer your neighbor, and thinking it seems as unremarkable as taking another bite of food. Without the words to describe your feelings, your understanding of yourself and your actions would be wildly different.

This is why we invented emotion words in the first place. By labeling our feelings, we can take responsibility for ourselves and understand our own experiences. Words like *joy*, *anger*, and *sadness* are ways to interpret and communicate our internal states with others. And we English speakers have taken this pretty far—we now have over three thousand emotion words at our disposal, with more being added yearly (think of *FOMO* or *anticipointment*). We are now more emotionally articulate than at any time in history.

But even with our impressive vocabulary, plenty of emotions still slip through the linguistic cracks. Take, for instance, that weird experience of being both attracted to and repulsed by someone at the same time. I once had two friends who embodied this emotional paradox. Like a modern-day Elizabeth Bennet and Mr. Darcy, they shared a deep mutual loathing laced with undeniable sexual tension. Despite their hatred, they couldn't stay away from each other and were always visibly aroused by each other's presence (and yes, they eventually hooked up, much to their confusion and everyone else's amusement). For years, I've scoured the dictionaries of every language I could think of searching for a word to describe this strange brew of desire and loathing; the usually reliable German and French came up short. And the term *ambivalence* just doesn't cut it. This type of "disglust" might be quite common, but it tends to fly under the radar because we don't have a word for it.*

This example also raises an intriguing question: How many of our emotions go unnoticed simply because we don't have the words to describe them? Of course, not every feeling needs a name—if I'm feeling just fine, I probably don't need to invent a word to describe it. But there are plenty of emotions that we ignore at our own peril. The less we recognize what's driving us, the more we risk being dominated by impulses we haven't consciously chosen, or at least chosen with the deliberate parts of our minds. If we want to see what's behind our actions, we'll need to know what's causing them.

The Joystick

Imagine your emotions working like the controller for a video game, what's often known, semi-ironically, as a joystick. Most controllers only have a few buttons, but even with four or six of them, you can make

* Thanks to Walter Mott Hupfel for this suggestion.

your game character do all sorts of extravagant moves. I've seen this firsthand. I sometimes play video games with my son, and he enjoys thrashing me in an obscenely violent one called *Street Fighter.* With a few well-timed pushes of the left-right and up-down buttons, he can execute a Spinning Piledriver that sends my poor, unfortunate avatar flying across the screen every time we play. There is no Spinning Piledriver button, but he can somehow pull off this move by hitting the right sequence of buttons.

Our emotions operate in much the same way. We all have "buttons," neurophysiological triggers that direct our behaviors. And just like in the game, these buttons can be pressed in different combinations to produce a wide range of outcomes. Hear a snake's ominous rattle? That presses a combination of buttons that prompt you first to freeze and then hightail it out of there. We label that combo "fear," but no fear button exists. Instead, it's just a sequence of potential routines. This is the emotional joystick in action.

When it comes to our complex brains, there are probably scores, if not hundreds, of "buttons," but to keep things manageable, let's imagine we're operating with a six-button joystick, the bare essentials needed to perform our own emotional version of a Spinning Piledriver.

First, we have the two most basic buttons: approach and withdraw. These are ancient, dating back to when our jellyfish ancestors started wiggling around in the primordial soup. They needed to move toward things like food and potential mates (approach) and away from danger (withdraw). These early instincts are still very much alive in us today. Sexual desire, hunger, and curiosity all come from various approach mechanisms; disgust, sadness, and fear are based on withdraw signals. And yes, we can feel both at once—like when you're eyeing that pint of ice cream in the freezer at 2 a.m., simultaneously craving it and knowing you really shouldn't.

Next, we've got pain and pleasure. Pain and pleasure are involved in nearly every emotion we experience. It's hard to think of any mood with no positive or negative value attached to it. But pain and pleasure aren't simple opposites; they're more like dance partners who occasionally step on each other's toes: Sometimes one leads, sometimes the other does, and sometimes both are moving in sync. Some people, for example, find pleasure in pain. For a sadomasochist, a brutal spanking might bring waves of ecstasy. Conversely, a tickle that goes on too long can turn a pleasant feeling into a miserable one. Although we tend to categorize our emotions as positive or negative, they often work in combination.

Finally, there are activate and calm, the buttons that regulate our energy levels. Activate gets us pumped up and ready for action, while calm soothes us to rest. These help maintain our energy and body temperature and control rhythms like sleep and hunger. Adrenaline is a prime example of the activate button in action. It cranks up our heart rate and prepares our muscles for a sprint. Conversely, calm kicks in after a long, stressful day, guiding us to that blissful state of relaxation and sleep, where everything slows down to its lowest gear.

These six buttons—approach, withdraw, pain, pleasure, activate, and calm—determine what we do and reveal much about who we are. The emotions we recognize, like happy, morose, or agitated, are just the labels we use to describe whatever buttons are being pressed at any moment. They are like Spinning Piledriver, a handy label we use to indicate which combinations of buttons are getting triggered.

And most of our emotions involve a lot of buttons. Take anger, for instance. The English word *anger* comes from the old Norse word *angr*, which initially referred to feelings of trouble, pain, or affliction. Aristotle described the Greek equivalent of anger, *orge*, as "an impulse, accompanied by pain, to a conspicuous revenge for a conspicuous slight . . . a certain pleasure must always attend it." Modern dictionaries define anger as a "strong feeling of annoyance, hostility, or displeasure."

From these definitions, we see that anger isn't just one thing—it's a complex mixture of different neurophysiological states. There's no single anger button in the brain, even if certain things seem to always piss us off. Instead, anger involves many different processes.

It starts with activation. Anger gets our adrenaline pumping and our heart racing. This rush makes anger compelling, like a surge of raw power. But anger also involves pain. When we are mad, we rarely feel good. Anger also triggers the approach button—we're usually drawn toward the person or thing that's ticked us off. And when we finally act on our anger, it often brings a strange sense of satisfaction, activating our pleasure and calm buttons. In other words, anger, much like sex, is an emotion that awaits some culminating relief and satisfaction.

The overlap between aggression and desire is also why many action movies resemble porn films (and vice versa). Think about it: A typical action movie has some loose plot about revenge. The hero gets angry and then embarks on different fight vignettes—one-on-one, one-on-two, group fights, and so on. Each fight escalates until it climaxes in slow-motion knockouts or massive explosions. It's not much different from how porn films deploy their own one-on-one and one-on-two sequences that culminate in explosive orgasms. The analogy holds because anger, like all our appetitive desires, builds up tension in anticipation of a deeper reward.

We could play this game with any emotion. Whether it's joy, misery, terror, or rage, it all boils down to a unique mix of motivational triggers. Hit the right combination, and you motivate a specific behavior. What feelings we're experiencing at any given moment are just the music of different buttons being pressed together, but most of these emotional processes are happening well below our ordinary awareness.

Before we move on, there are two other things worth noting about our emotions. First, they are energy states. All our emotion "buttons" modulate our energy somehow. Some, like approach or activate, crank it up; others, like calm or withdraw, turn it down. But in every case, our feelings are busy expending energy, so it's not surprising that we often use colors to describe them, like feeling blue when we're sad or seeing red when we're angry. Just as colors come from different energy frequencies, our emotions reflect varying energy levels.

Second, emotions are expressions of our vitality. When we feel an emotion, what we're feeling is the animating energy that makes us alive. Emotions are how we resist entropy and what set animals apart from everything else in the cosmos. Sure, stars and galaxies burn bright, but they don't have feelings. I find it helpful to remember this, especially when I'm in the throes of a harsh emotion. Whether it's the weight of shame, the pangs of hunger, or the ache of sadness, I try to remind myself that I'm experiencing something with a unique, cosmic significance. Our feelings are where we experience the life force most viscerally, and that's pretty special, even if it's not always pleasant.

Feeling States

This is also an excellent time to clarify a common confusion between terms like *emotion*, *mood*, *temperament*, and *personality*. They're often tossed around like synonyms, but each has distinct meanings, and each is important for understanding ourselves.

Let's start with emotions. Emotions are like a short strike of a piano key—you hit it, let go, and the sound quickly fades away. When one of your emotional buttons gets pushed, it's supposed to stay pressed only for a brief moment, just long enough to get you to do something like run away from that snake. At the first sound of the rattle, you might get a strong jolt of fear, but once you get away from the snake, the feeling quickly fades. Psychologist Jill Bolte Taylor suggests that these single-shot emotions typically last around ninety seconds unless something keeps them going. Afterward, your body starts looking for other signals to guide your behavior.

Moods, however, are like holding down that piano key for a long time. A mood is an extended motivational state, which is what happens when your emotion buttons get re-triggered again and again. Sometimes moods are set off by your surroundings—like the deep relaxation you might feel during a massage or the slow-burning indignation that builds when watching primetime cable news shows. But often, our moods seem to come out of nowhere, possibly due to hormonal changes or some unconscious impulse.

And this is where things get tricky. When a mysterious mood takes hold, it can completely warp your perception of the world. One of my favorite examples of this came when my son Ethan was five. He had awoken at two in the morning, screaming in terror about a monster in his closet. After checking the closet, under the bed, and everywhere else, I tried to convince him that he was safe, but he wasn't buying it. We ended up in a circular debate—me patiently explaining that monsters don't exist and him confidently insisting that they most certainly do. Finally, our argument ended when he offered the coup de grâce: "Well, Dad, if there is no monster in the closet, then why am I afraid?" Conceding to his impeccable logic, I spent the night sleeping on his floor. But I did learn a valuable lesson: Our moods are often just emotions in search of a convenient target.

Temperament, by contrast, is our emotional baseline, the average of all our moods and emotions over time. To go back to the piano metaphor, temperament is like your playing style. Some people always play slow and languorous, others fast and frenetic. Or, thinking of the joystick, it's the set points, the default levels on the activate, pain, and approach buttons.

Temperament plays a crucial role in flourishing, and all of this goes back to homeostasis. As I mentioned earlier, homeostasis refers to the balance of energy and activity within our bodies. All animals have a homeostatic set point—a natural energy and metabolism level their bodies strive to maintain. It's how order and vitality are balanced in the animal self. When we deviate from this set point, our bodies will engage in countermeasures to bring us back into line. You see this every day: When you're low on energy, you feel tired and hungry, which motivates you to rest or eat; when you're cold, you shiver to keep warm; when you're exhausted, you get sleepy. Many emotions are just our body's way of restoring our homeostatic balance.

The problem is that we can get stuck in emotional cycles that eventually alter our homeostatic levels. Let's use the example of anger again. It's an activating emotion that burns a lot of energy. In the short run, anger might empower you. It can help you stand up to a bully or fight against an injustice. But after you've acted on your anger, your body needs to cool down and your anger's pain needs to be released. This is why you only feel good once the anger is resolved.

But if you always get angry, it will become a habit, and you'll spend more and more time in a bad mood. Do this long enough, and your temperament will shift, and, next thing you know, you're a grumpy old man. This is partly what the Buddha talked about when he described dukkha—the persistent suffering from living in an unbalanced state. Freud might have called it neurosis, while others might describe it as being perpetually stuck in emotional turmoil. In any case, it's not a great way to live.

Ideally, your temperament should reflect an emotional level where you're expending just the right amount of energy to thrive. This is the homeostatic set point of your animal self. We can see this across the animal kingdom. Rabbits, for instance, are prey animals, and they're always ready to run. Using the joystick metaphor, we could say that rabbits have high set points on their activate and withdraw buttons. Sloths, by contrast, evolved a survival strategy centered on conserving as much energy as possible, and they have a high set point on their calm button. Each of these temperaments evolved to work optimally within their environments. If we want to optimize our selves, we'll need to recognize if our temperaments are best suited for our circumstance. We don't want to spend our days anxious like rabbits when nothing is looking to eat us, nor as immobilized as sloths when there's plenty of food.

The big challenge here is that the sources of our temperaments are often hard to know. A lot of our temperament is baked into our genes. Some folks are blessed with a sunnier disposition, while others tend toward chronic sadness or irritation. Studies on identical twins suggest that at least half of our temperament is hardwired into our genes, but the source of this genetic influence remains elusive. Part of this ambiguity arises from the sheer numbers of genes involved; psychologists estimate that at least seven hundred may be at play, although the specific ones that keep us cheerful or moody are still unknown.

To make things even more complicated, many of these genes might only get activated under certain conditions. If you suddenly find yourself in famine or war, your biology will shift as certain dormant genes now kick in. In other words, our temperament isn't the product of a single gene or even a set of genes but a mélange of genes that change depending on the situation. Gene editing might someday allow us to tweak our emotional baseline, changing us from a perpetually anxious or unhappy person into a blissful one, but for now, we're stuck with what we have.

The other challenge with temperament is that it is often hard to recognize. Temperament is our emotional baseline, always simmering in the background, so it's difficult for us to see. Usually, it's most apparent in another aspect of our character, our personalities. If temperament is about how we are likely to feel at any moment, personality is how we are likely to think and react to those feelings. Personality is our temperament with a thinking style layered on top. As a result, our personalities are usually more distinctive and visible.

In fact, one of the most common ways that people "know" themselves is through some personality classification scheme. From the four humors of ancient Greece to the Myers-Briggs Type Indicator, there are scores of methods that purport to tell us who we are and how we should live. The most scientifically reliable scheme comes from modern psychologists. They've developed the Big Five Inventory which claims our personalities are made up of five key dimensions that go by the acronym OCEAN:

Openness: How creative, curious, and adventurous you are.
Conscientiousness: Your level of organization, dependability, and responsibility.
Extraversion: Your sociability, friendliness, and outgoing nature.
Agreeableness: How compassionate, cooperative, and docile you are.
Neuroticism: Your tendency to be volatile, sensitive, and moody.

Numerous studies show that these five OCEAN traits are reliable predictors of how we will act in any given situation. For instance, I score very high in openness, so it's no shock that I've tried psychedelics, meditation, and many other avenues of self-exploration. I also score pretty low in conscientiousness, which is why my stuff is often scattered everywhere. So yes, the Big Five helps me know myself and gives me a label to explain some of my quirks.

The problem is, I'm not sure what else to do with this information. Knowing your short-term emotions and moods is extremely important for taking command of yourself in the moment. I often notice this when spiraling into a black hole, where everything seems terrible and doomed to stay that way. In those dark moments of the soul, when I'm projecting all my lousy feelings onto the world, it's helpful to remember that it's my mood talking, not reality. This detachment can keep me from making poor decisions, like stepping in front of a speeding truck or saying something I'd later regret in arguing with Thea. In other words, it's much easier to maintain your balance when you can recognize what's causing you to wobble in the first place.

But I'm not sure this type of self-awareness also works with personality inventories. One problem is their reliability. Many of them are notoriously bad at scoring people over time, and this is often because of our shifting moods. Sometimes, I feel introverted, and sometimes,

I'm sociable. Often I'm messy, but I'll occasionally catch the cleaning bug, much to my family's great delight. Where I score at any moment depends on the day. Another problem is that we often read into our personality tests only those things we want to see about ourselves—I'm more likely to identify as open because it coincides with a positive view of myself.

And then, there is the total use value of these labels. Some people may find a personality test a great way to "know" themselves, especially if they don't have any other tools at hand. Advocates of personality tests argue that knowing your traits can help you set realistic goals, find compatible partners, and make better life choices. For example, if you're an introvert or not agreeable, you probably shouldn't take a job in sales. But that doesn't mean a personality score can actually motivate you to change yourself. Most of the scientific research uses personality scores as predictors of people's behavior. Not surprisingly, they find that people who score high in conscientiousness and low in neuroticism tend to perform better at work.

The real question is whether knowing your own personality can help you change. In other words, if I know I score high in neuroticism or low in conscientiousness, can I use that to change my work behavior? For some people, this may be the case, but much of this depends on your mindset. Yes, I try to be neater around the house, but this is less because of my conscientiousness score and more because I don't want to annoy my family.

Ultimately, personality may not be destiny, but it can become prophesy. The real value in knowing your Big Five profile isn't just in labeling yourself, but in recognizing which patterns need attention. Research shows that when people consciously reflect on who they are and how they want to grow, they can change. The trick is to move from scorecard to strategy, to use personality awareness not as a label but as a launchpad. And, to do this, let's consider the most common reason we want to know our selves in the first place: Happiness.

18

Happiness

LIKE A MODERN-DAY CINDERELLA, MY FRIEND ELENOR endured a childhood of misery. With a mother and sister both grappling with borderline personality disorder, Elenor grew up in a home filled with emotional turmoil. Her father was often away, and when he was around, he seesawed between mania and depression. At age eleven, when her parents finally divorced, Elenor played the reluctant caretaker role for everyone.

But Elenor, ever plucky, decided that she would take matters into her own hands. She worked hard in school, got into an elite college, landed a great job, and married Nick, a wonderful and dynamic man who seemed like everything she had ever hoped for. For many years, it seemed like Elenor was living the "happily ever after" that her younger self had dreamed of.

But life, as it so often does, had other plans. Things started to unravel soon after their kids were born. Parenting, as it does for many couples, put a lot of pressure on her marriage and seemed to bring out the worst in Nick. Over time, he became withdrawn, obsessed over money and status, and left most of the caretaking to Elenor. They started arguing more, and Elenor questioned whether Nick still loved her. In the years that followed, things stayed rocky. There was constant tension in the house, they stopped having sex, and the fights sometimes got really bad.

Still, they worked hard to improve their marriage, and just when it seemed like things were getting back on track, a bombshell dropped: Nick was diagnosed with cancer, and it was bad. Nick tried every radical treatment available, and while these kept him alive, they came at a considerable cost. His body deteriorated, he became addicted to opioids, and mentally, he was a shadow of his former self. His personality became erratic, and he often lashed out in anger. Elenor spent the next six years shuttling him between hospitals, taking care of him and their family, and just trying to keep it all together. Eventually, Nick died.

Today, Elenor is a single parent raising three kids alone and trying to make sense of everything that has happened. And yet, remarkably, she is one of the most contented people I know. There is no bitterness, no self-pity, no gloom. Elenor is quick with a warm smile or a clever joke. She exudes a soft glow, a serene grace that hints at a greater transcendence. Even amid all the loneliness and challenges, Elenor seems to thrive.

Of course, Elenor is genuinely exceptional in this way. For most people, happiness is an elusive goal, something we're constantly chasing but rarely seem to catch. Part of the problem lies in our assumptions. We often believe that we can achieve happiness if we check off the right boxes. This was the case for me. I spent much of my early life thinking, "If I could just get that perfect job, earn a million dollars, or start dating Miss July, then I'll finally be happy." And I see this same mindset in a lot of people around me.

My friend, the psychiatrist Elizabeth Kieff, calls this the gold star illusion. We're taught as kids that the way to "win" in life is to collect our gold stars. We're supposed to get good grades, land a great career, find that perfect partner, and so on. We're led to believe that happiness is the permanent reward for doing all the right things.

There's just one hitch in this simple plan: Reality is constantly changing. As much as we want the world to be fixed and predictable, random events have a pesky way of intruding from unexpected places. Sickness arises, friendships fade, and sometimes we just wake up on the wrong side of the bed. As my friend Elenor knows all too well, reality doesn't just toss us softballs; it also throws some pretty wicked curves.

As a result, we tend to bounce through life, often craving something different from the present moment. We want our struggles to stop, our boredom to end, and a romance to sweep us off our feet. Over time, this adds up. If you were to look back at your life and tally all the hours you spent longing for something else, you'd probably find that your discontent took up years, if not decades, of your life. And that's not a great way to live. If we want to move past all this and start living better, we must find an alternative to the gold star illusion, a different pathway to well-being. We must overcome our habits of craving and aversion, and this requires us to reconsider two of the most important aspects of life: pain and pleasure.

The Pleasure Trap

The gold star illusion is rooted in our biology. Our animal selves are wired to feel pleasure from food, sex, and security; pleasure is thus a motivator, nature's way of rewarding us for doing the things that, in the wild, promote our survival. Our brains, always on the lookout for patterns and certainty, naturally assume that if we want to live happily ever after, all we need to do is set up the right conditions to provide a steady stream of pleasure.

The main driver behind all this pleasure-seeking is a neurotransmitter called dopamine. This little chemical increases the firing between specific neurons in your brain, making you want things. Dopamine primarily works as a surprise-success signal. In nature, it gets triggered when an animal stumbles upon something new and rewarding.

Imagine you're a monkey living in a banana forest. You spend your days munching on bananas, but they don't give you a lot of joy because they are familiar. Then, one day, you come across a mango. Oh, my (monkey) God! The novelty and sweetness of the mango triggers a massive dopamine surge, sending waves of intense pleasure through your little monkey brain. But this moment doesn't just make you happy—it retrains your brain. Instead of being content with bananas (which don't give you much dopamine), you only want to hunt for more mangoes (which do). You now forget those bananas, even if they're nutritionally good for you, because you want to relive the pleasure of the mango.

Dopamine works the same way in us. Whenever we encounter something new, surprising, and pleasing, we get a little dopamine. This is why novel experiences are often the most intense. The first time we eat dark chocolate, have an orgasm, or win a hand of blackjack is delightful because it triggers a big dopamine release. But dopamine isn't a satisfying hormone; it's a craving one. It always leaves us wanting more. This is why gambling is compelling, why we endlessly scroll through social media, and why video games and porn sites are addictive—they all trigger dopamine releases in us, which leave us craving that next dopamine kick.

But rather than making us happier, this does the opposite—it makes us miserable. This happens for a few straightforward reasons. For starters, pleasures always diminish over time. The first bite of a Recchiuti chocolate bar may be divine, but by the fifth bite, it's just another piece of chocolate, and that Hershey's bar you adored as a kid now tastes like brown corn syrup. The first line of cocaine is euphoric; the fifth line is a desperate attempt to stave off the void. In short, prolonged pleasure exhausts us. Great sex, stunning landscapes, and surfing perfect waves are all things we can eventually become numb to with overindulgence; well, maybe not perfect waves, but that's because they never last.

In other words, chasing pleasure is not the path to happiness; it's a trap. This goes back to our body's need for homeostasis. Too much pleasure messes with our body's chemistry because it disrupts our pleasure set points. As a result, we end up in self-destructive cycles. We need ever more drugs, sex, internet clicks, or whatever to recapture that sense of pleasure we once had. It's why addicts keep coming back for their next fix—they're no longer trying to get high; they're just trying to feel normal. Their reward network is damaged, and their pleasure set point is out of whack. When our pleasure "button" is over-triggered, it wrecks our entire temperament. Yes, it's a bummer, but it's also a fact of life: We aren't meant to always feel great.

But we often don't see this. Instead, we've become so habituated to our pleasures, so drawn to the allure of that next dopamine kick, that our lives become oriented around them. Any time we begin to feel slightly down or even just a little bored, the habitual craving kicks in, and the next thing we know, we're mindlessly picking up our phone or off to get another pint of ice cream. And, over time, these habits alter our temperaments and leave us with a hollow experience of being.

The Purpose of Pain

If chasing pleasure isn't the golden ticket to happiness, then maybe dodging pain is the way to go? Although this may sound logical, it is not good advice. Pain is both unavoidable and incredibly important. It's our body's way of telling us when something's wrong, like a broken leg that needs healing or a tooth that needs attention. Pain also acts as a powerful motivator, pushing us to do tough but necessary things. This is why it plays a role in many emotions: Anger's pain drives us to defend ourselves, sadness slows us down to reflect, and envy's sting motivates us not to settle for less. And, of course, there's the education we get from our most painful mistakes; nothing teaches quite like a good, hard fall.

But pain isn't just the flip side of pleasure; it's far more nuanced. While pleasure activates general reward networks in the brain, pain involves particular signals from various places throughout the body. Pain is usually triggered by special types of neurons called nociceptors. These nociceptors exist to relay precise information about injuries such as burns, cuts, and bruises. Nociceptors are also why pain tends to be localized, while pleasure is usually more of a holistic experience.

Pain also has another distinctive trait: It doesn't fade. No one suffers from chronic pleasure unless, of course, they live in California. Pleasure ebbs over time because the neurotransmitters behind it get depleted with overuse. Pain, on the other hand, doesn't lose its edge. If you break your leg, that pain sticks around to ensure you don't go hiking until it's healed. Pain doesn't diminish, because its job is to keep us informed about what's wrong until the issue is resolved. While we might grow accustomed to it, pain never loses its sting.

Yet even though pain is persistent, it's not supposed to be a constant signal unless something is seriously wrong. Yes, we might have lots of pain from cancer or a terrible injury, and it can be easy for us to get stuck in painful states of anxiety, depression, guilt, and stress, but that's not how we're supposed to live.

Despite its great power, pain is something we can control. This goes back to a hidden secret: Pain actually comes from our brains. Say, for example, you hit your thumb with a hammer. The awful pain you feel starts with those nociceptors that are registering the compression and bruising. But they are not creating the feeling of pain—they're just sending a particular neural signal to your brain. The excruciating pain in your thumb actually comes from your brain, taking in those messages and translating them as pain. In other words, pain is a matter of subjective interpretation by your mind. In this way, the brain is the ultimate source of our physical suffering. The pain signals from the body are really just unrefined sensations. It's the mind that distills them into motivations.

And here's where things get interesting. Like so much of our mental lives, our brain's ways of interpreting pain signals are partly learned, as are our reactions to them. Over time, we develop habitual ways of both experiencing and responding to pain. Sitting in the doctor's office, a tiny flu shot might become an agonizing impalement, an echo of an early childhood experience. Or we may run to the comfort of the liquor cabinet at the first whiff of a cold without even being aware that we're self-medicating.

But just as these habits are learned, they also can be unlearned. With the proper training, we can build up a high tolerance for pain by learning to control our reactions to it. The key is to gain awareness of your emotions and then establish some distance from them. Once we can recognize when we are compressed by fear, anger, or grief, we can then stop and see what the somatic experience of the emotion is like for us rather than simply acting on the urges impulsively. It's also why it's important for us to be able to recognize our feelings—by being able to label our emotions, we can cultivate greater equanimity.

This is something I've experienced firsthand through meditation. Sustained meditation can be challenging and inevitably involves some pain, even if it's just the discomfort of sitting still for hours on end. A big part of the contemplative practice is retraining yourself not to react to the pain but to observe it with calm detachment. Do this long enough, and you can start to reinterpret the pain. For example, a burning sensation might feel less like "burning" and more like an abstract tingling. The more you learn to see pain objectively, the easier it becomes to sit with it and observe its natural ebb and flow.

Advanced meditators can take this to extreme levels. Take the example of Thich Quang Duc, a Buddhist monk who gained international fame in 1963 when he set himself on fire in protest of the Vietnam War.

This act was immortalized in an iconic photograph by journalist Malcolm Browne. What's most remarkable about the photo is that Duc sits completely still, even as his flesh burns away. His contemplative practice was so deep that he could withstand unimaginable pain without flinching right up until his death. This type of equanimity is the key to self-optimization. Okay, maybe not quite this type, but you get the idea. Pain is a natural, inevitable, and crucial part of our existence.

In many ways, this is the secret to Elenor's grace. When I asked her how she managed to get through the past decade, she had some insightful observations. She said that when your dreams shatter and you lose everything, a kind of clarity kicks in. If the worst thing you fear has already happened, then you have nothing left to be scared of. For Elenor, this realization liberated her. She let go of the outsized expectations she had for her life and learned to coexist with extreme difficulty because, as she saw it, she had no other choice. This has filled her with a deep gratitude for what she still has. For Elenor, the path to flourishing wasn't found in living the dream but in surviving the nightmare that followed.

Four Tips for Living Better

So, how are the rest of us supposed to find happiness? Most people I know aren't too keen on spending years meditating in a Vietnamese monastery or taking care of a problematic spouse with cancer. Fortunately, you don't need to take such extreme measures. Over the past several decades, a vast amount of research has examined what factors promote a flourishing life. While the recommendations can range from keeping a journal to a daily gratitude practice, I'm going to highlight four of the most straightforward suggestions.

1) Avoid environments that are both painful and erratic.

As mentioned throughout this book, our animal self is a prediction machine. It craves comfort and safety, and while it can tolerate a fair amount of misery and threat, it needs to know what's coming next. When problems arrive in unpredictable waves, our bodies don't know how to adjust. Imagine, for example, a neighbor randomly blasting thumping house music at different hours of the night. Intrusions like this trigger the release of cortisol and norepinephrine—hormones that get your heart racing and your mind spinning.

If you knew the music always started at 11 p.m., you'd adjust, and while it might still annoy you, it wouldn't send your brain into a frenzy. But when the noise strikes randomly, your brain goes haywire. Our bodies don't like repeated, unpredictable shocks. It's why veterans often suffer from PTSD, why children bear deep scars from parental abuse, and why people living in dangerous neighborhoods frequently struggle with chronic stress—the unpredictability of violence fundamentally disrupts their natural temperament. To keep our emotional set points stable, we need to minimize unexpected traumas, no matter how small they may seem.

That's easy to say, but for many of us, this is a particularly tough challenge. If you're trapped in poverty, dealing with erratic or abusive family members, or stuck in a stressful job, it might not be so easy to smooth out your life. And let's face it, part of life is learning to live productively with discomfort, as I'll discuss later. But the key is to recognize when you're in a situation that's subtly torturing your mind.

So, how do we tackle this? While there's no one-size-fits-all answer, there are a couple of steps everyone can take. First, you must recognize whether you're in an unhealthy environment. Many times, we accept situations that harm us, whether it's an abusive relationship, a soul-crushing job, or even doomscrolling on our phones, because we think we have no choice or we're just used to it. This is why it's crucial to listen to your pain and figure out what it's telling you.

Second, you need to accept responsibility for making a change. Too often, we resign ourselves to awful circumstances, a form of learned helplessness akin to a lab rat trapped in a cage of our own making. A big part of flourishing is learning not to take crap from the world just because you cannot see any alternatives. You always have a choice; the key is finding the courage to make a change.

2) Adopt a positive mindset.

It is a long-established finding in psychology that in general, people feel better when they are in control of their circumstances. Yet even when we're not in control, our mindset becomes really important. If we *believe* that our actions result from our choices, regardless of our reality, we'll feel much better. The good news is that this is something we can cultivate ourselves. This idea is at the heart of Stoicism: Most of our experience in the world is shaped by the attitude we bring to it.

Consider that lousy job. You could think, "Ugh, I have to flip burgers again today" and then proceed to wallow in your misery. Or, you could approach the same job with a mindset like, "Today, I get to feed a lot of hungry people," or "This job helps me support the ones I love." These might sound like cheesy platitudes, but they can make a huge difference in your internal chemistry, keeping your emotional set point higher. It goes back to Marcus Aurelius and his Stoic, self-pep talks—living better inevitably means having a better mindset.

The hardest part of maximizing your autonomy is not letting your emotions dominate you. Emotions are natural motivational signals designed to make us act in particular ways, but they aren't precise or always accurate. Yes, we should pay attention to them and be aware of the information they contain, but we don't always need to act on them. We don't need to grab our phone anytime we feel bored, or open the fridge at the slightest whiff of hunger. We can coexist with our emotions, observing them with compassionate detachment.

I suspect this was one of Elenor's secrets. She's a powerful person and was fully committed to taking care of Nick and the kids. Instead of feeling like a victim of circumstance, she actively participated in her life. She was the one hounding hospital administrators, keeping her kids' spirits up, and cherishing any small joys the day might bring. Rather than passively accepting her situation, she found ways to empower herself. And she often did this calmly, not letting the roiling feelings inside her run the show. It turns out that positive thinking can lead to positive outcomes, even in the toughest of times.

3) Take on challenging but achievable tasks.

This is the idea of "flow." According to psychologist Mihaly Csikszentmihalyi, the more time we spend engaging in stimulating activities, the better off we become. To enter a flow state, we must find the right balance between skill and challenge. If a task is too hard, we'll feel anxious and discouraged, like trying to learn the piano by starting with Shostakovich's second concerto.

On the other hand, if the task doesn't challenge our skill level, we'll quickly get bored; no pianist wants to play only chopsticks. Flow comes when we find the sweet spot between our abilities and the task at hand, and we improve over time. Flourishing people are constantly exercising their competencies. The more we continue to do this throughout our lives, the greater our sense of fulfillment.

We can also take this advice in the inverse by asking if the things we are doing are actually helping us learn or feel good. If you're like me, you probably spend a lot of your day doing unproductive things. Consider social media. Is the time you spend there teaching you anything or helping you exercise a competency? Or is this simply "junk time" that provides a little hit of dopamine but isn't giving you anything more? Living better comes from spending more time learning new things and stretching our abilities.

4) Love other people.

One of the most common misconceptions about happiness is that it's something we can pursue on our own. But we are social beings through and through. Our fragile hominid ancestors didn't survive by going it alone; they stuck together in groups, and in doing so, they evolved all sorts of ways to stay connected. The social emotions persist in us—they are part of our evolutionary patrimony. The people around us deeply influence our feelings, moods, and temperaments, and we need to cultivate meaningful relationships to keep ourselves healthy.

This was another of Elenor's secrets. Like many people, she found great happiness in helping others. In caring for not just Nick and her children, but other cancer survivors, she tapped into one of the most surefire ways to gain life satisfaction—make things better for those around us. She let others help her, too. Throughout her ordeal, she leaned heavily on the support and nurturing of a wonderful group of friends. Elenor's grace and resilience didn't come from her alone; they were intricately woven into the love and care of those around her.

But, as with the rest of life, relationships can be very complicated. Other people have mixed effects on us. On the one hand, they can be incredibly uplifting. Think of someone comforting you when you're sad or helping to ease your anxiety when you're overwhelmed by stress. On the other hand, they can also be draining, pulling us away from our natural emotional balance—the crying child, the irritable spouse, the overbearing parent, the toxic colleague. As Jean-Paul Sartre famously said, "Hell is other people," mainly because of the emotional toll they can exact on us. Being around someone who is miserable, angry, or even overly cheerful can be exhausting precisely because their moods disrupt our emotional equilibrium.

The real secret to living well is maintaining healthy relationships. "Happy wife, happy life" might be an archaic cliché, but there's truth embedded within it: Our happiness is intimately tied to those we love. Our emotional well-being is dependent upon the well-being of others. No one can be happy if the people we care about are suffering, and nothing is as crucial to our flourishing as how we love and are loved in return. This last point is so important that it deserves a much closer look.

19

Love

LIKE MANY PEOPLE, I GREW UP UNDER THE CHARMING ILLUsion that the most important thing I could do in life was to find true love. Somewhere in the vast, chaotic world was my one perfect person—the Lennon to my McCartney, the rice to my beans, the one who would complete me. Once I finally found this person, I imagined a rapturous connection would sweep us away, our lives intertwining like a perfectly orchestrated rom-com. This person would be my lover, best friend, spiritual partner, therapist, and maybe the one who could finally figure out how to program the remote control. With life's quest complete, we could marry, have a beautiful family, and rest easy in the confidence that our woes would no longer haunt us.

Of course, reality was a bit more complicated. Throughout my teens and twenties, I went through a revolving door of relationships. Some lasted weeks, others months, and a few longer. Some were all about physical chemistry, others were intellectual, and a few were just weird. Along the way, I bruised a few hearts and got my own dinged up, too.

But through it all, there was a persistent undercurrent of dissatisfaction. The most intense passions often flared up in relationships that were doomed from the start—the married dancer or the too-free spirit I met on a Turkish bus. Meanwhile, my longer relationships seemed to fizzle out as soon as the inevitable realities crept in. Once my initial enthusiasm for the new romance began to wane, I would start second-guessing everything; the moment I no longer felt "completed," the red flags would start flying. Eventually I'd retreat into myself or push the other person away, and, unsurprisingly, the relationships would crumble. This cycle repeated itself more times than I care to admit, leaving me feeling painfully alone and wondering if I'd ever find that magic person who would finally fix everything.

It wasn't until after years of therapy, a lot of soul-searching, and a healthy dose of meditation that I finally let go of the illusion that there was one special person out there who would make everything magically right in my life. And wouldn't you know it? That's when I met the person I've been happily married to for over twenty years.

Perhaps it took two decades of dating to find this out. The lessons from my failed relationships gave me some great insights into what makes a successful one work, and these are lessons I've brought to my family and friendships as well. But more important, I was figuring out my shit, seeing how my own fears and hang-ups kept getting in my way. So, yes, I got my happy ending (or happy beginning, more accurately), but my life would have been much easier if I'd had a clearer idea of what love was from the start. And in this, I'm not alone.

Among all our emotions, none is as tempting, necessary, or mysterious as love. We tend to take love for granted as a straightforward concept. Love is, well, love, and everyone wants it. But once you start digging into what love is, it quickly becomes a puzzle. Love is a mass of contradictions. It is stimulating and soothing, erotic and nurturing, grounding and elevating. It promises certainty but often feels chaotic. It tempts us with pleasure but inevitably brings pain.

Part of love's mystery comes from the limitations of the English language. While other tongues often have dozens, if not hundreds, of words to express love's many dimensions (Sanskrit, for instance, supposedly has 267), we English speakers overuse just one. And we expect a lot from this beleaguered little word. It's supposed to capture connection and commitment, intimacy and nurturance, spirituality and unification, eroticism and pleasure—and that's just scratching the surface. As the clichés remind us, love has many "languages," takes many forms, and comes in many guises.

So, how on earth are we supposed to understand this baffling thing we call love?

The answer comes in distinguishing "love" from "loving." As the psychologist Erich Fromm observes, love is a noun and it encapsulates a set of complex feelings. It can range from the warm glow of deep connection to the fiery passion of raucous sex to the gut-wrenching pain of rejection. But at its core, love, like all emotions, is a motivational process—it's nature's way of nudging us to do certain things. And, contrary to the grand romantic narratives, these love feelings aren't meant to last forever; they're expressions of the moment, inevitably fleeting.

Loving, however, is a verb, and it's all about relationships. Like all relationships, loving comes with habits, patterns, and rules. When we struggle to find or sustain love, the issue usually isn't the feelings of love themselves, for there are lots of things that can trigger those feelings. Rather, the struggle is with relationships that generate those feelings. While love is about our individual experiences, loving is about the shared experiences we create together. If we want to have better relationships in our lives, it is useful to explore what is behind love, the feeling, and loving, the act of relating. For this chapter, we'll start with love.

I Feel Love

Throughout history, the task of deciphering love's mysterious terrain has usually been left to writers, musicians, and poets—the true masters of turning human emotions into lyrical enigmas. And if these creative souls are our most accomplished explorers, their preferred compass is usually the metaphor. Early Chinese poets, for instance, depicted love as a delicate, silky thread binding two people together. The Persian poet Rumi preferred to use the natural elements, as in love's fiery passion, airy bliss, and oceanic depths. The Roman poet Ovid took a more cynical approach, comparing love to warfare, slavery, and theft; clearly, this was a man who'd had his heart stomped on a few times.

And this metaphorical menagerie stays with us today. Consider pop music where love is a battlefield (Pat Benatar), a fire (Bruce Springsteen), the sunshine of life (Stevie Wonder), a wicked game (Chris Isaak), a healing (Marvin Gaye), a soft devastation (Billie Eilish), and so on. These metaphors are as familiar as they are poignant. If you've ever found yourself sobbing uncontrollably in your car to some super mournful ballad (I'm thinking of you, Joni Mitchell), then you know exactly what I mean.

Yet, for all their charm, I'm going to set aside these many poetic images and use a distinctly non-romantic metaphor to describe love. It might not be as alluring as a magic arrow or a gossamer thread, but it better captures love's many dimensions. It's the notion that love is a drug (Bryan Ferry) and we are all hopeless addicts (Robert Palmer).

The love-as-drug metaphor works on multiple levels. It starts with what happens in our brains when we feel love and when we're high on chemical substances. Those magical, heady feelings of love and those miserable, wrenching aches from love's loss both stem from an electrochemical stew bubbling away in certain parts of your brain. And, wouldn't you know it, the same hormones and neural networks light up when we indulge in drugs like cocaine, MDMA, and heroin. In other words, love is nature's way of getting us high without needing a shady back-alley transaction (although love sometimes involves that as well).

Like many other parts of us, this chemical connection traces back to our animal ancestors. As primates with complicated social lives, we've evolved a sophisticated neurochemistry to keep us together. Sometimes, this chemistry lifts us up; sometimes, it calms us down; and sometimes, it just keeps us balanced enough to survive another day. But make no mistake: Love feelings are the neurochemical rewards and benefits of connecting and cooperating with others. They nudge us to find suitable mates, invest in our offspring, care for the sick and injured, and feel deeply attached to our tribe. Love binds us in a way that promotes our collective survival, and it does this through a suite of powerful neurochemical triggers.

But the drug metaphor doesn't stop at feelings. The other reason love is like a drug is that we're wired to be dependent on it. Solitude is hazardous for any social primate in the wild, and none of our simian ancestors would have survived long in isolation. As a result, they evolved baseline feelings of loneliness, fear, and pain that are quickly triggered in the absence of social contact. Loneliness is the yin to love's yang, the necessary darkness to its light. It's nature's not-so-subtle way of saying, "Get back to the group, you fool, or something with sharp teeth is going to eat you!"

The same process occurs with us. As newborns, we are physiologically dependent upon a caregiver's touch. We come into the world with an innate love dependence. Our inborn set point is not sanguine and content; it is anxious, uncertain, and destabilized. As children, we can only find comfort and well-being if given nurturance and loving contact. An infant's breathing, heart rate, and basic hormonal flows are all designed to be co-regulated with its mother. Children who are denied such contact suffer deeply into adulthood. Like addicts in need of a fix, we need loving relationships simply to feel normal.

This dependence doesn't magically disappear when we grow up. We still need loving contact across our adult lives to keep our temperament steady and our energy in homeostatic balance. That's why being single can feel so challenging, and breakups can feel like the emotional equivalent of being punched in the gut (repeatedly). When we lose a friend or romantic partner, it's like losing our regular dose of emotional soma. Get dumped, and you'll feel like a junkie going through withdrawal: Your body is racked with pain, your soul is drowning in sadness, and your mind is plagued with hallucinations and compulsive thoughts. A little positive contact—a friendly hug or a supportive chat—can ease those symptoms, like methadone for the heart.

Conversely, this is also one of the great tragedies of drug addiction: Even if you kick the habit, you'll live in a chronic state of heartbreak because your chemical "lover" is with you no more. Most recovering addicts I know never fully get over their one great love, which, unfortunately, was either cocaine or heroin. So kids, don't do drugs, or at least the ones that make you feel outrageously and artificially good.

Our dependence on love is also why the most significant predictor of a flourishing life is the quality of our loving relationships. This isn't just some gooey Hallmark card sentiment; it's a cold, hard empirical fact. Numerous studies have shown that our ability to connect with others is the most crucial factor in helping us thrive.

One of the most convincing is an eighty-year research project that tracked two cohorts of young men who came of age in the late 1930s: one, a group of Harvard undergraduates (which included future president John F. Kennedy), and another, a group of Boston youth from troubled homes. The researchers kept tabs on them throughout their lives, interviewing them and their families every few years. Across hundreds of very different individuals, a remarkably similar pattern emerged. Those who were able to sustain loving relationships thrived; those who couldn't were far more likely to suffer from disease, alcoholism, drug abuse, and mental decline. It didn't matter how much success they had in business, how famous they became, or how many gold medals they won, if they didn't have healthy relationships, they suffered.

So how, then, can we find love? Funnily enough, this is a very modern question. For most of human history, loving relationships weren't discovered as much as they were assigned by the village elders, your parents, or the local matchmaker. Most people lived in tight-knit tribes where kinship and custom dictated everything, from who you married to how you had sex. These communities had bonding rituals, songs, and the occasional goat sacrifice to keep everyone in sync with the group. Think of it as a prehistoric rave, only with less thumping bass and more drum circles. The "drug" flow of their relationships was kept in steady dosage by rite and ritual.

Fast forward to today, and those tribal constraints have mostly disappeared. On the plus side, this means we have incredible freedom to choose who we want to be with, when we want to socialize, and how we want to relate to others. If we're feeling particularly misanthropic, we can choose not to relate at all; solitude is no longer the same death sentence it might have been for our hominid ancestors, at least in the short run. Instead of dealing with the hassles of actually relating to other people, we increasingly turn to technology. Feeling lonely? Check out Snapchat. Need a dopamine hit? Scroll through Instagram. Craving erotic stimulation? Welcome to the endless rabbit holes of Pornhub.

But surprise, surprise, none of these tech-fueled love proxies are a great substitute for the real deal. They might offer a quick fix, but they are a lot like trying to stave off hunger with cotton candy. The main problem with these technological stand-ins is twofold: regulation and addiction. Our digital delights are habit-forming precisely because they hijack our brain's natural mechanisms of pleasure and comfort. Once we get a taste, we keep coming back for more, and before we know it, we're chasing that dopamine dragon down a never-ending spiral of Likes, retweets, and artificially enhanced selfies.

Indeed, the more time we spend indulging in these virtual quick fixes, the more we deplete our dopamine reserves and throw our serotonin flows into disarray. Every moment we spend glued to our screens, obsessing over our latest high score or crafting the perfect Instagram caption, is time we're not spending on actual human interaction. Instead of these technologies being self-affirming, they often become self-destructive, leading us further away from the authentic connections that truly sustain us. To see how this all works, let's focus on one of the most potent love feelings we know: eros.

Eros

Of all our natural love feelings, perhaps none are more potent than eros. When I use the term *eros*, I don't simply mean eros, the erotic; I mean eros, the feeling of vitality. Eros is the love feeling that lights us up, the natural equivalent of caffeine, ecstasy, or cocaine. Sometimes, this feeling is sexual, but eros goes beyond just getting physical. It's the excitement that any intriguing person can spark—the inspiration from a great teacher, the warmth of an unexpected compliment, the thrill of a casual flirtation. These are the feelings that animate and elevate us. They entice us with delicious emotional waves of activation and pleasure. They call forth the energy within. Eros is what makes romance seductive and spending time with friends fun.

Eros is one of our most powerful "natural" drugs, and it's no wonder we're obsessed with it. And thanks to neuroscience, we now know a fair bit about the chemical processes behind it. Those erotic feelings of lust, excitement, and elation come from a cocktail of hormones like dopamine, serotonin, testosterone, estrogen, and oxytocin. Release the right mix of these chemicals in your brain, and you'll be aching, panting, and downright crazy with desire.

And that, ironically, is the simple part. The bigger mystery is what triggers those chemicals to flood our brains in the first place. Until recently, nobody knew. Before the 1940s, scientists didn't pay much attention to erotic behavior, and anyone who did was often viewed with suspicion, like Freud, or simply as a pervert. Then along came Alfred Kinsey. A biologist by training, Kinsey was a respected entomologist who made a name for himself studying gall wasps (an unlikely subject to make one's name with, but, hey, that's biology). In 1938, when he was asked to teach a course on marriage and family at Indiana University, he realized there was almost no solid research on human sexuality. Intrigued by this glaring gap, and perhaps by the fact that he and his wife had an open marriage, Kinsey began systematically surveying people about their sexual preferences.

And what he found upended the conventional wisdom of the day, which held that sexuality was a pretty straightforward affair between conventional, heterosexual pairs copulating infrequently and only in the missionary position. Instead, Kinsey's research (and the waves of studies that followed) revealed that our erotic triggers are both subjective and often idiosyncratic. Some folks are drawn to short, hairy construction workers; others to skinny, moody Asians; and many to something else entirely. Despite the almost endless variety, there are some common factors that consistently shape our desires, and they tend to fall into one of three categories: biology, social context, and life history.

Some erotic triggers are baked right into our genes. What usually gets us going are signs of reproductive fitness: physical health, youthfulness, symmetry, and vitality. These cues can vary somewhat by sex and orientation. For example, heterosexual males are often turned on by shiny hair, ample breasts, and a small waist-to-hip ratio. Heterosexual females, on the other hand, are frequently stimulated by markers of status, strength, and resources: "Tall, dark, and handsome" is indeed a thing, but wealth, talent, and fame don't hurt, either. Evolutionary biologists suggest that such traits signal fecundity and access to resources, something that any reproducing primate would want in a mate. Similar patterns hold in same-sex attractions as well.

But while biology explains some of our desires, it doesn't account for all of them. This is because erotic feelings also depend on our surroundings. Eros, like anything of value, is influenced by supply and demand. What we find sexy or exciting usually depends on what's available. Singles are generally pickier at the start of the party than they are by the end; a chiseled body stands out more at the grocery store than at the gym.

Eros is also shaped by our culture. What's sexy in South Korea might not be in Botswana, and vice versa. Sure, we Americans may be attracted to that handsome stranger, but he's generally more alluring in a tailored suit than with a bone through his nose, at least for most people. This tendency is most evident in our fantasies and porn preferences, where internet users gravitate toward themes that are both familiar—moms and dads, cheerleaders and athletes, teachers and bosses—and culturally specific. For instance, Pornhub users in Utah are far more likely to type in the search term "Mormon" than, well, anywhere else; and yes, of course, there is such a thing as Mormon porn.

Added to the mix are the many complications stemming from our unique psychology. Our erotic triggers aren't just hardwired into us from birth; they are shaped by our early experiences. These influences can range from childhood associations, like the comfort of mommy's nightgown, to the smells of our early companions, which tend to become a turnoff in adulthood, a phenomenon known as the Westermarck effect. Childhood teaches us how to channel our sexual energies, and these lessons stick with us throughout life.

One of the oddest examples of this was the popularity of flagellation in Victorian Europe. It turns out that whipping and spanking were highly sought after in nineteenth-century brothels. Dickens's London, for instance, was teeming with all manner of dominatrices. Historians believe this popular fetish was the by-product of the severe corporal punishment common in elite private schools. Evidently, if you spank a British schoolboy enough in childhood, he'll see it as a path to sexual fulfillment as an adult.

The big challenge comes in balancing eros and our relationships. Eros wells up from the deepest part of our life force. As Freud observed, eros is our first love feeling, and it stays strong within us throughout our lives. A flourishing life gives eros its proper expression. But not everyone can access it. Some people were raised in traditions that shamed them for their sexual feelings, others were sexually traumatized in childhood, and some were simply unclear about their sexuality. A big part of knowing ourselves is understanding our erotic triggers.

Sexual self-knowledge, however, can be a tricky business. After all, how do we know which of our sexual triggers are truly innate and which ones were programmed into us by our upbringing? There's no easy answer. Sexual feelings are both powerful and intimidating, and as Freud noted, society demands we keep them well-regulated. A big part of exploring who you are is being open to peering into the murky and often threatening wellspring of your erotic desires and being willing to deal with whatever you find there.

The other great challenge with eros comes in our relationships. The term *erotic relationship* is something of an oxymoron, and this comes down to the nature of desire. The urge and excitement of eros are partly fueled by dopamine, which thrives on novelty, like a monkey discovering a ripe mango. While we crave the safety and certainty that come with commitment, eros is enhanced by variety, spontaneity, and mystery. It's far easier to get excited by that alluring stranger because of their mysterious potential, but even the most passionate relationships become normalized over time. It's like eating an exquisite meal—the first bite is full of wonder and joy, but with time, it becomes a familiar pleasure, and eventually it can feel mundane.

Some try to resolve this dilemma by bouncing from one partner to the next. Addicted to the rush of sexual novelty, they're always looking for a new high. But serial hookups, like all our dopaminergic pleasures, can lead to diminishing returns. Or worse, people let their unresolved issues guide them into problematic sexual relationships. For example, it's common for people who were sexually abused as children to seek out abusive partners in adulthood; like a Victorian aristocrat, they unconsciously conflate sexual energy with pain and degradation. Our sexiest relationships may give us a significant charge at the beginning, but they can also end up causing us harm in the long run.

So, how do we sustain eros in healthy, stable relationships? Or, as the brilliant author and couples' therapist Esther Perel asks, "How can we continue to want what we already have?" Beyond trying obvious things like shaking up your routines with vacations, costumes, or role playing, Perel suggests that the long-term answer lies in opening up to unknown parts of our partners. It's about embracing the idea that your partner is a separate person with their own inner world, which can reignite intrigue and attraction. If we want to sustain the spark of the erotic, we need to relinquish the comfort of the familiar. The challenge, according to Perel, is that we too often conflate intimacy with eroticism. While sex can help foster intimacy, intimacy can sometimes dampen our desire. And to understand why, we need to explore the process of loving.

20

Loving

I SOMETIMES WONDER IF MY FRIEND TRISTAN MADE A DEAL with the devil. Tall, charming, and ridiculously handsome, he has an almost otherworldly charisma. His effect on women is astounding. I've never seen anyone else command the kind of adoration that he does. Once, we were chatting at a Christmas party when a stunning woman he barely knew approached him. Sporting a set of toy reindeer antlers and a sultry smile, she cooed, "Tristan, can't you see that you're making me horny?" Nothing like this ever happens to anyone else I know.

But a devil's bargain is never fair, and it's particularly cruel for Tristan. Despite all his allure, Tristan is incapable of sustaining a meaningful romantic relationship. Well into his fifties, he remains alone and genuinely perplexed about why. His problems usually begin after a few dates. Whenever he starts getting close to someone, a paralyzing fear grips him. He doesn't want to feel this way, and he's missed out on being with some truly amazing women, but it's as if some inner, alien force kicks in, pulling him away from the connection he desperately wants. Oddly enough, most of the women he dates can see this, and rather than feeling rejected, they often feel compassion for him. I've never known anyone to be so beloved by the very people they've dumped.

Tristan's case is extreme but also illustrative, because who among us hasn't struggled with love at one time or another? When we're young, this often means bouncing from one relationship to another; as we get older, we may struggle to maintain that spark in our marriages and friendships. And many people don't even get this far. One recent survey found that roughly one-third of Americans experience intense feelings of loneliness every week. Something is wrong with how we relate to each other. If we want to optimize ourselves, we'll inevitably need to focus on our relationships.

Yes, But Do You Like Me?

Think for a moment about the people you like most in this world. I'm not talking about your casual friends or some distant celebrity, but the people who really get you—those you could spend hours talking with or feel comfortable with even in silence. What is it about these people that makes them unique? Why do we like them so much more than anyone else?

We usually believe that the answer is something specific to that particular person. Bob is fun and perpetually coming up with some new adventure; Carol is big-hearted and generous; Alice is hilarious and a delight to be with; and Ted is solid and always ready to listen. Everyone we like seems to have a special quality about them, and we think this is the reason we like them.

But this is only part of the story. While we might be able to come up with any number of explanations for why we like any one person, it's not *really* why we like them. After all, plenty of other people in the world probably have these same traits. The real secret to our successful relationships is intimacy.

The word *intimacy* has been part of the English language for about five hundred years, tracing its roots to the Latin word *intimus*, meaning "inside" or "innermost." And it's this feeling of inner connection that ultimately defines our closest relationships. Intimacy is where we see each other beyond the personae, ego postures, and identities that usually come between us and other people. It's recognizing each other at a deeper, core level.

This experience has a neurochemical basis. Intimacy arises when our brains are flooded with serotonin, oxytocin, GABA, and a dash of dopamine—the hormonal recipe that makes us feel at one with another person. If eros is about the pleasure of wanting, intimacy is about the satisfaction of having.

The secret of intimacy lies in recognizing that loving is not a thing but a process, and a very dynamic one at that. Our relationships need to be sustained with regular input. Like spinning tops, the more energy we put into them, the smoother they turn. And while they may coast on their own momentum for a while, if we don't give them regular attention, they will begin to wobble and eventually fall over. To keep close, we must continually reengage.

Loving usually follows a distinct pattern, a cycle of intimacy. We build feelings of connection, or stimulate flows of serotonin, oxytocin, GABA, and dopamine if you want to be technical about it, by repeating a three-step process, over and over and over again with suitable people:

Establish mutuality. The first step in building intimacy is finding things you share in common. "You like knitting? I like knitting." "You're from Texas? I'm from Texas!" The more significant things you share, the closer your bond becomes. This is why shared politics, religion, language, and sense of humor play such crucial roles in our relationships. Intimacy rests on the foundation of sameness—how we are both alike and mutually distinct from the rest of the world.

Share vulnerability. The next step in building intimacy is to reveal parts of yourself that are not visible on the surface. Yes, we may hold common interests, but a deeper connection comes from sharing what's inside. This could be a secret longing, a guilty pleasure, or any part of yourself that someone wouldn't know from superficial interaction. It's the secret sauce behind bonding games like Two Truths and a Lie. When we reveal our inner side, particularly our flaws, secrets, and doubts, we invite others to share a deeper experience of being.

Give affirmation. Once we express a vulnerability, the next step in the cycle of intimacy is providing affirmation. This can range from a simple compliment to a general declaration of love and commitment. The point is not simply to make other people feel better but to make them feel heard and seen. Affirmations are vital for letting the vulnerable person know that whatever they share is okay, and that knowing their inner life does not diminish our affection or make us want to leave. It is a way of giving us confidence that others will be there for us.

We build true connections by going through this cycle of mutuality, vulnerability, and affirmation. And the deeper we go into the cycle, the stronger this connection becomes.

In a now-famous article called "36 Questions That Lead to Love," *The New York Times* suggested that you could do this with anyone.* The questions start by getting people to share less obvious facts about themselves. For example, you're invited to describe how you'd like to be famous or what you think makes a perfect day. As the list progresses, it ventures into more revealing questions that encourage you to share your most terrible memory or describe your relationship with your mother. And sprinkled throughout are prompts to compliment the other person, where you tell them something you like about them. What the questions are really doing, though, is guiding you through the cycle of intimacy.

But if building intimacy is so straightforward, why does sustaining it seem so difficult?

One sticking point is affirmation. People often struggle to recognize when their partner is communicating their vulnerability. I see this in my marriage. Sometimes, Thea will share a frustration at work or anxiety about a problem, and my first response is, "Well, why don't you do something to fix it?" Instead of being helpful, this only makes her more upset. While I think I'm being reasonable, I'm being tone-deaf. At that moment, Thea isn't looking for advice—she's looking for support. And this is often the case. When people share their problems with us, they're sharing vulnerabilities. And when we share our vulnerabilities, we're not seeking solutions, we are seeking comfort.

Another major barrier to intimacy is our fear of expressing vulnerability. The researcher and writer Brené Brown describes this point extremely well. According to Brown, one of the biggest obstacles to intimacy is that we falsely conflate vulnerability with weakness. We tend to think that our problems are particular to us and that no one else has them. So, instead of sharing our fears, shame, or insecurities, we bottle them up.

---

* This study was based on research by psychologist Arthur Aron.

This has two unfortunate consequences. First, it cuts us off from other people. Intimacy is a reciprocal process that only deepens if both parties share their vulnerabilities. When one person is vulnerable and the other is not, the relationship becomes one of dependency, not intimacy.

Second, by keeping our vulnerabilities hidden, we give them greater power. This is especially true with feelings of shame, particularly around sex or other "immoral" things. The more we hold on to our shame, the more it isolates us from others. We can then spiral into a shame-isolation cycle, where we feel unlovable because of our shame and, in turn, keep ourselves removed, thwarting any chance for love.

The fear of expressing vulnerability is particularly acute for American men. Our culture emphasizes strength and certainty as the hallmarks of true masculinity. Real men, we are told, don't experience anxiety or self-doubt; they are always confident and assertive. So it's unsurprising that American men suffer more from loneliness and social isolation. The irony is that this perception is entirely backward. Sharing vulnerability is a sign of true strength and courage, a willingness to show confidence in your whole self, warts and all. Rather than making you powerless, sharing vulnerability makes you powerful.

Here is one of the most critical points in this book: The true enemy of intimacy is fear. If we struggle to connect with others, it's usually because we fear getting too close. Much of this fear is rooted in childhood. While this might sound like a Freudian cliché, it's a concept with substantial empirical support. Some of the most valuable insights into this concept come from the pioneering work of psychologists John Bowlby and Mary Ainsworth.

Their idea, known as attachment theory, is straightforward: Our early experiences in childhood are vital in shaping how we love as adults. It starts when we are toddlers. As we begin exploring the world, we are incredibly vulnerable and need assurance that we will be kept safe. Children who receive steady and attentive love from their parents develop greater confidence in venturing out and meeting new people, always knowing that a protective embrace is there for them to return to. They have a firm grounding in the knowledge that they are loved and that connecting with others is safe—a secure attachment style, as Bowlby and Ainsworth call it.

Many people, however, don't get healthy, loving experiences as children. Perhaps they had parents who were distracted, negligent, or inconsistent, leading to an anxious attachment style. In this case, the child is scared to venture out independently because they are never sure if their caretaker will be there when they return. Or they may have had parents who were abusive or intolerant of mistakes and emotions, which often results in an avoidant attachment style, where the child doesn't trust anyone and keeps to themselves. Worse yet, they may have had parents who alternated between being abusive and inattentive, creating an anxious-avoidant attachment, which seesaws between fearfulness and withdrawal.

The challenges don't end in childhood. The attachment styles we develop as children carry into adulthood, shaping how we interact with others in ways we might not even recognize. For example, people with anxious attachment styles tend to be emotionally needy and demanding. They constantly seek reassurance and are terrified their partner will leave them. Yet, they often don't see themselves this way. Instead, they blame others for their problems—this partner doesn't meet my needs, or this friend doesn't get me. Often, these individuals will choose romantic partners who will likely leave them or find ways to sabotage their relationships, unconsciously validating their chronic fears.

Avoidant types, on the other hand, tend to be cold and distant. They have trouble opening up and sharing their inner lives, leading to more transactional than intimate relationships. As a result, they are often out of touch with their emotions, carrying around feelings of pain and shame that prevent them from finding the connection they long for. These individuals struggle with closeness; their relationships tend to stay limited. Occasionally, they may open up, tantalizing their partners with a glimpse of connection, but they usually retreat into their habit of staying within themselves.

One of the most valuable things about attachment theory is that it can help us identify the challenges in our loving relationships. Many people are surprised to discover they score high on either the avoidant or insecure scales. Learning about our attachment patterns can be eye-opening. It's easy to overlook when we're acting withdrawn or needy—such emotional habits might feel like our "normal." Seeing ourselves in comparison can help us put our struggles in perspective and guide us in shifting our behavior.

This kind of self-correction, however, requires effort. Sustaining intimacy doesn't come easily for many people. I know that when I'm feeling avoidant, the last thing I want to do is reach out to another person. Sometimes, the only thing that pushes me to fight against my isolating tendencies is knowing that I have obligations to the people around me and myself. It's up to me to push through my limitations, even when I want to hide in front of the TV with a pint of ice cream. But for those with real fears of connection, this effort is crucial to sustaining intimacy.

Transcendent Loving

If you had lived in almost any other time or place, the concept of "happily ever after" with a romantic partner would have been virtually unheard of. This was because relationships were largely involuntary. You probably lived in a small village, clinging to your tribe for survival. You spent most of your time with kin, and your social life was strictly divided along gender lines—women mainly stayed at home, while men were often away. Marriages were arranged for economic factors rather than romance, and you didn't look for deep emotional or sexual fulfillment from your spouse. Divorce was rare and highly shunned. Your extended family was the center of your social world, and your love was defined by circumstance, forcing you to make the best of it.

Today, things are very different—at least in the industrialized West. Most of our relationships are largely discretionary. It's up to us to figure out who we want to love and how much we want to love them. Consider our romantic partners. Rather than being married off by sixteen (as is common in many traditional cultures), this might be when we start dating. We might spend the next twenty years "shopping around" for different partners among possibilities. We can have "starter marriages," divorce without stigma, or choose not to marry at all.

But it's not just romantic life that's becoming increasingly voluntary—

nearly all our social ties are as well. We pick our own friends, decide how much time to spend with our families, and choose how social we want to be. Thanks to social insurance and changing social expectations, we don't always need to take care of aging parents or destitute relatives. Our loving relationships are things we decide for ourselves; commitment is an individual choice.

However, all this freedom has created a dilemma. It starts with a less-than-romantic inevitability: *Loving requires effort.* Although we may get swept up in fantasies of "happily ever after," loving is demanding work. Worse, the rest of the world doesn't exist to satisfy our infantile needs. Our love partners aren't always waiting with champagne and roses. Friends and family can be inconvenient and sometimes downright annoying. Young children are relentlessly needy; teenagers are chaotic and moody; and aging parents can be exasperating.

So, amidst all the challenges of love, what keeps us together? The answer to this question is transcendent relationships. If erotic relationships are about our own pleasure and intimate relationships are about shared connection, then transcendent relationships are about our deliberate intentions. They are based less on our immediate feelings and more on our values and aspirations.

Transcendent love is often described as committed love, but we must be careful here, as the two aren't necessarily the same. Many people are in committed relationships that are pretty dysfunctional—think of couples who stay together "for the kids" despite their bitterness. Committed relationships can also be codependent: staying with an emotionally distant partner because they tolerate our bad habits, or remaining with an abusive one because they validate our shame. But this is commitment in the hollowest sense. It's not genuinely loving.

Transcendent relationships, by contrast, are rooted in a conscious intention to expand our capacity for love. These are the relationships we cultivate to rebalance order and vitality within ourselves. Of course, commitment plays a significant role in this process. We go beyond our immediate needs when we bind ourselves to others with vows to stay faithful, kind, and present. But commitment is just the vehicle, because what truly matters is its intention. In transcendent love, we engage with others conscientiously, guided less by fleeting emotions and more by an aspiration to live better through opening ourselves up to others, often by putting their needs ahead of our own.

The most blatant example of transcendent love is with our children. This might sound strange at one level, for we often think it's natural to love our kids. But this isn't always the case. Kids can be bratty, annoying, and awful. The real reason we don't abandon them is they have an incredibly powerful natural weapon: They're cute. Adults find their large eyes, little round faces, and disproportionately big heads on little bodies to be irresistibly adorable. This cuteness is nature's way of protecting kids from the blowback of their innate horribleness. But even with these formidable defenses, we adults inevitably project our anxieties, insecurities, and resentments onto them. At its worst, parenthood can become a battleground where we play out our unresolved issues on our children.

At its best, parenthood expands us, pushing us beyond our everyday habits and self-obsessions. In the sleepless nights spent holding a feverish child or on days when gentle patience with a toddler's wanderings is needed, we transcend our own issues. When approached with deliberate care, these moments allow us to express a vitality usually hijacked by our petty egotism. In other words, transcendent love isn't just about showing up and going through the motions—it's about striving to rise above ourselves.

In adult relationships, transcendent loving often means deliberately confronting our limitations. Let me share a few examples of people I've known who have done this. Steve married Carrie right out of college. At first, their relationship was all about the physical connection. When they started dating, they couldn't keep their hands off each other, and that erotic thrill seemed enough. But after they got married, Steve became more focused on work and emotionally checked out. The only times he and Carrie connected were during sex, which became less and less frequent. Over time, this left Carrie feeling abandoned, and she eventually had an affair. The marriage ended, and Steve felt wounded and betrayed for a long time. He was ashamed, angry, and deeply caught up in a narrative where he was the victim.

However, in the years that followed, I noticed a shift in Steve. He began examining his habits of withdrawal and came to recognize his role in the marriage's failure. If he wanted to have a successful relationship in the future, it was up to him to open up, even if that didn't come naturally. Twenty years later, he's happily remarried and enjoys a real emotional connection with his new partner—but this didn't happen by chance. It came from a lot of hard work to overcome his tendencies to withdraw.

Or take a different case. Dana is bright, beautiful, and super sexy. When we were younger, she had no shortage of boyfriends—typically roguish actors and musicians. But she never stayed with them for long; inevitably, one problem or another would arise, and the sizzle would fizzle. Then she met Ozzie. He was short, chubby, and balding, definitely not her usual type. But he made her laugh, readily shared his feelings, and was always genuinely present. While her earlier boyfriends provided plenty of passion, Ozzie offered intimacy. Even so, Dana felt a lot of ambivalence. Was this shlubby guy the one she was meant to be with? Eventually, she decided he was. When I asked her how she overcame her initial reluctance, she said she had figured out some ways to "eroticize Oz" (a phrase I've always loved), and that was enough.

As both stories illustrate, transcendent love is about expanding our capacity for eros and intimacy. It's about pushing through our limitations and finding better ways to connect with those around us. But on a deeper level, transcendent love is, for lack of a better word, a spiritual endeavor. It's about tapping directly into the life force that animates us. As I described earlier, we all have an effervescent energy coursing just below our conscious awareness. Love feelings are one way we access that energy, piercing through the thick layers of habit and distraction that keep us from knowing our essential being.

Transcendent love is about taking on the quest to connect with that energy for ourselves. It's about taking responsibility for cultivating our love feelings. Or, to borrow a well-worn metaphor, it's about learning how to "get high on your own supply." Transcendence requires expanding our consciousness and seeing alternative ways of loving that go beyond our ordinary habits.

This is also why transcendent love is central to many religious traditions. Christianity, for example, calls on us to experience God through love. The first epistle of John (4:7–8) says, "Let us love one another, for love comes from God. Everyone who loves has been born of God and knows God. Whoever does not love does not know God because God is love." In Buddhism, this is expressed through compassion for all living beings. The Metta Sutta says, "Even as a mother protects her only child with her life, so with a boundless heart should one cherish all living beings, radiating kindness over the entire world."

In both traditions, love is something one cultivates from within. In Christianity, this is typically done through good deeds and prayer; in Buddhism, it's expressed through "loving-kindness" meditation, where one "takes in" all the world's suffering and sends forth salutations of peace and compassion. Both practices are about getting past our selfish and self-centered preoccupations and sharing a nurturing empathy with others.

This type of spiritual practice is often described as selfless love, but as you can probably guess, I don't think that's the best term, because there's no way we can really be without a self. It's why I prefer the term transcendent love. It's loving as self-correction. It doesn't matter whether it is our children, lovers, or even the most challenging person we know, by expressing love and compassion for others, we're compelled to overcome our own limitations. It forces us to reconfigure the balance between order and vitality within the self. And this reveals the ultimate target of transcendent love: ourselves.

"Self-love" is an easy idea to dismiss. It can sound hokey, onanistic, or self-indulgent; and sometimes it is. We can use self-love as an excuse to avoid facing uncomfortable truths. But ultimately, self-love is about learning how to approach our fears, pains, and hang-ups with tenderness and compassion.

Let me offer another personal example of this. Many years ago, I was on a meditation retreat, grappling with a lot of internal and diffuse pain that had no clear target. After struggling with this ache for a long time, I had an idea. I visualized this pain as a wounded little boy. As I observed this miserable creature, I decided to try an experiment. I imagined comforting him in the way I might comfort my children. Almost immediately, the pain within me began to ease, and the more I did this, the better I felt. This was revelatory, for here was self-soothing at a really deep level. It occurred to me that this is also what it means to "be your own best friend." It's about approaching all your negative qualities with love.

Transcendent love is how we get past our egoistic selves. It's a way of connecting with feelings of love that are unconditional and independent of our personae. It's where we don't need an identity or anything special about us to feel loved—we are just loved. It's how we provide ourselves the experience of feeling cherished, a deep union with a life source that is warm, radiant, and boundless. While we often think we need to be "worthy" to experience such love, the fact is that these feelings already exist within us. They're nestled within our deeper layers of self. The life force gives us our love feelings. We just need to make ourselves open to it.

The challenge, however, is that our minds throw up a lot of obstacles along the way. Finding the ability to love ourselves is often tricky, especially if we're caught up in habitual cycles of pain, anxiety, or depression. We instinctively think we'll find love and happiness by meeting our ego needs rather than moving beyond them. We often get so distracted by our melodramas that it's hard to stay in a place where we can practice this kind of compassion, either toward others or ourselves. The key to transcendent loving is in figuring out where the roadblocks lie.

21

Recognition

MY FRIEND HANNAH IS AN ABSOLUTE DELIGHT. WHIP-SMART, warm, and lovely, she radiates an effervescent charm that could make even the grumpiest of souls crack a smile. She is one of those rare people who combines wholesome goodness with a lively curiosity, someone who is dependable yet always up for a wild adventure. Whether she's generously helping refugees or joyfully dancing at a party, she sails through life with a luminescent grace. Or, as another friend aptly describes her, Hannah is simply "a blessed ray of fucking sunshine."

But even the sunniest days can have their clouds, and beneath Hannah's glow lurks a darker side. She loves her job as a teacher, but she has a nagging feeling that she should have a career with more prestige. She adores her husband, but she can also criticize him quickly, ready to swoop down on his missteps like a hawk spotting a mouse. She's a stickler for rules and a bit of a control freak regarding routines: Her house must be spotless, her children exceptional, and her arguments always right. This impulse not only distances her from the rest of the imperfect world but also causes her stress. For all her radiance, there's often a palpable tightness to her, a simmering tension just beneath the surface. Hannah is plagued by a nagging itch, a feeling that even the best things in her life aren't quite as good as they could be. Yet, this is not a problem that's easy for her to see—after all, what could possibly be wrong with wanting the best?

We're all a bit like Hannah in our ways. We all have great qualities. Most people are generally kind and helpful and want to make the world a better place. But beneath these good intentions lie the flaws, mental habits, and emotional cycles that trap us in misery. They can show up as uncontrolled rage, listless fatigue, or any other dysfunctional mood. We obsess over that jerk at work, worry incessantly about the kids, or endlessly spin some other tale in our heads. And because we usually take these thoughts and feelings as literal representations of the world, we believe them to be genuine truths. But they're not. Our stories are just how our minds try to map and predict what's happening around us; they're not precise depictions of reality.

In previous chapters, we've seen how these processes operate, so we might know all of this in theory. But, in practice, we usually don't even see our imbalances. This is particularly ironic, considering how easy it is for us to see everyone else's. We all know someone who drinks too much, stays with that awful girlfriend, or is self-defeating in their anxieties, yet always seems to have a pitifully transparent excuse for their miseries. Other people's issues are so obvious, but when it comes to our own, we're often blind.

Why is this the case? I see three explanations. First, when it comes to ourselves, we tend to focus on the symptoms of our imbalances rather than their cause. Take our ordinary thoughts. Most of the time, we're trapped in the story of the moment: the next task, the pressing fear, the latest indignation. We take whatever thought or impulse pops into our brain as the truth, often a truth that's threatening, dissatisfied, or just plain unsafe. We believe catastrophe is imminent, we're terrible people, or we're the only ones who are always right. We rarely see the more important fact that our thoughts are not precise representations of reality.

Second, we often use unhelpful terms to describe what's going on with us. Even if we recognize when something's off, we use the wrong story to explain it. It's like we're a tribe that lives in the shadow of a volcano. We exist in perpetual fear, never knowing when an eruption might happen. So, every year, we sacrifice a few teenagers to our Vulcan gods. This causes us a lot of pain, but we believe it's necessary for our survival. So we keep doing this until some free thinker comes along and explains the realities of plate tectonics (although it's likely we would also throw him into the volcano as a heretic).

Obviously, this is a stylized metaphor—for the record, no cultures actually threw teenagers into volcanoes, at least not as sacrifices—but we all do something similar. We may feel chronically anxious or agitated, but we're stuck, because we don't have the right words to describe what's really happening. We continue to punish ourselves because we see no alternative. And what's worse, we often reject the people who can see things clearly. Have you ever made the mistake of telling a friend they shouldn't marry that awful fiancé they're always complaining about? Then you know exactly what I mean. But the problem remains: We won't find better solutions until we can accurately describe our imbalances.

Third, which are the best words to use? We don't always know. Today, we enjoy an incredible variety of ways to diagnose our problems. We've already explored some of these, with concepts from psychoanalysis, neuroscience, and Buddhism, but this barely scratches the surface. Before us sits a vast collection of religions and mysticisms, psychological theories, philosophies, self-help books, psychotropic medications, and more, all of which promise us some pathway to the optimal life. Like diners at a spiritual salad bar, we can now pick and choose from a cornucopia of offerings: Combine your psychoanalytic theory with some tantric spirituality, throw in a serving of astrology, and top it all off with a sprinkle of Adderall. The possibilities are endless.

So, which approach is most useful? There is no easy way to know. No single system will describe all our problems, nor can any single system provide all the solutions. We are far too complex for that. What works for one person might not be best for another, and I certainly don't have a one-size-fits-all prescription. Yet it's important to recognize that nearly all the ways we identify our problems are going to be flawed, and some of them might even be harmful. So let's consider the challenges of the most common ways we know our imbalances.

The Root of Our Problems

Life's biggest challenges usually arise from a combination of three sources: something we're born with, something we've learned, or something in our circumstances. Like everything else about us, our woes emerge from the marriage of nature, nurture, and environment, and if we want to get past our problems, we must figure out which one is which.

We'll get into nurture below, since it's the most complicated, but, for now, let's start with nature and environment. You may come into this world as a curious introvert or a fidgety optimist, but either way, many of your quirks are genetically predetermined. Perhaps you're born with a disease, an awkward personality, or a slow metabolism. If you're unlucky in the genetic lottery of life, there will be some problems you have to endure. Your challenge will be to learn acceptance of who you are.

However, many of these innate "problems" are really just circumstantial. This stems from a rather self-evident truth that's easy to forget: Flourishing depends on how well our traits match our environment. An obsessive personality might be a terrible hindrance for a preschool teacher but a great blessing for a computer programmer. Sickle cell anemia may cause heart disease in America but protect you from malaria in Africa. The truth is that much of what's a problem isn't intrinsic to us but a misalignment between us and our surroundings.

Yet, we usually don't see this. We're conditioned to believe that we should be able to thrive under any circumstance; all it takes is a positive attitude, a can-do spirit, and maybe a motivational quote or two slapped on the background of a mountain sunrise. If we're struggling to succeed, it's a sign that something is fundamentally wrong with us, like defective products rolling off the assembly line of life. But clearly, this tough love approach doesn't always work. If you're an alcoholic, it's probably wise to avoid bars; if you have low self-esteem, don't date narcissistic assholes. As the writer James Clear artfully observes, "Environment is the invisible hand that shapes human behavior." Blindly thinking you can be impervious to your circumstances is a recipe for disaster.

The tricky fact of life, of course, is that not all circumstances can be either seen, avoided, or changed. You may be born in poverty or in a war zone. Maybe you need to take care of a sick or aging family member. Sometimes, the only jobs we can get in the moment are unsatisfying ones. Life is not always peaches and cream, and some of our most rewarding activities, like parenting or loving others, will inevitably be difficult. Here lies a fundamental dilemma: How, in the words of the serenity prayer, can we learn to accept what we cannot change, gain the courage to change what we can, and find the wisdom to know the difference?

Answering this question may be one of life's greatest challenges, and it's something that we have to do again and again. Often, we seek answers from some outside authority who can tell us what's wrong or where the problems lie. But we need to be careful. What looks like the definitive explanation for our issues may be an illusion or even compound our problems. While it is essential to recognize our problems, we should be mindful that we're using the right vocabulary. Let's consider three examples.

1) The Supernatural

Throughout history, organized religion has been the most common way people have apprehended their woes, and for most of the world, it remains so today. Yet, in the modern era, religion is often not a reliable guide. And the problem with religion goes back to its origins. Religion's primary function has been to bind people together in shared beliefs and usually to regulate sex and structure social relationships. It did not arise to solve each individual's problems. Sure, religions might dangle the promise of eventual salvation like a heavenly carrot, but their true purpose is to weave people together into a single moral fabric. Religious codes were written to keep everyone in line for the collective good of the tribe, not to help its members achieve individual enlightenment. Here again, "know thyself" means "know thy place." This is why religions are usually so intolerant of heresy and get downright violent toward other sects—nonbelievers threaten the very organizing principle of the group.

As a result, religions often give us imprecise diagnoses of our problems. In most religious systems, your struggles are seen through the wide-angle lens of faith. For example, as a Roman Catholic, I was taught from a young age that I was born in sin. Jesus sacrificed himself to atone for my flaws, which, in retrospect, seems like very passive-aggressive behavior. My priest said that the best thing I could do in life was to emulate Christ; any deviation from this ideal was a sign of my inner depravity. So, naturally, all my youthful problems were viewed through the lens of the Church's teachings. If I was suffering, it was a sign of God's displeasure with my sins.

For billions of people worldwide, this type of story remains the primary way they understand themselves. Sometimes, it's genuinely helpful. This is especially true in periods of hardship and grief when faith can be a great comfort. Most faiths contain profound truths about the deeper nature of our being. My early Catholic faith, for all its problems, taught me some valuable lessons on patience, love, and forgiveness. And I've met a lot of wise and compassionate priests and ministers who offer their parishioners great insights on living better.

But for many people, religion is often not a helpful framework for truly comprehending what's wrong. Maybe their faith has acquired too much mythological or doctrinal baggage. The Bible may have lots of inspirational and uplifting passages, but its stories don't explain how to treat bipolar disorder, why I have heart disease, or even how to handle a dysfunctional relationship. Too often, our religions say we should keep throwing teenagers into the volcano when, in truth, we know the realities of plate tectonics, and this contradiction doesn't work for us.

Take my friend Hannah. Her mother was devoutly Christian, and Hannah, eager to please as a child, was a fervent believer. She offered daily prayers to God and spent several days a week at her Baptist church. But Hannah has a vibrant and adventurous spirit, and by high school, she started to butt heads with her church's teachings. This caused her a lot of emotional turmoil. She often felt that she was failing to measure up to some exacting standard of perfection. For Hannah, this was the beginning of a restless dissatisfaction that her Christianity only made worse, telling her that her anxieties were rooted in her own sinful desires. Eventually, she left her faith, not just because it made her feel terrible about herself, but because it was no longer helping her live better.

Similar hazards exist in other supernatural schemes that promise to tell us who we are and how we should live. Horoscopes, enneagrams, tarot cards, and the like all claim to have authoritative systems that map out our strengths and weaknesses. All we need to do is fill out a questionnaire or type in our birthdate, and voilà, the mysteries of the universe will be revealed. Yet, these systems are fraught with problems.

A classic example is astrology. It traces its roots back four thousand years to the stargazers in ancient Babylon and perhaps goes even further back in China, so it's much older than nearly all our current religions. It bounced around Asia and Europe for centuries until the ancient Greeks added the twelve constellations we know today. And it's extremely popular. Millions of Americans rely on astrologists to tell them who they are or what they should do, like cosmic therapists with a penchant for glittery robes.

The problem with astrology, tarot readings, and even personality tests, however, is their unreliability. This isn't simply because of the tenuous link between the alignment of the planets this week and my relationship preferences. Instead, it's just in the sweeping nature of their claims. I'll give a simple example. I was born on July 6, a birthday I share with the Dalai Lama, Sylvester Stallone, Frida Kahlo, the rapper 50 Cent, and George W. Bush. Here we are, Cancers one and all. But does this simple fact mean I have more in common with this motley crew than the rest of the planet? As much as I'd like to think so, this is clearly not the case.

Horoscopes are written in such a vague way that they are applicable to nearly anyone. Consider a typical description of Cancers: "Happily ensconced in your protective shell, you are secure enough to face life's greatest challenges. Although you don't seek out problems, when difficulties arise, you always work hard to overcome them." Sounds good, but don't most people feel this way about themselves? They do. When I posed a similar statement on a public opinion survey I gave a few years ago, 90 percent of people said it described them "well" or "very well," regardless of their astrological sign.

Worse, it's far too easy to use these diagnostic schemes to rationalize our dysfunctions. Too often, we select only those ideas that fit our preexisting stories and reject those that don't, so they only tell us what we already want to hear. We concoct an image of Allah, the Buddha, or a Sagittarius to accommodate our problems rather than addressing them. Jesus's rage at the Pharisees justifies my chronic anger, his turning water into wine excuses my alcoholism, and so on. When it comes to supernatural systems, what looks like a diagnosis can all too often be a self-serving indulgence. If we want to see our imbalances more objectively, we'll need to find a more empirical method.

2) Psychiatry

When identifying psychological problems, nothing is more authoritative than the *Diagnostic and Statistical Manual of Mental Illness, Fifth Edition*, commonly known as the *DSM-5*. Published by the American Psychiatric Association, it covers more than three hundred significant disorders, ranging from dementia to video game addiction and everything in between. If psychology is modernity's religion, then the *DSM-5* is its Bible. Professionally speaking, it's the encyclopedia of our shit.

So, what could be better if we're searching for a diagnosis of what's wrong with us? Yet, here again, you should approach the *DSM-5* with the same caution you'd use when approaching a restaurant with a great exterior—it might look inviting, but you have to be careful about what's actually being served inside.

It starts with its curious history. The *DSM-5* originated from a government effort to classify the population. Back in the 1840s, officials with the US Census Bureau decided it would be a swell idea to start tabulating data on "idiocy and insanity," a label that, incidentally, was also applied to nearly all enslaved people at the time. Realizing these two terms were a bit too broad, they began elaborating on these categories to include things like melancholia, mania, and dementia. Thus, the official "scientific" labeling of our problems had begun.

Fast forward to the late 1940s. Tens of thousands of veterans were coming home from World War II with combat trauma. The US Veterans Administration wanted some help treating these soldiers but had no clear way to categorize who was sick and who was not. The American Psychiatric Association heeded the call. It convened meetings of its top professionals and forged a compendium of all the mental health problems they were diagnosing. This became the first edition of the

DSM. Over the past seventy years, it has been revised four more times, expanding and updating its list of what it considers to be all our possible mental disorders.

The *DSM-5*, however, has its controversies. Much like the Bible, the *DSM* was compiled by a group of people with a mixed set of perspectives and motives. It's also a living document, getting continually updated. Every few years, panels of psychologists and doctors decide what gets put in and what gets left out, which inevitably invites debate. It is not always clear what will get counted as "disorders" and what might be the quirks of normal behavior. For example, homosexuality was initially classified as a disorder in 1952 and was only taken off this list in 2013.

Given this history, it's essential to remember what the *DSM-5* can and cannot tell us. The *DSM-5* is primarily a document used to define normality and deviance. It was designed to help governments and doctors classify people who were not functioning well in their social environments. It was not intended as a tool to help "normal" people optimize themselves nor even to comment on whether the problem lies with the person or the environment itself. For people who are struggling with debilitating mental illness, the *DSM-5* can be of great service, especially if their symptoms are glaringly obvious. If someone is getting blind drunk every night or regularly exposing their genitals in public, then something is wrong, and the *DSM-5* might be able tell you what's behind it all.

But when it comes to common mental problems that have been given the labels of depression, general anxiety, or obsessive-compulsive disorder, the symptoms are often fuzzy or unclear. One of the most damning critiques of the *DSM-5* is that many of its diagnoses are simply unreliable. When people are tested at one time, they receive one diagnosis; when retested, they are given a different one. All of this stems from the difficult task of determining normal versus abnormal behavior.

Take the case of Hannah. Although she feels a lot of pain, Hannah is usually quite cheery. Her life is filled with all the markers of success: a good job, a beautiful family, and excellent health. The types of problems she struggles with may not show up on the *DSM*'s radar because it is primarily concerned with severe issues; it isn't an especially reliable guide for nagging yet functional imbalances like the dissatisfaction of always wanting more. In other words, when it comes to more garden-variety problems, the *DSM-5* is not often the best authority.

I've experienced this firsthand. When I started therapy again in my thirties, my health insurance needed an official diagnosis. Since there wasn't a classification for "anguished heartbreak" in the *DSM-5* (and still isn't), my therapist used the catchall diagnosis of "adjustment disorder." Although this generic term was technically correct, it didn't capture the essence of my problem, which was that I was not adjusting well to my unexpected singleness. It didn't describe why I chose to be in a relationship with such an unreliable person or why I did the things I did to push her away. In short, "adjustment disorder" really didn't say very much about the real sources of my heartache; it was like diagnosing a broken leg as "dysfunctional limb syndrome."

The same goes for Hannah. If she went to a psychiatrist, the doctor might say she was okay. After all, she gets on well in the world, and the *DSM* doesn't have a listing for "chronic dissatisfaction disorder." Or perhaps a more zealous doctor would diagnose her with a related syndrome, like anxiety or OCD. But these don't describe her problems. What's worse, with a misdiagnosis, Hannah would probably be given a prescription and sent on her semi-merry way.

And this raises the thorny issue of treatment. These days, most mental health issues are addressed with pharmaceuticals. And there's no denying modern pharmacology has made leaps and bounds in the last fifty years. For people grappling with severe conditions like hallucinatory schizophrenia or bipolar disorder, medication can be a lifesaver. Even for less acute issues, meds can be incredibly useful. Just look around—half your friends are probably popping pills for anxiety, depression, insomnia, or that mysterious itch they've yet to diagnose correctly. And the best part? It's all so wonderfully convenient. Why waste time on a therapist's couch when you can swallow a little yellow pill and get back to scrolling on Instagram?

However, for all their benefits, these medications have a significant shortcoming: They don't address the root of our problems. In reality, most pharmaceuticals are designed as short-term solutions to alleviate the symptoms of our more acute issues, not as vehicles for exploring the murky depths of why we're suffering in the first place. So, even if Hannah started taking antidepressants, she'd probably still feel that gnawing pain; it just might be a little more muted, like putting a silencer on a very persistent, very annoying internal alarm. In short, modern pharmacology might be able to dampen the volume, but it can't change the tune.

This reveals the hazard of medicalizing our problems: It becomes a convenient way of sidestepping the hard work of finding long-term solutions. The *DSM-5* is very much symptom-oriented in its approach to health. What was initially meant to be a stopgap measure has quietly become the go-to fix for all our woes. The fact that nearly one in four Americans is now taking some form of prescription medication for their mental health is a pretty solid clue that something's amiss in how we're living our lives.

I see this with my students. Here they are, the best and brightest of their generation, yet most are medicated up to their eyeballs. These magic pills might help them cope with the crushing demands of our society's peculiar definition of success, but very few are questioning those definitions in the first place. And the same goes with the rest of us. Most people I know are taking more and more pills to keep running faster on the treadmill without ever stopping to ask why they're sprinting like hamsters in the first place. If we truly want to flourish, we must find a more holistic approach to understanding our problems beyond just slapping a Band-Aid on a bullet wound.

3) Therapy

In my other life as a political scientist, I conduct many surveys. Measuring public opinion is a tricky business, more art than science. There's always some ambiguity in how you frame questions and measure responses. Yet, in thirty years of doing this work, I've discovered one hard-and-fast rule: Never ask people to explain *why* they hold certain attitudes. Why? Because most people are terrible judges of their own minds. Ask them why they're against, say, abortion rights or raising taxes on the rich, and you'll get a response that sounds like a mixtape of cable news soundbites or, worse, a shrug and an "I don't know." As

I often tell my students, the job of a survey is to measure what people think; the job of the surveyor is to figure out *why*.

The same principle applies when it comes to understanding our problems. We're all pretty clear on *what* we believe—this plays out in the endless loops of stories we tell ourselves day in and day out—but figuring out *why* we think what we do? Now, that's a trickier proposition. And it's notoriously hard to do on our own. Sure, there may be some rare enlightened guru meditating in a cave who's got it all figured out, but for the rest of us mere mortals, we usually need someone else to help us see our problems clearly.

This need for outside perspective goes back to how our brains are wired. In our formative years, we learned how the world works, and these lessons were encoded in our brains through synaptic patterns—neural highways that later shaped our thoughts and consciousness. Most of these patterns are deeply ingrained and largely reflexive. We may update them as we learn new things (or unlearn old ones), but mentally speaking, we are creatures of habit.

The hitch is that many of these mental highways aren't exactly ideal for traveling through our adult lives. My friend, the therapist Kato Wittich, has a wonderfully compassionate term to describe this problem: *survival strategies*. Most of our mental issues arise from the mismatch between the survival strategies that worked for us as children and the way we live today.

Say, for example, you were someone who grew up with an abusive, alcoholic parent. As a child, you never knew if the person you depended on would be loving or hurtful, angry or checked out. To survive, you quickly learned ways to navigate this emotional minefield. Maybe you coped by becoming a mini mind reader, always trying to anticipate and soothe their moods. Or perhaps you became an expert at hiding, shutting yourself in your room, and learning to mistrust everyone.

These survival strategies got etched into your neural architecture as firmly as knowing how to read or ride a bike. And like those everyday skills, your survival strategies became your go-to responses, the patterns you act on without realizing it. As a result, you might spend the rest of your life unconsciously replaying the same strategies. Perhaps you end up being too accommodating to people who don't deserve it, or maybe you isolate yourself from the world entirely. In those moments, you're simply reactivating your childhood survival strategies, like an old, worn-out vinyl record that keeps skipping back to the same track.

The problem is that we need to be made aware of when we are doing this. Normally, we get so caught up in our reactions, so absorbed in the stories playing out in our heads, that we don't even notice when they've become obsolete. Our minds cling stubbornly to outdated routines, not just because they're familiar but because we genuinely believe these strategies are still crucial for our survival on a deeper, primal level. We mistakenly think we need our bad habits to keep us alive.

I see this dynamic clearly with Hannah. Her parents were loving, sure, but her father had a temper that rivaled a teapot on full boil, and her mother was often lost in her reveries. The old farmhouse where she grew up, alongside her four siblings, was a jumbled mess—think "quaint rustic charm" meets "hurricane aftermath." For Hannah, the instability of her environment was a daily threat, so she often retreated to the sanctuary of her room, where she could impose some order on the chaos.

The emotional toll of her father's frequent outbursts left her with a chronic sense that life just didn't measure up. This wasn't due to any objective shortfall but probably stemmed from her unmet need for a connection with her parents. Her adult feelings of inadequacy—the nagging sense that nothing is ever quite good enough—echo the survival strategies she developed in childhood: finding comfort in the tidiness of her space and striving to prove herself worthy of attention and affection.

Like ours, Hannah's challenge is finding alternative ways of living. In the short run, she copes by doing yoga, losing herself in fiction, and exploring art and nature. These activities offer a temporary reprieve, creating space to live differently. Other people take more radical measures like psychedelic trips, meditation retreats, or even the occasional deep dive into books about how to know yourself.

These methods can be enlightening, but inevitably, the old habits resurface. That's where other people come in. There's nothing quite as effective as having someone who can compassionately call you on your bullshit. Sometimes, this comes from those around us, like an honest friend, a thoughtful priest, or perhaps even a particularly astute bartender. But it's essential to keep our ordinary relationships in perspective. Expecting the people we love to hold up a mirror to our flaws constantly isn't fair to them or us. If we want to confront our issues head-on, there's nothing like a professional.

Enter therapy. As I've mentioned before, therapy is perhaps the most useful way to interpret your stories and identify your survival strategies, the constant mental habits that may trap you in unhealthy patterns. In our WEIRD (Western, Educated, Industrialized, Rich, and Democratic) epoch, it is the most efficient way to understand and cope with your own individual issues, and there are many different approaches. But, like any intervention, therapy also has its hazards, and it's important to recognize them up front.

For many, therapy starts as a revelation. I've met many people who are positively giddy when they begin seeing a shrink. Suddenly, they see things about themselves they never could before. They unearth hidden patterns of behavior and their connections to the past. They begin to recognize their part in the problems they've been blaming on others. This often leads to significant life changes. They end a toxic relationship, quit that soul-sucking job, or stop hating themselves quite so much. In short, they begin to correct the mismatches between who they are and where they are. All this comes from having an intelligent, compassionate outsider who reflects their problems back to them in a new light.

But after a few months, the excitement inevitably wanes. The once-frequent updates about their latest breakthroughs taper off, and they settle into the more mundane work of digging deeper into their psyche. After a year or so, the earth-shattering revelations become fewer and farther between, and therapy sessions start to feel like rehashes of the same old stories. Herein lies the question that haunts psychotherapy today: How effective is it at solving our problems?

There's no simple answer. At its best, therapy can help us become aware of our inner processes, allowing us to recognize the outdated survival strategies that cause us suffering. This recognition is crucial. Instead of being completely caught up in our interpretations, we learn to view them more objectively. For example, say you find yourself seething with anger at a sibling who's once again borrowing money from your parents. In therapy, you might realize that this anger isn't just about the money—it's tied to old patterns where your sibling always seemed to take advantage of you. The current feeling is essentially a replay of past experiences. So, instead of being consumed by rage, therapy offers you some perspective, allowing you to think, "Oh, this is just an old demon being woken up. It's not the full reality."

But at some point, recognition alone isn't enough. If we want to live better, we'll want more than just insight. It means breaking free from the mental habits that keep us misaligned. And it's not clear if therapy alone can do that. Therapy may be great for helping us see our problems and not letting them dominate us, but it's less clear how much therapy can solve them. There's also the risk that we have a crappy therapist (there are a lot of them out there) or that we use therapy to tell us what our ego wants to hear. I know plenty of intelligent people who either manipulate their therapists or use therapy as a weekly validation session. If we genuinely want to transcend our issues, we'll need to take the next step—we'll need to figure out how to let go.

22

Letting Go

WHEN DO YOU FEEL LIKE YOUR BEST SELF? FOR ME, IT'S USUally first thing in the morning, after a night of great sleep. In those brief, liminal moments before I open my eyes, sparkling energy courses through me. I float in blissful serenity, my mind unencumbered by any pressing thoughts—it's a wondrous way to be. Eventually, however, this feeling ends. Some notion or another will barge into my mind, interrupt my reverie, and send me down a gully of plans and worries, and this semi-agitated state usually holds me for the rest of the day.

My cat, by contrast, doesn't seem to have this problem. She spends her days in rapturous ease, lounging about the house in deep contentment, a picture of purring enlightenment. The Buddha might have said that existence is suffering, but clearly, he never met my cat. Yet why does my cat live so much better than I do?

The answer is partly in our different ways of being. My cat was born with a fixed mental template, one that's similar to all other cats. She lives fully in her animal self. I, on the other hand, am configured differently. I can't enjoy my days simply lying in the sun or sleeping curled up in a cute little ball. Partly, this is because of everything I have to do, like hold a job, take care of my family, and feed the cat. But these mundane realities don't account for our differences, for these tasks aren't so demanding. In fact, I usually enjoy them. Instead, some part of me is thwarting any possibility of living in purring ease.

In this, I'm not alone. I know few people who sustain my cat's radiant equanimity. Maybe they live in some remote Greek village or Himalayan valley where everyone eats yogurt, lives into their nineties, and enjoys an existence free of worry. But such Shangri-las are the exception. Most people exist in varying states of perpetual dissatisfaction, even after their basic needs are met. Just look at the staggering rates of anxiety, depression, and drug abuse in America today. Despite all our wealth and comfort, something is clearly off with us. So, who or what is at fault?

To find an answer, we can start with the usual suspects: the daily barrage of bad news, the hollow promises of consumerism, and the erosion of traditions that once connected us to the Earth and each other. Yes, our modern way of living has its perks (electric lights, the internet, and, let's not forget, the sweet, sweet blessing that is ice cream), but none of these are helpful for spiritual enlightenment. Then there are the more personalized demons: the boutique neuroses, custom-tailored ego trips, and emotional thunderstorms that roll in without warning. When it comes to our imbalances, the wobbles can come from both within and without.

However, these obvious villains are actually the minor henchmen, for there's a bigger mastermind behind all our disquiet: language. Yes, our old frenemy, language. The advent of language was indeed a mixed blessing for our species. On the one hand, it gave us the power to dominate the food chain, create art, build civilizations, and comprehend the cosmos. On the other hand, it's responsible for warping our natural processes, turning us into creatures who overthink and overanalyze until we're tangled in neurotic webs of our own making. It wasn't knowledge that cast us out of the Garden of Eden; it was language.

And language's most cunning trick? It messes with our sense of time and self. Language loves to yank us out of the present moment, pushing us into the past with endless "what ifs" and thrusting us into the future with a million "what nows." The torrent of words in our heads traps us in stories of what was or what might be, leading us to believe in life's greatest fiction: that there's a solid, unchanging "me" at the center of it all, a constant protagonist in the ever-unfolding drama of life.

So, how do we keep the very thing that defines our humanity from being our own worst enemy? If you look across the world's spiritual traditions, you'll find a relatively straightforward answer: Leave your words behind. Although it's important to use words to recognize and label our problems, at some point, we'll need to put down our mental dialogues and embrace the much more challenging task of living fully in the moment. Nirvana, it turns out, is not a place you can talk your way into.

If our purpose in life is to optimize this self, then we are going to have to start experiencing the world less through words and more through direct sensory experience. It turns out we need far less of ourselves than we commonly think. Most of our thoughts, identities, and dramas are unnecessary for living well. As with my cat, we can learn to flourish when we exist in a way not so defined by all our mental constructs and cogitations.

Adventures in Stretching

The phrase "letting go" is deceptive. At first glance, it conveys an image of surrender, giving up all effort and responsibility while the world goes on without you. But when the great wisdom traditions talk about letting go, they're not suggesting that you spend your days kicking back with a bong and the PlayStation. Spiritually speaking, letting go is more like an intense workout for the soul. It's a vigorous, sweaty engagement with life that demands strength, courage, and a hefty dose of concentration. It's not a passive surrender; it's an energetic confrontation with our discomforts and blockages.

Because this type of letting go is counterintuitive, we often need some guidance on how to do it. And there is no shortage of techniques: Therapy, psychedelics, self-help books, and even great works of philosophy all provide insights on how to actively transcend your imbalances. But among all these methods, there is one that I have found most useful in my ordinary life. It's an ancient Asian practice that has a rich philosophical tradition, and it's also recently become very popular in the West. It is yoga.

Now, I know what you might be thinking: Yoga?!? Really?!? Cue the eye-rolling.

I get it. My first impression of yoga was not a good one. It came from a PBS show that aired on Sunday mornings during the 1970s when I was a kid. It featured a dull woman in an all-black leotard who spoke in a slow, monotonous voice. Her stretches were weird, the vibe was dreary, and the whole thing smelled faintly of patchouli and regret. To my young mind, yoga seemed like the exercise equivalent of carob.

At a casual glance, yoga may not seem much better today. The American yoga scene is filled with ditzy influencers posting about their chakras and pitching overpriced yoga gear, not to mention the abundance of self-proclaimed gurus boasting they have *the* foolproof method for achieving enlightenment. It's easy to dismiss yoga today as another trendy way to advertise your spiritual superiority, show off your toned body, or become suckered by some New Age scam. From this perspective, yoga does not seem like a genuine way to find transcendence. But rejecting yoga for its distinctly American excesses is unfair, for yoga is far more than simply looking great in your Lululemons, even if they are remarkably flattering.

It starts with the word itself. *Yoga* is a term that traces back five thousand years to the Indus River Valley civilization. It is often translated as "yoke," but that's not its only meaning. Yoga also connotes ideas like alchemy, diet, discipline, and even constellation. Over the centuries, these many meanings of yoga encompassed a broad array of spiritual techniques, including breathing, meditation, and moral rules for living. They were often intertwined with Vedic philosophy, Ayurvedic medicine, and supernatural ideas like chakras and Brahman. The physical exercises we know as yoga in the West, or "asanas" as they are called, are only a tiny part of a much greater set of spiritual practices evolving in South Asia over thousands of years. So, when it comes to yoga, there's actually a lot to explore.

However, I'm going to keep things simple. I'm not going to extoll the benefits of Zumbayoga or unpack the arcane and supernatural beliefs of Vendantic thought. I'm not going to suggest some weird breathing techniques or make claims about aligning your chakras. Nor will I boast about how yoga has made me a better person. Instead, I'm just going to share four simple lessons that my very ordinary yoga practice has taught me about letting go.

Lesson 1: Letting Go Is a Continual, Active Process.

I was twenty-eight when I took my first yoga class, and, to be honest, it wasn't inspired by any great spiritual longing. It was 1995, and I was holed up in a big, drafty house in Oakland, California, with a bunch of other starving graduate students. My life was a mishmash of academic career anxiety, poverty, and enough stress to compress a diamond. My coping strategy was simple: exercise like a maniac. Every day, I'd bike, run, or lift weights as if I could somehow sweat out my fear of failure. My body, however, had other plans. I was constantly plagued by a stiff neck and a back that often went on strike. Muscle spasms would ambush me at the worst times, often leaving me bedridden.

One day, one of my roommates—a cute one, of course—suggested I join her for a yoga class. Still haunted by the image of that drab woman in the black leotard, I had some doubts. But desperation and the opportunity for flirtation were powerful motivators to my young mind, so I tagged along.

Yoga turned out to be nothing like I expected. The biggest surprise was how physically challenging it was. Instead of passive stretching and dull poses, yoga was a sweaty exercise in vigorous counteraction. It was as intense as my most strenuous workouts, and I always came away drenched in sweat.

The kind of yoga I practice is called Vinyasa, which typically translates as "flow yoga." It involves a sequence of movements linking one pose to another, often in coordination with the breath. In Vinyasa, you move up to one pose on an inhale and then move into another on an exhale. My yoga practice is pretty simple. I don't do any contorted, acrobatic positions; instead, most of my poses are some variation on either a forward bend or a twist with an occasional headstand, pushup, or backbend thrown in.

Within this simple routine, however, a lot is going on. With yoga poses, you don't just extend, you engage. You actively flex one set of muscles to release others. For instance, to stretch your hamstrings, you contract your quads; to loosen up your back, you firm up your abs. In yoga, strength and flexibility must be developed together. Strength alone makes one tense and subject to spasms and strain. Flexibility doesn't come from lying around like a noodle either; it comes from vigorous effort to find release.

The same push-pull principle applies when dealing with our mental and emotional baggage. Most of our dissatisfactions come from habits of mind, deeply ingrained patterns of thinking that lock us into cycles of tension and stress. In other words, we usually carry around a psychic stiffness, not unlike the tightness in our shoulders. Our bad moods and neurotic compulsions are the mental equivalent of muscle spasms, just as our muscle spasms often arise from our negative thoughts and neuroses. It's all connected, like some bizarre symphony where misplaying in the cello section screws up the woodwinds.

If we want to break free from these recursive loops of stress and tension, we must actively engage with them. This is what both yoga and meditation are all about—regularly counteracting our unhealthy physical and mental habits with mindful effort. It starts with just showing up, day after day, even when you'd rather hit the snooze button. I try to practice yoga every morning for at least forty minutes. Some days, it's like dragging myself through molasses, and some days, I miss. But I never finish a yoga session feeling worse than when I started. And if I miss a session, I'm usually a lot more stressed and cranky the rest of the day.

The same thing holds with life in general. Most of the time, we are driven by neurotic compulsions that lock us in loops of stress and anxiety, hoping that if we change something around us, the distress will go away. We believe that if we can nail that next promotion, shed those last ten pounds, or get our spouse to stop leaving their socks everywhere, everything will magically fall into place.

The reality, though, is that the same neuroses that drove us to chase those goals aren't going to evaporate once we've achieved them. Mental habits are stubborn like that. They don't just vanish because you finally snagged that corner office or flattened your stomach. It's up to me and me alone to loosen the grip of all my bad mental routines, and this is something I need to do every moment of every day. Self-optimization is a vigorous and continuous activity that never ends.

It starts with an active commitment to see things as they are, not simply as we want them to be. It means facing each moment in all its colors, not merely the ones we like, what the Buddha called right intention and right effort. Unflinching acceptance of the truth is the first task of the transcendent self.

These words may sound like vague platitudes, but they are the most profound wisdom I know. Self-optimization is about fully embracing our experience in each moment, warts and all. It's about learning how not to freak out when things go wrong. It's about not needing to distract ourselves with screens, junk food, or a stiff drink whenever we feel a little off. The more we can sustain this active acceptance of life's complexity, the more natural it feels. And, of all the things I've tried—and, as you can probably guess by now, I've tried a lot—yoga and meditation have been the best instructors on how to do this.

Lesson 2: Letting Go Is an Act of Courage.

Many years ago, I studied with a yoga teacher who would end each session by telling us to "have courage." At the time, I wasn't doing anything heroic, and this advice puzzled me. Courage? For what, getting a salad instead of a cheeseburger? Eventually, though, I came to understand what she meant, and it was neuroscience that provided the answer.

As I've mentioned throughout this book, our brains are hyperactive prediction machines, constantly trying to map out and anticipate reality. These mental routines, the neural grooves within our brains, help us navigate through ordinary life. And while some of these routines are useful, many are not. Think of all the energy we waste on worries that never materialize or the hours we spend fuming over things that happened years ago. These inefficient mental patterns keep us from living better.

So why do we cling to so many negative and unproductive thoughts? Here's where fear barges in. Our mental routines make the world legible to us. They give us the comforting (albeit false) impression that we know what's going on, even if what's going on is a horror show of our own making. Giving this up increases our uncertainty, and this is terrifying for us. It's like George and his honey wagon—we hold on to our miseries because we're scared to open ourselves up to greater unknowns. Our brains crave clear maps of the world, and when things get blurry, the fear kicks in.

When my yoga teacher urged us to "have courage," she was nudging us to face this fear head-on rather than retreating to our old, dysfunctional routines. But to do this, we need to appreciate what courage really is. We often think of courage as some elevated state, the moment when the hero of a story draws upon their superpowers to vanquish the evil villain. From the outside, courage seems electric and transcendent, an infusion of glowing power.

In real life, courage is a horribly uncomfortable state of being. Courage requires coexisting with all kinds of terrible feelings that are churning away inside of you. When we live with courage, we live with the knowledge that the optimal life is not one without fear or pain, because fear and pain are as natural as sleeping and breathing. Fear and pain are just our self's way of sounding the alarm when something's off. If we constantly run away from fear and pain or try to shove them into the nearest closet, we're cutting ourselves off from vital information.

Courage is about living in a way so that your fear and pain don't dominate you, either in guiding all your actions or triggering you to retreat into a numbing distraction. It's about tolerating life's many ambiguities without reflexively pulling back at the first sign of discomfort. Courage is about observing all of these terrible feelings with some detachment rather than letting them own us. It is about accepting that you don't know when the pain will end or when you will figure it all out. And most importantly, *courage is something we can learn.*

In yoga, we teach ourselves courage by intentionally relaxing into challenging poses. This could be holding a deep knee bend or a plank pose for a long time, even as your body is quivering, and your mind is suggesting, "Hey, we better check the phone." But instead of giving in, yoga teaches you to relax in the discomfort. You don't try to silence the voice or ignore the impulse; you let them be, coexisting with them as best as you can. Sometimes it works, and sometimes it doesn't, but the intention remains: How can I investigate these crappy feelings rather than letting them own me?

And here's the funny thing—the more you can coexist with the pain with equanimous detachment, the better you eventually feel. This is the genius of the contemplative practice. Somewhere in the misty past, a brilliant yogi like the Buddha figured out that the less you react to your negative feelings, the more open your consciousness becomes. This equanimity generates that wonderful glow at the end of an intense yoga or meditation session—a radiance that floods you when you learn to relax with what is.

Similar processes also happen in other techniques of self-optimization. Take therapy. Most of the actual work in therapy involves not just identifying your problems but learning how to better coexist with them. Say, for example, you're one of those people who can't hear your partner mention a past lover without descending into a spiral of jealousy, the kind that makes you wonder if they're secretly planning to elope with that cute waiter who they smiled at with a little too much enthusiasm. Instead of seeing the reality of what might be a perfectly happy relationship, your mind gets hijacked by these wild, anxious fantasies, and you're trapped in a loop of anxiety and self-hatred. It's not exactly a recipe for domestic bliss.

Enter your therapist, who, armed with a box of tissues and a carefully cultivated look of concern, helps you start to see these patterns not as the rock-solid truths you feel them to be but as the mental projections they are. You dig into your past, figuring out when these pesky thoughts started and why they keep appearing like uninvited guests at your emotional dinner party. Therapy is all about recognizing these demons for what they are—typically, some outdated survival strategies that made sense when you were young but are now just messing with your adult life.

Once you've got a handle on what's haunting you, the next step is figuring out how to live with these demons without letting them take over the entire house. This usually involves the counterintuitive move of engaging with your negative feelings instead of fleeing from them like they're trying to sell you a Florida time-share. It's not enough to declare, "Hey, I'm done with jealousy and insecurity!" as much as we'd like it to be that simple. We don't have that kind of control over our minds, which have a knack for doing their own thing. Instead, it's about learning to recognize when you're off-kilter and getting curious about what's going on.

The Buddhist writer Pema Chödrön offers some really great advice on how to do this. She says we always need to be on the lookout for what pain and discomfort are trying to tell us. Our worst moments can be our best teachers, even if they feel more like grumpy substitutes in the short run. I find this perspective helpful when I'm trying to coexist with a painful or difficult emotion. When I'm distressed, I try to step back and repeat to myself: "This moment is a perfect teacher, this moment is a perfect teacher." It's a way of gaining some equanimity and keeping open to what my more uncomfortable self-processes are trying to communicate rather than simply running away from them.

In other words, self-optimization requires mustering up the courage to both acknowledge and come to peace with your problems. It doesn't mean banishing your inner demons to some dark, fiery pit or letting them be the boss; it means accepting that they are part of the self, figuring out how to live better with them, and maybe even offering them a cup of tea. And, remarkably, the more you practice this, the quieter these demons eventually become.

Lesson 3: Your Thoughts Do Not Define You.

During yoga sessions, I often find myself floating away on a river of thoughts, even when I'm supposed to be focusing on my breath and body. One moment, I'm in downward dog, and the next, I'm mentally replaying that aggravating argument I just had with Thea or worrying about how well my next lecture will go.

This, of course, is just how the egoistic self works. When it isn't occupied with something truly attention-grabbing, it starts to wander off like a toddler in a toy store—curious, reckless, and self-absorbed. The ego dislikes being ignored. It wants your attention, and is constantly bugging you with nagging, inane demands. And, at some level, this is its job. Remember, the ego is there to help us get what we want from other people. When it doesn't have anything urgent to work on, it starts rehashing unresolved stories, digging through old plot lines like a soap opera that it just can't quit, trying to figure out what it can do in the future. And, because the mind is a creature of habit, the ego gravitates back to the same tired episodes of past dramas and future anxieties.

Here's where the vigorous activity of yoga comes into play. One of the most important ways we can push back against our egoistic habits is by creating space between our ordinary consciousness and the thoughts in our heads. Instead of being fully occupied with whatever dramas our minds are concocting, we can open up some distance between our experience of the moment and the narrative chatter trying to hog the spotlight. We can begin to renegotiate our contract with our minds.

This is something I have experienced in both yoga and meditation. Whenever I catch myself lost in thought, I try to gently acknowledge it with something like, "Oh, look, there you go, thinking again." Then, I let go of the thought and return my attention to my breath or the pose I'm holding. But sometimes, the thought grips me tight. In those cases, I find it helpful to briefly engage with the thought itself. I'll ask myself, "Is this thought helping anything?" More often than not, the answer is a resounding no, and that makes it easier to let it go.

The same approach applies to the rest of our lives. We spend most of our waking hours in a mental fog, wandering through self-conjured fantasylands that aren't nearly as exciting as we'd like to believe. These daydreams aren't just about our fears and hopes—they include the biggest illusion of all: that we have a singular self. Much of the time, our minds not only evoke distorted pictures of reality but also fabricate an illusory experience of being. This "me," with all my identities, ego needs, and fragile conceits, is as much a mental invention as the fantasies and anxieties my mind generates about the world in general. It's like a one-person theater production, where I'm playing all the roles, writing the script, sitting in the audience, and forgetting that none of it is real.

Instead of getting caught up in these egoistic dramas, we can carve out some space between our consciousness and experience of self. Just as I can question whether my thoughts are helpful or appropriate, I can ask the same questions about my consciousness. In other words, I can pause and ask, "Is this particular 'me' really helpful right now?" And once again, the answer is usually no.

This may sound like a weird idea, but it gets to the heart of the Buddha's teachings on nonattachment. Our minds crave certainty. They want something tangible to latch on to, whether it's a possession, a fantasy, or even a comforting idea. We like to box up reality, slap a label on it, and assume that's the whole story. We cling to our images about ourselves or a limited type of consciousness, thinking that we are this one particular way, a "me" with a capital M, that is fixed and unchanging.

But this is where we fool ourselves. We are not static entities. Instead, we're beings of energy, and energy, by its very nature, never sits still. It's constantly shifting, pulsating, and flowing from one moment to the next. Our consciousness is really just a bunch of electrical impulses coursing through the innumerable neurons within our bodies. And these neurons are just collections of proteins and molecules in constant motion. Everything that we perceive as "real" is an interpretation of a small fraction of information from a far more subtle and dynamic reality underneath it all.

This feeling of being "me" is just a particular way that our life force, the energy system that comprises us, is negotiating with reality, pushing back against the entropic stream of the universe. All of the living things that comprise us, the trillions of cells, mitochondria, and microbes, are part of this same life process that's been resisting entropy on Earth for roughly four billion years. Our experience of self, our fears of death, and our craving for certainty are all parts of this entropy-resisting process.

A similar process occurs in our ordinary lives. In practice, self-optimization means constantly resisting a kind of personal entropy, the slow decay of our vitality and potential. The more we get locked into mental routines from the past or get caught up in future expectations of either doom or glory, the less alive we are in the present moment. If we can figure out how to live with less distraction, less judgment, and less habit, we can expand our own "potential for something to happen." If we stay open to the possibilities of living beyond the thoughts in our heads, we can cultivate flexibility and resilience to engage with life more fully.

Most of the time, this means recognizing that the vast majority of our thoughts and self-images are really not that necessary. Instead, we can strive to reorient our ordinary experience where our minds are both intentional and unbound by words. In my experience, contemplative practices like yoga and meditation have been extremely useful in helping me do all of this.

Lesson 4: Living Well Only Happens in the Present.

My first yoga teacher was this amazing guy named Rodney Yee. Muscular and statuesque with a long ponytail, he combined the intense athleticism of a gymnast with the lithe grace of a ballet dancer. He was no dull hippie in a leotard—he was more like a radiant demigod, a true embodiment of what you'd imagine when you think of someone who's found some secret pathway to flourishing. Not surprisingly, Rodney would later become a colossal yoga celebrity with best-selling DVDs, an enraptured female following, and the inevitable scandals that come with all of this. But when I first walked into his class in Oakland, California, he was just this badass guy who seemed to hold some secret key to a better life.

And one of these keys, weirdly enough, ran through the area behind my knee.

Let me explain. At the start of every class, Rodney would have us spend about fifteen minutes focusing on a tiny body part. Often, this was an area we usually didn't think much about. One day, it might be the tops of our necks; the next, it would be our feet; and on some occasions, it was the back of the knee. We'd then go through our regular yoga routine, keeping focused on what was happening in these obscure body regions while we did our various poses. At first, this seemed weird, but eventually, Rodney's logic became apparent. After several weeks, I began stitching all these little awarenesses into a richer overall body consciousness. Instead of living solely in my head, as I typically do, I started living more in my arms, torso, legs, and the area behind my knee.

We can take a similar approach to the self. Most days, we mentally exist in only a tiny part of our being. Our attention is caught up with planning the grocery list for tomorrow's dinner or worrying about that too-casual comment about Pornhub that our teenager made last night. Our minds rarely stay in the present because they always try to predict the future and learn from the past.

The ultimate aim of self-optimization is to cultivate a fuller experience of each moment. And while this may sound like a New Age trope, it's based on a simple truth: The present moment is the only time that truly exists. The past is gone, and the future hasn't happened yet. Only the present holds all the beauty and luminescence of life. And the more attention we can pay to the small elements of our current moment, the knee-pits of life, the richer our experience of the moment becomes.

Today, this is often described as mindfulness. Mindfulness is the practice of being more fully aware of your sensations, thoughts, and feelings without filtering it through some preconceived judgment. It's truly tasting your food without just shoveling it down. It's stepping away and observing whatever story is running through your head. Mindfulness is experiencing your emotions as somatic energy states rather than allowing them to completely compress you.

This is where a contemplative practice is invaluable. Absent any kind of spiritual discipline, there are few forces in our lives that will nudge us toward embracing the moment. The stresses of family, the temptations of consumerism, the distractions of the internet—all of these are taking us away from the now. Yoga and meditation are techniques that retrain us, helping us to both expand our consciousness and find some space from the relentless pressures of our cravings, aversions, and other distractions from the moment. This is how we get more in touch with the deeper energy flow that comprises us.

But even if you're not inclined to twist yourself into a pretzel with yoga or spend weeks in silent meditation, there's one straightforward, ever-present tool that can always connect you with the moment: your breath. It's the one part of your conscious existence that's free of all the mental clutter—no thoughts, no emotions, just the pure, unadulterated act of breathing. Your breath just is, always happening as long as you live. It's like a secret escape hatch from the mental hamster wheel.

Whenever I'm caught up in some challenging emotion—say, fretting about that awkward joke I made at the party last night or obsessively worrying about my children's future—I've found that simply returning my attention to my breath is a game-changer. By clearing my mind and gently resting my awareness on the natural flow of breathing, something magical happens: I start to exist more fully in the present. And the more I focus on my breath, the faster all those problems fade away.

This mindfulness isn't just some woo-woo concept; it's the simplest key to living better. The more we become aware of all the parts of us contributing to this moment, like the breath, the body, the sensations, the more expansive our consciousness becomes. It's like upgrading from a dingy motel room to a luxurious hotel suite with a panoramic view. Suddenly, you're not stuck in the cramped confines of your mind; you're living in the whole, rich expanse of the present. And in this space, a remarkable new experience of being emerges, one that's more radiant, contented, and a little bit closer to the enlightened state of my cat.

Final Thought

So this brings us to the end of the tour. This, of course, isn't the end of the journey. If anything, it's just a brief stop—a chance to catch your breath and maybe check out the view before diving back into the wild, ever-changing adventure that is you. Knowing yourself is less like reaching a final destination and more like exploring a never-ending amusement park full of twists, turns, and the occasional haunted house.

If you're itching to dig deeper into any of the ideas we've wrestled with here, I've included a list of books in the Further Readings section that have both informed my thoughts and been invaluable in my own explorations. I hope they can be useful for you as well. Either way, I thank you for staying with me to the end. May the rest of your life's journey be full of wonder, radiance, and, most importantly, laughter. For, as the old saying goes, "To truly soar high, one must first let go of the weight of taking things too seriously."

Acknowledgments

For all the isolation of writing, any book is a social creation, and this is especially the case here. I'm greatly indebted to the many remarkable people who have helped shape it. My gratitude begins with my students at the University of Chicago, who gamely explored many ideas with me and bravely shared their own stories along the way. As a teacher, I could not ask for any better. The University of Chicago and my colleagues in the Department of Political Science have been incredibly supportive, not only with generous leave but in allowing me the freedom to wander across many different fields in my teaching and writing.

My agent, Matt McGowan at Goldinlit, took a chance on a sketchy idea and found it a home at Liveright. My editor, Peter Simon, has been everything an author could want from a publisher—showing patience, faith, and incredible editorial judgment. His stamp is everywhere on the manuscript. Diane Durrett and Rebecca Springer provided invaluable copyediting.

While writing, I enjoyed excellent feedback from some remarkably generous and attentive readers, including John Britton, Rachel DeWoskin, Henry Flores, Schuyler Frautschi, Neil Kostic, and David Scharff. Andrea Morales, the producer of my podcast, *Nine Questions with Eric Oliver*, was also a valuable sounding board and enabler of much exploration.

This book was also shaped by wonderful conversations with Jackie

Acho, Laurie Anderson, Susan Augustine, Bill Ayers, Chris Bache, Laura Berman, Susie Britton, Oliver Burkeman, David Christian, Jim Cohen, Ryan Coyne, Adrian Danzig, Harriet De Wit, Nick Eply, Sarah Hammerschlag, Dan Hooper, Mott Hupfel, Elizabeth Kieff, Tom Levinson, Amy Owen, Richard Owen, Maxwell Ryan, Oliver Ryan, Anil Seth, Andrew Solomon, Rebecca Schanberg, Rosanna Warren, Kato Wittich, and Richard Wrangham. Their insights and wisdom are sprinkled throughout this work.

I survive on the invaluable support from my friends and family. I'm especially grateful to Ed and Lorna Goodman, Renee and Craig Dalton, Elaine Sivcoski, Brenda and Dave Bergen, Barnonia, my Hyde Park community, and the wonderful folks at the Corkins Exchange.

Most important was the incredible support, editorial acumen, and brilliant insights of my wife, Thea Goodman. Her love paves all roads.

Further Readings

Here is a brief list of some of the many works that have shaped the contents of the book's various chapters. To keep this group manageable in length, I've selected only a few books that would be most accessible to a general reader. I owe these authors (and the many authors I did not list) a great deal of gratitude.

Introduction

The Ego Trick by Julian Baggini delves into the concept of the self, questioning whether it is an illusion and how it is constructed.

The Self Illusion: How the Social Brain Creates Identity by Bruce Hood. A compelling exploration of how our sense of self is created by our brain and shaped by society.

Sources of the Self: The Making of the Modern Identity by Charles Taylor. A thorough examination of how modern historical developments have shaped notions of identity.

The Denial of Death by Ernest Becker explores how our awareness of mortality has shaped human psychology and the concept of the self.

Chapter 1: Essence

The Elegant Universe: Superstrings, Hidden Dimensions, and the Quest for the Ultimate Theory by Brian Greene. A compelling introduction to string theory and the fundamental nature of the universe, touching on concepts of energy and the essence of reality.

A Brief History of Time by Stephen Hawking examines the nature of the universe, including discussions on energy, time, and the fundamental particles that make up everything, making it a perfect complement to the atomic and energetic discussions in this chapter.

Zen and the Art of Motorcycle Maintenance: An Inquiry into Values by Robert M. Pirsig investigates the concepts of quality and essence, weaving existential musings and scientific thought. One of my all-time favorite novels.

The Big Picture: On the Origins of Life, Meaning, and the Universe Itself by Sean Carroll. Carroll's exploration of the big questions about life, the universe, and everything ties in directly with the chapter's exploration of energy, entropy, and the nature of reality.

Big History by David Christian offers a modern origin story that starts with the beginning of the universe. I've assigned this book in my class for many years.

Chapter 2: Self

What Is Life? With Mind and Matter and Autobiographical Sketches by Erwin Schrödinger. This classic work theorizes about the concept of life from a physicist's perspective, particularly focusing on the idea of negative entropy and the molecular basis of life. It helped guide the later discovery of DNA.

The Vital Question: Energy, Evolution, and the Origins of Complex Life by Nick Lane examines how energy flows within living organisms and how these processes have driven the evolution of life.

Every Life Is on Fire by Jeremy England explores life's origins and its relationship to the laws of thermodynamics.

The Origins of Life: From the Birth of Life to the Origin of Language by John Maynard Smith and Eörs Szathmáry. A wonderfully comprehensive work that discusses various theories about how life originated on Earth, providing context for the chapter's exploration of LUCA and the early stages of life.

From Bacteria to Bach and Back: The Evolution of Minds by Daniel Dennett explores the evolution of consciousness and how simple biological processes like those seen in LUCA have given rise to complex minds relevant to the discussion of self and life processes.

Chapter 3: Purpose

Man's Search for Meaning by Viktor E. Frankl. A classic study from a Holocaust survivor, Frankl's exploration of finding purpose in life, even in the most challenging circumstances, provides a deep philosophical perspective that aligns with the chapter's exploration of purpose beyond religious doctrine.

The Evolving Self: A Psychology for the Third Millennium by Mihaly Csikszentmihalyi examines how individuals can evolve by finding meaning and purpose, integrating the various layers of self.

Nicomachean Ethics by Aristotle. Terence Irwin's translation is accessible and widely recommended for readers who want to understand Aristotle's ideas on eudaemonia, virtue, and the good life. It's a foundational text in philosophy, exploring the principles of living well and achieving happiness through virtue.

Chapter 4: Foundations

A Short History of Nearly Everything by Bill Bryson. This may be my favorite nonfiction book of all time. A wonderfully engaging story about the history of modern scientific thinking written with Bryson's charming and witty style, it is an inspiration for this book.

The Immortal Life of Henrietta Lacks by Rebecca Skloot tells the story of HeLa cells, the first immortal human cells ever grown in culture, exploring their impact on science and our understanding of cellular biology.

The Gene: An Intimate History by Siddhartha Mukherjee offers an in-depth exploration of genetics, the role of DNA, and how our understanding of genes shapes our identity, directly complementing the chapter's discussion on DNA and cellular processes.

The Telomere Effect: A Revolutionary Approach to Living Younger, Healthier, Longer by Elizabeth Blackburn and Elissa Epel. This book discusses the role of telomeres, the protective caps on our DNA, in cellular aging and health, offering insights into how lifestyle choices impact our cells and longevity.

Chapter 5: Evolution

The Origin of Species by Charles Darwin. The foundational text on evolutionary biology, Darwin's work lays out the theory of natural selection and the evidence supporting it, making it essential reading for understanding evolution.

The Selfish Gene by Richard Dawkins is a seminal work on evolutionary biology that discusses how genes drive the behaviors of living organisms.

The Tangled Tree: A Radical New History of Life by David Quammen discusses the revolutionary discoveries in molecular biology that have changed our understanding of evolution, particularly the idea of horizontal gene transfer, which complicates the traditional tree of life.

I Contain Multitudes: The Microbes Within Us and a Grander View of Life by Ed Yong explores the role of microbes in our bodies and how they influence our health, behavior, and evolution, directly complementing the chapter's discussion on the microbiome and the interconnectedness of life.

Chapter 6: Animal

What Evolution Is by Ernst Mayr offers a clear and accessible explanation of evolutionary theory, making it an excellent resource for understanding the foundational concepts of evolution discussed in this chapter. His insights into how animals evolved to navigate their environments resonate with the chapter's discussion on the development of coherence and sentience in animals.

Internal Time: Chronotypes, Social Jet Lag, and Why You're So Tired by Till Roenneberg. Roenneberg's work on circadian rhythms and the internal clocks that govern our daily lives provides a scientific basis for the chapter's exploration of how the animal self is anchored in time.

The Ancestor's Tale: A Pilgrimage to the Dawn of Evolution by Richard Dawkins takes readers on a reverse chronological journey through evolution, explaining how species have diverged from common ancestors. This book aligns well with the chapter's exploration of our evolutionary history and interconnectedness.

The Moral Molecule: How Trust Works by Paul J. Zak. In a great overview of oxytocin and its role in human behavior, Zak shows how this "moral molecule" fosters trust and social bonding, reinforcing the idea that we are deeply interconnected with others through biological mechanisms.

Sociobiology: The New Synthesis by Edward O. Wilson. Wilson's pioneering work in sociobiology explores how social behaviors in animals, including humans, are deeply rooted in biology.

Chapter 7: Language

The Language Instinct: How the Mind Creates Language by Steven Pinker is a foundational work in understanding the cognitive basis of language. He explores how language is an innate human ability shaped by evolutionary pressures.

The Recursive Mind: The Origins of Human Language, Thought, and Civilization by Michael Corballis explores how recursive thinking—a key feature of human language—enables complex thought and communication.

The Principles of Psychology by William James. This seminal work on psychology lays the foundation for understanding the distinction between the "I" and the "Me." His insights into the development of self-consciousness through language remain influential in the field.

Oh, What a Blow That Phantom Gave Me! by Edmund Carpenter. Carpenter's anthropological work examines the impact of introducing modern media to isolated cultures, such as the Biami people.

The Symbolic Species: The Co-Evolution of Language and the Brain by Terrence Deacon. This work explores the co-evolution of human language and brain structure, providing a biological perspective on the emergence of symbolic communication.

Chapter 8: Morality

On the Genealogy of Morals by Friedrich Nietzsche explores the origins and development of moral concepts, particularly the shift from "master morality" to "slave morality."

The Goodness Paradox: The Strange Relationship Between Virtue and Violence in Human Evolution by Richard Wrangham discusses the evolution of human aggression and the domestication of our species. It supports the chapter's argument that human morality and social norms emerged as strategies for managing intragroup violence and promoting cooperation.

Hierarchy in the Forest: The Evolution of Egalitarian Behavior by Christopher Boehm. Boehm's anthropological study examines how early human societies managed power dynamics and maintained social order through moral codes.

The Anatomy of Disgust by William Ian Miller. This exploration of disgust as a moral emotion sheds light on how feelings of guilt, shame, and self-loathing are culturally constructed.

Discipline and Punish: The Birth of the Prison by Michel Foucault. Foucault's analysis of the evolution of modern disciplinary systems provides a theoretical framework for understanding how morality and social norms are enforced through internalized self-regulation.

Chapter 9: Ego

The WEIRDest People in the World: How the West Became Psychologically Peculiar and Particularly Prosperous by Joseph Henrich. This terrific book explores the cultural evolution of WEIRD (Western, Educated, Industrialized, Rich, and Democratic) societies and their unique psychological traits.

The Presentation of Self in Everyday Life by Erving Goffman. Goffman's sociological analysis of how individuals manage their self-presentation in social interactions offers valuable insights into the performative aspects of the ego.

Chapter 10: Psyche

The Ego and the Id by Sigmund Freud. Of Freud's many works, this is the clearest description of his theory of the mind.

Civilization and Its Discontents by Sigmund Freud. This is a book I've assigned for decades, a great description of how morality is necessary for civilization and what it does to us.

Freud: A Life for Our Time by Peter Gay. Gay's comprehensive biography of Freud provides deep insights into how Freud's personal experiences and historical context influenced his development of psychoanalytic theory. This biography is essential for understanding the connections between Freud's life and his ideas on repression.

The Politics of Psychoanalysis: An Introduction to Freudian and Post-Freudian Theory by Stephen Frosh explores Freudian psychoanalysis's political and social implications, particularly in relation to repression and power dynamics. His analysis provides a critical lens through which to view Freud's theories in a contemporary context.

Freud: In His Time and Ours by Élisabeth Roudinesco offers a modern reevaluation of Freud's contributions to psychology, including his concepts of repression and the unconscious. This text is particularly useful for understanding how Freud's ideas have evolved and been interpreted over time.

Chapter 11: Archetypes

The Archetypes and the Collective Unconscious by Carl Jung. This work is a cornerstone of Jungian psychology, where Jung elaborates on his theory of archetypes and the collective unconscious. It's essential for understanding how Jung perceived the deep, universal patterns that shape human experience across cultures and time.

The Hero with a Thousand Faces by Joseph Campbell popularizes the concept of the monomyth or the hero's journey, which draws heavily on Jungian archetypes. This book is useful for anyone interested in how these universal stories manifest in various cultures and in modern storytelling.

Archetypal Dimensions of the Psyche by Marie-Louise von Franz. A close collaborator of Jung, von Franz's work delves into the practical application of Jungian archetypes in therapy and self-exploration. Her insights help bridge Jung's more abstract ideas with real-world psychological practice.

Archetype: A Natural History of the Self by Anthony Stevens offers a comprehensive introduction to Jungian archetypes, linking them with evolutionary biology and the psychology of the self. This book is an excellent resource for understanding how Jung's ideas align with contemporary science.

Chapter 12: Transcendence

Wherever You Go, There You Are by John Kabat-Zinn. This book is foundational for understanding mindfulness in the context of modern living. It explores the concept that true transcendence involves being fully present, rather than seeking escape from reality.

The Heart of the Buddha's Teaching: Transforming Suffering into Peace, Joy, and Liberation by Thich Nhat Hanh. This volume offers a comprehensive overview of Buddhist teachings, including the Four Noble Truths and the Eightfold Path, with practical guidance on how to apply these teachings to modern life for achieving transcendence.

Mindfulness: A Practical Guide to Awakening by Joseph Goldstein. Goldstein's book delves into the principles of mindfulness and meditation, drawing from Buddhist teachings to guide readers toward greater self-awareness and spiritual awakening.

What the Buddha Taught by Walpola Rahula. This is a book I use in my classes to teach about Buddhism. It is a classic and offers a clear and straightforward description of Buddhism.

Chapter 13: Thinking

Incognito: The Secret Lives of the Brain by David Eagleman. Eagleman's exploration of the unconscious mind reveals how much of our thinking and decision-making occurs outside of conscious awareness. His work aligns with the idea that much of our cognitive processes are hidden beneath the surface.

Vision: A Computational Investigation into the Human Representation and Processing of Visual Information by David Marr. This groundbreaking work on vision provides a computational model for understanding how the brain processes visual information. Marr's theories are foundational for studying perception and how our brains construct a coherent visual experience from raw sensory data.

Phantoms in the Brain: Probing the Mysteries of the Human Mind by V. S. Ramachandran and Sandra Blakeslee delves into neurological case studies to explore how the brain constructs reality. Their book is particularly relevant for understanding how perception can be altered by brain damage or dysfunction, offering insights into the brain's role in creating our subjective experience.

Descartes' Error: Emotion, Reason, and the Human Brain by Antonio Damasio. In this influential book, Damasio argues that emotions are integral to reasoning and decision-making, challenging the traditional view of emotion as separate from rational thought. His work is essential for understanding the connection between cognition, perception, and emotion.

How the Mind Works by Steven Pinker explores the cognitive and evolutionary mechanisms underlying human thought, perception, and emotion. Pinker's work provides a broad overview of how the brain functions, making complex topics in cognition accessible to a general audience.

Chapter 14: Intention

Thinking, Fast and Slow by Daniel Kahneman. Kahneman's exploration of the dual processes of thinking—System 1 (fast, intuitive) and System 2 (slow, deliberate)—is crucial for understanding how our brains process information and make decisions. His work highlights the biases and heuristics that shape our perception of free will and decision-making, which ties directly into the concept of self-efficacy and intentionality discussed in the chapter.

Who's in Charge?: Free Will and the Science of the Brain by Michael Gazzaniga. This work on the neuroscience of free will challenges traditional notions of autonomy and control over our actions. Gazzaniga explores the brain's modular structure and how different parts contribute to our sense of agency, offering a scientific lens through which to view the limitations of free will discussed in the chapter.

Mindset: The New Psychology of Success by Carol Dweck. Dweck's concept of "growth mindset" aligns with the ideas of self-efficacy and the power of intention. Her research into how our beliefs about our abilities shape our actions and potential for success is directly relevant to the discussion of how reordering our thoughts can lead to personal transformation.

Surfing Uncertainty: Prediction, Action, and the Embodied Mind by Andy Clark delves into the predictive processing model of the brain, which posits that much of our cognition is based on the brain's attempts to minimize prediction errors. This model helps explain how our brains create mental shortcuts and why our perceptions and intentions are often shaped by unconscious predictions rather than deliberate thought.

Behave: The Biology of Humans at Our Best and Worst by Robert Sapolsky. Sapolsky examines the many factors—genetic, environmental, and social—that influence human behavior, bridging neuroscience and behavioral science.

The Master and His Emissary: The Divided Brain and the Making of the Western World by Iain McGilchrist. This book explores how the two hemispheres of the brain shape our experience of the world, impacting everything from culture to individual perception.

Chapter 15: Consciousness

The Conscious Mind: In Search of a Fundamental Theory by David J. Chalmers. Chalmers explores the "hard problem" of consciousness, addressing why and how physical processes in the brain give rise to subjective experience.

Consciousness Explained by Daniel C. Dennett. Dennett offers a comprehensive account of how consciousness can be understood as a natural phenomenon, presenting a materialistic view that challenges traditional notions of the mind.

Being You: A New Science of Consciousness by Anil Seth discusses the latest research in neuroscience and cognitive science to offer a new understanding of how consciousness arises from the brain's interactions with the world.

The Ego Tunnel: The Science of the Mind and the Myth of the Self by Thomas Metzinger. This book explores the idea that our sense of self is a kind of illusion created by the brain, proposing a new way of thinking about consciousness and identity.

The Origin of Consciousness in the Breakdown of the Bicameral Mind by Julian Jaynes presents a controversial theory that consciousness, as we understand it today, only emerged in humans within the last few thousand years, following the breakdown of earlier mental structures.

I Am a Strange Loop by Douglas Hofstadter investigates the concept of the self and consciousness, proposing that our sense of self is a complex, self-referential loop within our minds.

Chapter 16: Enlightenment

The Doors of Perception by Aldous Huxley. Huxley's classic exploration of his experiences with mescaline offers insights into how psychedelics can alter perception and consciousness and how they relate to mystical and spiritual experiences.

How to Change Your Mind: What the New Science of Psychedelics Teaches Us About Consciousness, Dying, Addiction, Depression, and Transcendence by Michael Pollan. Pollan examines the history, science, and therapeutic potential of psychedelics, providing a comprehensive overview of their role in altering consciousness and promoting psychological healing.

The Psychedelic Experience: A Manual Based on the Tibetan Book of the Dead by Timothy Leary, Ralph Metzner, and Richard Alpert. This book serves as a guide for navigating the psychedelic experience, drawing parallels between the effects of psychedelics and the spiritual journey described in the Tibetan Book of the Dead.

The Psychedelic Explorer's Guide: Safe, Therapeutic, and Sacred Journeys by James Fadiman. Fadiman offers practical advice and insights on how to safely and effectively use psychedelics for personal growth, therapy, and spiritual exploration.

The Varieties of Religious Experience by William James. Although not specifically about psychedelics, James's classic work on the nature of spiritual experiences provides a foundational understanding of the mystical and transcendental aspects of consciousness that psychedelics often evoke.

Chapter 17: Emotions

The Emotional Brain: The Mysterious Underpinnings of Emotional Life by Joseph LeDoux. LeDoux offers a deep dive into the neuroscience of emotions, explaining how our brains process emotions and how these processes influence our behavior and decision-making.

Emotional Intelligence: Why It Can Matter More Than IQ by Daniel Goleman. Goleman's seminal work explores the concept of emotional intelligence, emphasizing the importance of understanding and managing our emotions for personal and professional success.

The Feeling of What Happens: Body and Emotion in the Making of Consciousness by Antonio Damasio. Damasio explores the relationship between emotions and consciousness, offering insights into how emotions contribute to our sense of self and our experiences of being.

Why We Feel: The Science of Human Emotions by Victor Johnston. Johnston offers a comprehensive overview of the evolutionary basis of emotions, explaining how emotions have developed to guide our behavior and help us navigate the complexities of social life.

The Nature of Emotion: Fundamental Questions edited by Paul Ekman and Richard J. Davidson. This collection of essays by leading researchers in the field tackles fundamental questions about the nature of emotions, including their definition, origins, and role in human life.

Chapter 18: Happiness

Flourish: A Visionary New Understanding of Happiness and Well-Being by Martin Seligman. Seligman, a pioneer in positive psychology, presents his theory of well-being, which goes beyond happiness to include other aspects like meaning and engagement.

The How of Happiness: A New Approach to Getting the Life You Want by Sonja Lyubomirsky. Lyubomirsky offers a research-based guide on practical strategies to increase happiness in daily life.

Stumbling on Happiness by Daniel Gilbert. This book delves into the quirks of human psychology and how our minds often misjudge what will make us happy.

The Art of Happiness: A Handbook for Living by the Dalai Lama and Howard C. Cutler. A blend of Tibetan Buddhist wisdom and Western psychology, this book explores how to cultivate happiness through compassion and mindfulness.

The Conquest of Happiness by Bertrand Russell. Written by the great philosopher, this classic work examines the causes of unhappiness and offers advice on how to overcome them.

Flow: The Psychology of Optimal Experience by Mihaly Csikszentmihalyi introduces the concept of "flow" as a key to achieving happiness and fulfillment through deep engagement in activities.

Chapter 19: Love

The Art of Loving by Erich Fromm. This classic text explores the nature of love and its importance in human life. Fromm distinguishes between different types of love and emphasizes that love is an active, intentional practice rather than a passive state.

Mating in Captivity: Unlocking Erotic Intelligence by Esther Perel explores the complexities of desire in long-term relationships and offers insights into maintaining eroticism while fostering emotional intimacy. One of my all-time favorite books.

The 5 Love Languages: The Secret to Love That Lasts by Gary Chapman is a practical guide to understanding the different ways people express and receive love, which can improve communication and satisfaction in relationships.

Why We Love: The Nature and Chemistry of Romantic Love by Helen Fisher examines the biological underpinnings of romantic love, focusing on how neurotransmitters like dopamine and oxytocin influence our feelings and behaviors in relationships.

The Course of Love by Alain de Botton. De Botton's novel offers a philosophical and psychological exploration of love, chronicling a couple's relationship and the challenges they face in sustaining love over time.

Chapter 20: Loving

Wired for Love: How Understanding Your Partner's Brain and Attachment Style Can Help You Defuse Conflict and Build a Secure Relationship by Stan Tatkin provides practical advice on how understanding your partner's attachment style can enhance intimacy and relationship stability.

The Power of Attachment: How to Create Deep and Lasting Intimate Relationships by Diane Poole Heller explores healing attachment wounds and creating secure, fulfilling relationships through practical exercises and therapeutic techniques.

Radical Acceptance: Embracing Your Life with the Heart of a Buddha by Tara Brach combines Buddhist teachings with psychology to explore self-love and compassion, offering a pathway to healing attachment wounds through mindfulness.

Love for Imperfect Things: How to Accept Yourself in a World Striving for Perfection by Haemin Sunim. Sunim, a Buddhist monk, provides gentle guidance on self-acceptance and love, emphasizing spiritual practices to cultivate inner peace and transcendent love.

How to Be an Adult in Relationships: The Five Keys to Mindful Loving by David Richo blends psychology and spirituality to offer insights into adult attachment and how to cultivate mindful, loving relationships that transcend ego and fear.

Chapter 21: Recognition

Staring at the Sun: Overcoming the Terror of Death by Irvin D. Yalom. Yalom explores existential psychology, focusing on how the recognition of mortality can lead to a more meaningful life.

The Untethered Soul: The Journey Beyond Yourself by Michael A. Singer. Singer offers a spiritual perspective on how to recognize and let go of the thoughts and emotions that hold us back.

Atomic Habits: An Easy & Proven Way to Build Good Habits & Break Bad Ones by James Clear. This book provides practical advice on recognizing and changing the small habits that shape our lives.

Daring Greatly: How the Courage to Be Vulnerable Transforms the Way We Live, Love, Parent, and Lead by Brené Brown. Brown's exploration of vulnerability and courage highlights the importance of self-awareness in personal growth.

The Power of Now: A Guide to Spiritual Enlightenment by Eckhart Tolle. Tolle emphasizes the importance of living in the present moment, helping readers recognize the mental patterns that cause suffering.

The Four Agreements: A Practical Guide to Personal Freedom by Don Miguel Ruiz. Ruiz's work provides a framework for recognizing and transforming limiting beliefs and fostering personal freedom and happiness.

Chapter 22: Letting Go

Letting Go: The Pathway of Surrender by David R. Hawkins. Hawkins provides a comprehensive guide to the process of letting go, exploring how to release negative emotions and achieve a state of peace and freedom.

The Art of Living: Vipassana Meditation as Taught by S. N. Goenka by William Hart. This book offers insights into the practice of Vipassana meditation, focusing on mindfulness and the art of living in the present moment. As a Vipassana meditator myself, I found this book to be a great description of the thinking behind the practice.

Yoga and the Quest for the True Self by Stephen Cope blends yoga philosophy with modern psychology, offering insights into how yoga can help us.

The Wisdom of Insecurity: A Message for an Age of Anxiety by Alan Watts. One of my favorite thinkers, Watts explores how our quest for security and certainty in life often leads to anxiety, and he offers insights on how embracing uncertainty can lead to a more peaceful and fulfilling existence.

When Things Fall Apart by Pema Chödrön. Another book that I assign to my students and one that I've given to more people than I can remember. A wise, soulful, and compassionate guide to living better with uncertainty.

Index

Note: Footnotes are indicated by *n* after the page number.